STECK-VAUGHN

GED

Mathematics

EXERCISE BOOK

DOROTHY McMURTRY

STECK-VAUGHN®
C O M P A N Y
ELEMENTARY · SECONDARY · ADULT · LIBRARY

About the Author

Dorothy McMurtry is the Dean of the Adult Learning Skills Program at Kennedy-King College, one of the seven colleges within the City Colleges of Chicago, Community College District 508. Ms. McMurtry supervises Adult Basic Education, GED, and English as a Second Language instruction for 10,000 students annually. She plans and implements staff development activities for 110 adult educators and other academic support personnel. In addition to these responsibilities, she serves on a number of advisory boards for literacy and workforce preparation initiatives.

Staff Credits

Executive Editor: Ellen Northcutt
Supervising Editor: Tim Collins
Design Manager: John J. Harrison
Cover Design: Rhonda Childress

ISBN 0-8114-7369-4

Copyright © 1996 Steck-Vaughn Company.

0 1 2 3 4 5 6 7 8 9 DBH 01 00 99 98 97 96 95

☰Contents

Unit 3: Geometry 76

Simulated GED Test A 96

Simulated GED Test B 107

Answers and Explanations 118

Answer Sheet 156

≡To the Learner

The *Steck-Vaughn GED Mathematics Exercise Book* provides you with practice in answering the types of questions found on the actual GED Mathematics Test. It can be used with *Steck-Vaughn GED Mathematics* or *Steck-Vaughn Complete GED Preparation*. Cross references to those two books are supplied for your convenience on the exercise pages. This exercise book contains both practice exercises and two complete simulated GED tests.

≡Practice Exercises

The GED Mathematics Test tests your math skills and problem-solving ability in three content areas: arithmetic, algebra, and geometry. The practice exercises are divided into the same three content areas by unit. The arithmetic unit covers the basic operations in three application areas: number relationships (whole numbers, fractions, decimals, percents, exponents, and scientific notation), measurement (including perimeter, area, volume, rate of motion, and rate of interest), and data analysis (calculating mean, median, ratio, and probability and interpreting graphs, charts, and tables). The algebra unit presents converting context into symbolic language, combining and simplifying like terms, setting up and solving equations, inequalities, and quadratic and linear functions. The geometry unit includes parallel and perpendicular lines, triangle theory, coordinate system, distance problems, and the Pythagorean relationship.

The units include practice in the skills needed to complete the GED Mathematics Test successfully, including ratio and proportion, an operation that can be used to solve approximately one-third of the questions on the GED Test.

Steps for solving word problems and identifying missing and extraneous information can help you identify correct solutions to problems. Solving set-up problems is a special type of GED test item. This book provides practice in answering problems that ask you to identify the best method to solve a problem but don't ask for a numerical solution.

≡Simulated Tests

This exercise book contains two complete full-length Simulated GED Mathematics Tests. Each Simulated Test has the same number of items as the actual GED Test and provides practice with similar item types as are found on the GED Test. The Simulated Tests can help you decide if you are ready to take the GED Mathematics Test. To get the most benefit from the Simulated Tests, take each test under the same time restrictions as you will have for the actual GED Test. For each test, complete the 56 items within 90 minutes. Space the two tests apart by at least a week.

The GED Mathematics Test is divided into three content areas: **arithmetic, algebra,** and **geometry.**

Approximately 25% of the items on the GED Test require you to identify the best method to set up a problem for solution. A short reading passage precedes two-thirds of the items, while a graphic stimulus precedes one-third of the items. Approximately 15% of the items involve using a formula from the given formula page (found on the inside back cover of this book).

Illustrations

Approximately one-third of the items relate to a drawing, chart, map, or graph. Practice with illustrations is essential to develop the skills to interpret information presented on the GED Mathematics Test. Always read the title, key, and any other information associated with the illustration before answering any questions.

Analysis of Performance Charts

After each Simulated Test, an Analysis of Performance Chart will help you determine if you are ready to take the GED Mathematics Test. The charts give a breakdown of test items by content area (measurement, number relationships, data analysis, algebra, and geometry). By completing these charts, you can determine your own strengths and weaknesses as they relate to the mathematics area.

Correlation Chart

The following chart shows how the sections of this exercise book relate to the sections of other Steck-Vaughn GED preparation books. You can refer to these other two books for further instruction or review.

CONTENT AREAS	Arithmetic	Algebra	Geometry
BOOK TITLES Mathematics Exercise Book	Unit 1	Unit 2	Unit 3
Mathematics	Unit 1	Unit 2	Unit 3
Complete Preparation	Unit 7, Arithmetic	Unit 7, Algebra	Unit 7, Geometry

Unit 1 Arithmetic

Whole Number Concepts

Directions: Compare the following numbers. Write >, <, or = between the numbers.

1. 324 _____ 432
2. 973 _____ 973
3. 1,036 _____ 1,008
4. 560 _____ 5,600
5. 2,779 _____ 2,769

6. 400 _____ 430
7. 6,325 _____ 6,394
8. 12,992 _____ 12,991
9. 180,000 _____ 18,000
10. 85,063 _____ 85,630

Directions: Write each set of numbers in order from smallest to largest.

11. 293; 392; 932; 923; 329 _____
12. 480; 844; 804; 408; 488 _____
13. 5,631; 6,531; 5,316; 6,315; 6,153 _____
14. 705; 7,005; 750; 7,500; 7,050 _____
15. 19,482; 9,842; 98,421; 18,429; 8,914 _____

Directions: Round each number to the given place.

Round to the nearest ten.

16. 19 _____
17. 731 _____
18. 2,945 _____

Round to the nearest hundred.

19. 4,505 _____
20. 32,098 _____
21. 683,257 _____

Round to the nearest thousand.

22. 5,527 _____
23. 12,206 _____
24. 499,820 _____

Round to the nearest ten thousand.

25. 37,800 _____
26. 855,399 _____
27. 702,906 _____

Round to the nearest hundred thousand.

28. 493,600 _____
29. 1,253,378 _____
30. 5,402,186 _____

Round to the nearest million.

31. 3,176,942 _____
32. 95,681,300 _____
33. 462,500,000 _____

 See Also — Mathematics Complete Preparation — Unit 1, Lesson 1 — Unit 7, Whole Numbers Operations

≡Estimating with Whole Numbers

You can use estimation to help find the answer to some multiple choice problems. First, round the numbers given in the problem. Then, use the rounded numbers to estimate the solution. Eliminate any of the choices that are not close to the estimated solution.

Example: Allen's weekly pay is $297. How much will he make in one year (52 weeks)?
(1) $ 1,485
(2) $10,544
(3) $13,824
(4) $15,444
(5) $18,324
Round $297 to $300. Round 52 weeks to 50 weeks. Multiply the rounded numbers. $300 × 50 = $15,000. Allen earns about $15,000 in one year. Option (4) is the only answer close to $15,000.

Directions: Estimate each answer. Eliminate any of the choices that are not close to the estimate. If there is more than one choice remaining, you may need to find the exact answer.

1. Last Friday night a local theater sold a total of 592 tickets at $6.00 each. How much money did the theater make on tickets last Friday night?

   (1) $3,000
   (2) $3,125
   (3) $3,552
   (4) $3,950
   (5) $9,472

2. Light travels at a rate of 186,282 miles per second. If it takes 11 seconds for light to travel from a certain star to Earth, about how many miles away is the star?

   (1)   18,600
   (2)   186,000
   (3)   1,860,000
   (4)   2,046,000
   (5) 20,460,000

3. A manufacturer of CDs finds that one out of every five hundred CDs produced in her factory is defective. If the factory produces 29,000 CDs in one day, about how many are defective?

   (1)   6
   (2)   60
   (3)   600
   (4)   6,000
   (5) 60,000

4. Two years ago in Bay City, 3,452 people took the GED test. Last year 2,807 took the test. What was the decrease in the number of people taking the GED test?

   (1) 1,655
   (2) 1,405
   (3)   745
   (4)   655
   (5)   645

▦Whole Numbers: Computation Practice

<u>Directions</u>: Enter your answers to the following problems on the lines provided.

Example: What is the sum of 125 and 75? _____200_____

1. What is the product of 144 times 23? _____

2. What is the difference between 24,593 and 10,638? _____

3. What is the sum of 37,454; 41,345; 49,496; and 22,738? _____

4. If you divide 896 by 32, what is the quotient? _____

5. Find the product of 9,675 times 326. _____

6. What does 90,000 minus 82,575 equal? _____

7. What is the quotient of 230,400 divided by 36? _____

8. What is the total of 861; 495; and 827? _____

9. What is the product of 8,622 times 393? _____

10. Add 946; 30,306; 58,275; and 67,580. _____

11. What is the difference between 658,235 and 621,791? _____

12. What is the sum of 7,478 and 9,757? _____

13. If you multiply 5,763 times 472, what is the product? _____

14. What is the quotient of 355,416 divided by 502? _____

15. Add fourteen, eleven thousand, and five. _____

16. Subtract seven thousand fifty-nine from eight thousand three hundred eleven.

    _____

17. Multiply two hundred three by one hundred eleven. _____

18. Divide seven hundred thirty-six thousand two hundred fifty-four by twenty-four.

    _____

See Also   Mathematics   Unit 1, Lesson 2
                Complete Preparation   Unit 7, Whole Number Operations

Directions: Choose the best answer to each item.

1. On a word processing test, Lydia typed 694 words in 15 minutes. On that same test 6 days later, Lydia typed 753 words in 15 minutes. By how many words did Lydia's speed improve from the first test to the second test?

   (1) 49
   (2) 53
   (3) 59
   (4) 69
   (5) 71

2. Town and Country Video rents 3 video movies for $5.00. In one week Town and Country Video had rented 675 videotapes. How much money did Town and Country Video record in rental receipts?

   (1) $ 225
   (2) $ 675
   (3) $ 725
   (4) $1,125
   (5) $1,500

3. The Appleton School District has 8 elementary schools and 2 senior high schools. The average enrollment at the elementary schools is 356 students per school, while the average enrollment at the high schools is 1,307 students per school. What is the total student enrollment in the Appleton School District?

   (1) 1,663
   (2) 2,614
   (3) 2,848
   (4) 5,462
   (5) 10,456

4. In the month of July, which has 31 days, an average of 2,118 people visited the Museum of Science and Industry each day. The museum was open each day of the month. How many people visited the museum during July?

   (1) 14,826
   (2) 25,416
   (3) 59,304
   (4) 63,540
   (5) 65,658

5. In 1985, the United States Patent Office granted 4,600,602 new patents. This is 641,197 fewer patents than the number of patents issued in 1980. How many patents were granted in 1980?

   (1) 3,205,985
   (2) 3,959,405
   (3) 4,600,602
   (4) 5,241,799
   (5) Not enough information is given.

6. In a recent school board presidential election for the Meadow Ridge School District, Agnes Hancock received 3,121 votes. Her opponent, Andrew Sawyer, received 2,374 votes. By how many votes did Hancock defeat Sawyer?

   (1) 447
   (2) 477
   (3) 497
   (4) 747
   (5) 774

Directions: Choose the best answer to each item. Most problems have more than one step.

Items 1 and 2 refer to the following passage.

A mail carrier recorded the number of pieces of mail she delivered during a one-week period. Her route covered 3 miles with 63 scheduled delivery stops. The mail carrier's record of deliveries by day was: Monday, 531 pieces; Tuesday, 116 pieces; Wednesday, 285 pieces; Thursday, 432 pieces; Friday, 157 pieces; and Saturday, 480 pieces.

1. What was the total number of pieces of mail delivered by the carrier for the week? Round your answer to the nearest hundred.

   (1) 1,900
   (2) 1,974
   (3) 2,000
   (4) 2,100
   (5) 2,200

2. What is the difference between the number of pieces of mail delivered on the heaviest delivery day and the sum of the two lightest delivery days?

   (1) 531
   (2) 415
   (3) 299
   (4) 258
   (5) 116

3. A craft store sold 450 silk-screened T-shirts. The total sales amount was $7,000. If 200 shirts were sold for $18 and another 200 shirts were sold for $14 on sale, at what price per T-shirt were the last 50 sold?

   (1) $ 2
   (2) $ 8
   (3) $10
   (4) $12
   (5) $14

4. Robbins Community Center has 108 men and 72 women interested in playing in the softball league. If each team has 12 players, how many teams will be in the softball league?

   (1) 10
   (2) 12
   (3) 15
   (4) 16
   (5) 18

Item 5 refers to the following drawing.

Section A	?	
Section B	36 in.	72 in.
Section C	24 in.	

Note: Not drawn to scale

5. The magazine racks in the Freeport Library have adjustable shelves. If the shelves are inserted as indicated in the drawing, what is the height of section A?

   (1) 12 in.
   (2) 24 in.
   (3) 36 in.
   (4) 48 in.
   (5) 60 in.

6. Mr. and Mrs. Arnold borrowed $7,000 from their bank to finish the basement of their home. They must make monthly payments of $258.45 for 3 years to repay the loan. How much interest will the Arnolds have paid when the loan is repaid?

   (1) $ 230.00
   (2) $ 687.00
   (3) $1,208.70
   (4) $2,304.20
   (5) $2,908.55

Items 7–10 refer to the following information.

Ms. Espinoza opened a savings account with $75 when she got a new job. The balances in her account for the first 6 months are:

Month	Deposit	End-of-Month Balance
April	$75	$ 75
May		125
June		180
July		225
August		265
September		340

7. In what month did Ms. Espinoza deposit the smallest amount of money?

(1) May
(2) June
(3) July
(4) August
(5) September

8. What was the total amount of money deposited in Ms. Espinoza's account for the 5 months after her initial deposit of $75?

(1) $265
(2) $253
(3) $221
(4) $202
(5) $201

9. In what month did Ms. Espinoza deposit the most money?

(1) May
(2) June
(3) July
(4) August
(5) September

10. In October, Ms. Espinoza withdrew $135. In November, she deposited $60. What was her balance at the end of November?

(1) $ 0
(2) $145
(3) $150
(4) $265
(5) $535

11. On Stan's hiking map 1 inch equals 50 miles. How long will the actual trail be if the trail on the map is 3 inches long?

(1) 15 miles
(2) 50 miles
(3) 150 miles
(4) 300 miles
(5) 1,500 miles

12. The Toucan Restaurant served twice as many adults as children one week. If 450 adults were served, how many children were served?

(1) 900
(2) 450
(3) 300
(4) 225
(5) 45

13. If Elma's Cleaning Service can clean one floor of an office building in 90 minutes, how long will it take the service to clean 6 floors? (Hint: 60 minutes = 1 hour)

(1) 6 hours
(2) 7 hours
(3) 8 hours
(4) 9 hours
(5) 10 hours

14. Hinds Nursery started the year with an inventory of 5,000 pots. In January 1,320 pots were used, in February 1,485 pots were used, and in March 2,109 pots were used. About how many pots were left?

(1) less than 75
(2) between 75 and 125
(3) between 125 and 200
(4) between 200 and 275
(5) over 275

Steps for Solving Word Problems

Directions: Read this explanation carefully. Then practice solving the word problems on pages 11–12.

You probably are comfortable performing these basic mathematical operations.

Examples:

1.
$$\begin{array}{r} 50 \\ + 97 \\ \hline 147 \end{array}$$

2.
$$\begin{array}{r} \$117.35 \\ - 52.99 \\ \hline \$ 64.36 \end{array}$$

3.
$$\begin{array}{r} \$1.04 \\ \times \quad 14 \\ \hline 4\,16 \\ 10\,4 \\ \hline \$14.56 \end{array}$$

4.
$$\begin{array}{r} \$.13 \\ 8\overline{)\$1.04} \\ \underline{8} \\ 24 \\ \underline{24} \end{array}$$

When the same numbers are used with words to form word problems, you may find it helpful to follow the steps listed below. Study the following word problems. The underlined key words give you clues about which operation to use to solve each problem. The solutions are shown above.

Example 1: Elizabeth worked in the packaging department of Wilson's Hosiery Company. To complete an order for one store, she needed 50 pairs of beige pantyhose and 97 pairs of black. What was the total number of pairs of pantyhose needed to complete this store's order?

Example 2: Sylvia's account at People's Gas Company had a credit balance of $117.35. Her March heating bill was $52.99. What will be the balance in her account after the deduction for the March bill?

Example 3: Joe owns a mobile hot dog stand. He ordered 14 pounds of hot dogs to sell at the ball park. If each pound costs $1.04, how much money will fourteen pounds of hot dogs cost?

Example 4: There are 8 hot dogs to a pound. What is the average cost per hot dog if one pound costs $1.04?

Each of the above word problems can be easily solved by using the following steps.

STEPS FOR SOLVING WORD PROBLEMS

1. Read the problem carefully and underline key words. Be sure you understand the information you are given and what you are being asked to find.
2. Identify all the facts.
3. State what you want to know.
4. Decide what computation operation or operations can be used to solve the problem.
5. Estimate the answer.
6. Carry out the operation(s) to find the exact answer.
7. Review your work by checking against the estimate.

Now reread Example 3 that you first saw on the preceding page.

Joe owns a mobile hot dog stand. He ordered 14 pounds of hot dogs to sell at the ball park. If each pound costs $1.04, how much money will fourteen pounds of hot dogs cost?

Step 1: Read the problem carefully and underline key words (how much, cost).
Step 2: The facts are
    A. The hot dogs cost $1.04 per pound.
    B. He will buy 14 pounds of hot dogs.
Step 3: You want to know the cost of 14 pounds of hot dogs.
Step 4: When all items being purchased are the same price, multiply the price by the number desired to calculate the total cost.
Step 5: To estimate, round $1.04 to $1.00 per pound for the hot dogs. Multiply 14 pounds times $1.00. The exact answer will be at least $14.
Step 6: Perform the operation.

$$
\begin{array}{r}
\$\ 1.04 \\
\times\quad 14 \\
\hline
4\ 16 \\
10\ 4\quad \\
\hline
\$14.56
\end{array}
$$

Step 7: Review your work to make sure you have not made an error in performing the computational operations. The estimate is $14.00 and the exact answer is $14.56.

Example 5: Beck's Bookstore bought 30 boxes of pocket dictionaries for $720. If there were 20 dictionaries in each box, how much did one dictionary cost?
Step 1: Read the problem carefully and underline key words (how much, cost).
Step 2: The facts are
    A. Thirty boxes of dictionaries cost $720.
    B. Each box contained 20 dictionaries.
Step 3: You want to know the cost of one dictionary.
Step 4: To find the cost of one dictionary, first determine the total number of dictionaries by multiplying the number of boxes times the books per box. The second operation will be division because all the dictionaries are of equal value.
Step 5: Use estimation to determine that the dictionaries cost a little more than a dollar each because the total amount is $720 and the total number of dictionaries is 600.
Step 6: Perform the operations to find the exact answer.

$$
\begin{array}{r}
30\quad \text{boxes} \\
\times 20\quad \text{dictionaries per box} \\
\hline
600\quad \text{dictionaries}
\end{array}
$$

$$
\begin{array}{r}
\$1.20 \\
600\overline{)\$720.00} \\
\underline{600}\quad \\
120\ 0 \\
\underline{120\ 0}
\end{array}
$$

Step 7: Finally, review your work to make sure you have not made any errors in performing the computational operations. The estimate of a little more than $1.00 per dictionary was reasonable. The exact answer is $1.20 per dictionary.

Directions: Solve the problems using the steps outlined on the preceding pages. When the problem has more than one operation, separate the problem into steps. Choose the best answer to each item.

1. Maria has two jobs. Her annual salary on her full-time job is $17,532, and on her part-time job she earns $6,468 annually. What is her monthly income?

   (1) $ 539
   (2) $1,460
   (3) $2,000
   (4) $3,234
   (5) Not enough information is given.

2. On Sunday, the Super Store recorded the following sales: 15 refrigerators, 36 electric toasters, 20 washing machines, 5 clothes dryers, 24 video recorders, and 48 radios. What was the total number of items sold?

   (1) 140
   (2) 148
   (3) 158
   (4) 160
   (5) 168

3. Brian's car payment is $169 per month for 3 years. If Brian paid $750 down, what is the total cost of his car?

   (1) $3,096
   (2) $3,846
   (3) $6,834
   (4) $6,903
   (5) $8,112

4. Bleacher seat tickets to the college baseball game cost $4.50 each. How many tickets were sold by the South Side Boosters if they collected $900?

   (1) 100
   (2) 150
   (3) 200
   (4) 250
   (5) 300

5. A video recorder costs $259, and Ann pays $25 down on the purchase price. If Ann makes 6 equal payments after the down payment, what must she pay each month?

   (1) $49
   (2) $45
   (3) $43
   (4) $41
   (5) $39

6. During the first four days of operation, the Contemporary Shop made $1,321 on Thursday, $950 on Friday, $1,529 on Saturday, and $1,734 on Sunday. To the nearest hundred dollars, how much money did the store make in its first four days?

   (1) $4,800
   (2) $5,200
   (3) $5,500
   (4) $5,600
   (5) $6,000

7. The telephone rate between two zones is $.25 for the first 5 minutes and $.10 for each additional minute. How long was a phone call if the total charge for the call was $2.25?

   (1) 10 min.
   (2) 15 min.
   (3) 20 min.
   (4) 25 min.
   (5) 75 min.

 **Solving Word Problems II**

Directions: Solve the following problems using the steps for solving word problems. Most problems have more than one step. Choose the best answer to each item.

1. The Union Land Development Company divided a tract of land into 15 equally valued lots to build homes in the Canterbury Subdivision. The tract of land was valued at $150,000. What was the value of each lot?

   (1) $ 1,050
   (2) $ 1,500
   (3) $10,000
   (4) $10,500
   (5) $15,000

2. Four bricklayers from the Emerald Construction Company laid 63,240 bricks in a six-day period. If each bricklayer laid an equal number of bricks, how many bricks did each bricklayer lay each day?

   (1) 7,405
   (2) 3,952
   (3) 3,545
   (4) 2,635
   (5) 2,258

3. Regal Square Apartments has 14 floors. Each floor of the building has 4 apartments, and each apartment has 8 electrical outlets. How many outlets are there in the building?

   (1) 26
   (2) 32
   (3) 112
   (4) 448
   (5) 512

4. Aaron budgeted $3,600 for rent, $780 for utilities, and $1,800 for food for the year. How much is his monthly budget for these expenses?

   (1) $ 450
   (2) $ 515
   (3) $ 618
   (4) $3,090
   (5) $6,180

Items 5 and 6 refer to the following passage.

The Miller Vending Machine Company purchased 15 cases of potato chips at $7.99 per case to fill its snack machines. Each case of potato chips had 36 three-ounce bags which sold for 50 cents per bag.

5. If all the bags of potato chips were sold, how much money was collected from the vending machines?

   (1) $ 7.50
   (2) $120.00
   (3) $150.15
   (4) $195.00
   (5) $270.00

6. What was the profit to the nearest dollar made on the sale of the 15 cases of potato chips?

   (1) $120
   (2) $150
   (3) $195
   (4) $250
   (5) $270

7. The Wet Pet Shop ordered 475 goldfish for its grand opening giveaway. If each customer received 3 fish, how many fish were left after 105 customers visited the store?

   (1) 60
   (2) 80
   (3) 150
   (4) 160
   (5) 300

≡ Missing and Extraneous (Too Much) Information

Some problems cannot be solved because some piece of needed information is missing. Some problems include information you do not need to find the answer. You must be alert when reading each problem to determine what information you need and whether this information is provided.

Example 1: To wallpaper an entire bedroom, Jeff needs 880 square feet of wallpaper. If a roll of wallpaper covers 75 square feet, how much money does Jeff need to purchase the wallpaper for this room?

Using the steps for solving word problems on pages 9 and 10, solve the problem above.

Step 1: Read the problem carefully and underline key words (how much).
Step 2: The facts are
    A. 880 square feet of wallpaper are needed.
    B. One roll of wallpaper covers 75 square feet.
Step 3: You want to know:
    How much money is needed to purchase the wallpaper?
Step 4: Review your facts. This problem cannot be solved because you are not given an important piece of information: the selling price of the wallpaper per roll.

It is equally important to be able to recognize that some problems have <u>too much</u> information. Sometimes it is not necessary to use all the numbers that appear in word problems.

Example 2: The Booster Club sponsored a dinner dance to raise money to buy team uniforms. Eighty couples attended the dance at $28 per couple. After paying the expenses for the dance, the club was able to buy half of its team's uniforms which cost $15 per uniform. How much money was collected before expenses?

Follow the steps below.

Step 1: Read the problem carefully and underline key words (how much).
Step 2: The facts are
    A. Eighty couples attended the dance.
    B. Each couple paid $28.
    C. Uniforms cost $15 each.
    D. The club could buy $\frac{1}{2}$ of the uniforms after expenses.
Step 3: You want to know: How much money was collected before expenses?
Step 4: Only one operation is necessary. Eighty couples attended and each paid $28. Multiply the price of the ticket by the number of couples attending the dance.
Step 5: Round $28 up to $30. The estimated answer is:
    $30 × 80 = $2,400.
Step 6: Carry out the operation to find the exact answer:
    $28 × 80 = $2,240
Step 7: Review your estimated answer against the exact answer.
    Those answers should be similar.

Two pieces of information are included in the problem that are <u>not</u> necessary to answer the question asked. The unnecessary information was the cost of the uniforms and the club's ability to buy half of the uniforms they needed.

 **See Also**

Mathematics	Unit 1, Lesson 3	
Complete Preparation	Unit 7, Solving Word Problems	
		Unit 1: Arithmetic **13**

≣Missing Information Practice

<u>Directions:</u> Each problem below is missing information. Write on the lines below the missing information that is needed to solve each problem.

1. The city advisory council has 150 representatives. The representatives are Republicans, Democrats, and Independents. Forty-five of the representatives are Democrats. How many of the representatives are Independents?
    To determine the number of Independents, the missing piece of information is

    _____ .

2. An inheritance of $8,000 is to be shared equally by the members of the Marble family. What is each family member's share?
    To determine the dollar amount for each family member, the missing piece of information is

    _____ .

3. The Beverly Cycle Shop recorded sales of $4,567 for the total number of bicycles sold in June. What was the average cost per bicycle?
    To determine the average cost per bicycle, the missing piece of information is

    _____ .

4. Franklin drove 548 miles on his vacation in September. How much was spent on gasoline?
    To determine the cost of the gasoline, the missing pieces of information are

    A. _____ .

    B. _____ .

5. The McLaren Child Parent Center had two separate budgets, one for books and one for recreational expenses. The sum of the two budgets was $4,600 for 12 months. By the end of the fifth month, a total of $2,800 was left. How much money was left for books for the last 7 months?
    To determine the money left for books, the missing pieces of information are

    A. _____ .

    B. _____ .

6. Regina purchased 3 one-gallon cartons of milk, 5 cans of dog food, and a four-pound can of coffee. How much change should Regina receive from the checkout clerk?
    To determine the amount of change that Regina should receive, the missing pieces of information are

    A. _____ .

    B. _____ .

≡ Extraneous Information Practice

<u>Directions:</u> Each problem below has too much information. Identify the extra information, and then solve the problem. Write your answers on the lines provided.

1. Last year the annual property taxes for the Myers' house were $1,055, the insurance was $325, and the interest was $1,578. What was the average monthly cost for insurance and taxes?

   The extra information is _____ .

   The answer is _____ .

2. The Philly Florist delivered flowers to the hospital. The costs were $15.95, $17.98, $24.35, and $25.45. The driver was paid $5 per hour. What was the total cost of the flowers delivered to the hospital?

   The extra information is _____ .

   The answer is _____ .

3. Norma applied for a new position at the hospital. Her annual salary is $15,750. The new position has an annual base salary of $18,750. Norma must pay $325 for union dues. What is the amount of the difference between the two salaries?

   The extra information is _____ .

   The answer is _____ .

4. The Norphlets are remodeling their kitchen. They decided to purchase their appliances from Bass Appliance Store. The stove, refrigerator, and dishwasher cost $1,675. The other remodeling cost of $3,144 is to be financed over a two-year period with equal monthly payments. What will be the monthly payment for the remodeling job?

   The extra information is _____ .

   The answer is _____ .

5.

	Times	Tribune	USA Daily
Monday	523	288	151
Tuesday	536	254	79
Wednesday	511	352	87
Thursday	524	323	123
Friday	537	357	147
	2,631	1,574	587

   How many more Times were sold than USA Daily for the five days?

   The extra information is _____ .

   The answer is _____ .

Order of Operations

Which solution gives you the correct answer for $6 + 4 \times 3$?

Solution A	Solution B
$6 + 4 \times 3 =$	$6 + 4 \times 3 =$
$10 \times 3 = 30$	$6 + 12 = 18$

Only Solution B gives you the correct answer. Because it is possible to solve the problem and calculate two different answers, mathematicians agree that rules are needed so everyone evaluates the problem the same way. The rules that follow are the rules for solving problems like these. The rules are called the Order of Operations.

> **Order of Operations**
> 1. First, evaluate operations within parentheses.
> 2. Next, evaluate operations with powers and roots.
> 3. Perform multiplication and division operations from left to right.
> 4. Perform addition and subtraction operations from left to right.

Note: If the problems do not have parentheses or powers and roots, then start with the third rule.

Directions: Use the rules described above to solve the following problems.

1. $3(7 + 4) - 18 \div 9$

2. $\dfrac{5 \times 4 + 2}{17 - 2 \times 3}$

3. $6(7 - 5) + 4$

4. $14 + 28 \div 7$

5. $\dfrac{5 \times 6 + 2}{12 - 4}$

6. $8 + 4 \times 2$

7. $(5 + 3) \times (8 - 3)$

8. $25 \div 5 + (7 + 2)$

9. $28 \div 4 + 28 \div 7$

10. $\dfrac{27}{9 - 2(3)}$

11. $8(2 + 9) - 40$

12. $7 + (4 + 2) \times 3$

13. $\dfrac{(6 - 2)}{(3 + 1)}$

14. $5 + 2 \times 4$

15. $\dfrac{8}{2} + \dfrac{18}{6}$

16. $6(3 + 7) - 4(4 - 2)$

17. $\dfrac{21}{(5 - 2)}$

18. $36 + \dfrac{12}{6}$

19. $9 \times 9 + 3 \times 4$

20. $100 - 2 \times 50$

21. $(8 + 9) \times (4 + 3)$

22. $\dfrac{(3 + 7 + 10)}{(2 + 3)}$

23. $\dfrac{63}{9} + 4$

24. $\dfrac{55}{11} \times \dfrac{81}{(3 + 6)}$

≡ Set-Up Problems

Many problems on the GED Mathematics Test require you to identify the correct way to set up a problem rather than to work out the solution. Practice learning how to set up word problems will improve your ability to solve other problems.

Setting up a problem involves being able to write correct mathematical expressions when given written information. Study the following examples.

Written Information	Mathematical Expression
1. the amount earned after working 40 hours per week at \$5 per hour for 10 weeks	$40 \times \$5 \times 10$
2. the average time worked per day if you worked 5 hours Monday, 7 hours Tuesday, and 6 hours Wednesday	$\frac{5 + 7 + 6}{3}$
3. the cost of 2 cans of tomatoes if they sell for 3 for \$2.	$\frac{\$2}{3} \times 2$

Approximately 25% of the problems on the GED Mathematics Test are set-up problems like the example below.

Example: Elliot saved \$15 in January, \$35 in February, and \$45 in March. Which expression could be used to find the average amount Elliot saved each month?

(1) $\$15 + \$35 + \frac{\$45}{3}$

(2) $\frac{\$15 + \$35}{3} + \$45$

(3) $\frac{\$15 + \$35 + \$45}{3}$

(4) $\frac{\$15}{3} + \$35 + \$45$

(5) $\$15 + \frac{\$35}{3} + \$45$

Finding the average amount Elliot saved requires you to add the three amounts and divide the total by 3. Although there are addition and division operations in each of the answer choices, only option (3) indicates the correct order of operations.

Options (1), (4), and (5) show adding three numbers, but only one of the numbers is divided by 3. Option (2) shows the sum of two numbers divided by 3.

Since you are not required to find the solution, stop after you have identified the correct set-up.

 **See Also** | Mathematics   Unit 1, Lessons 10 and 11

≡ Set-Up Problems Practice

Directions: Write a numerical expression for each of the exercises below on the lines provided.

Example: One yard of fabric costs $4.98. Find the cost of 5 yards of the same fabric.
Numerical Expression: $5 \times \$4.98$ or $5(\$4.98)$

1. Marcus earned $110 a day for 5 days. Write a numerical expression which shows Marcus's hourly wage if he worked 40 hours per week.

   Numerical Expression: _____.

2. An elderly aunt died and left $1,500 to be divided among three nieces. One niece is to receive $375, and the second niece is to receive $700. Write a numerical expression to show how much the third niece is to receive.

   Numerical Expression: _____.

3. Elena bought 5 pounds of grapes at 59 cents per pound and 4 pounds of ground beef at $1.69 a pound. If she gave the clerk $20, write a numerical expression to represent the change that she should receive.

   Numerical Expression: _____.

4. One dozen eggs cost $1.09. Write a numerical expression to show the cost of 1 egg.

   Numerical Expression: _____.

5. Steve earns $19,500 annually. Floyd earns $1,100 per month. Write a numerical expression that shows how much more per year Steve earns than Floyd.

   Numerical Expression: _____.

6. Carson's Department Store makes a profit of $12.50 for each Stylewise watch that is sold. Write a numerical expression to show the number of watches that must be sold to make a profit of $150.

   Numerical Expression: _____.

7. A sixty-minute television program has 5 commercial breaks. Each break lasts 2 minutes. Write a numerical expression that shows the actual length of the program.

   Numerical Expression: _____.

8. A bolt of fabric contained 30 yards of fabric. The store sold twenty-seven yards of the fabric at the regular price of $3 per yard. The rest was sold at the sale price of $1 per yard. Write a numerical expression that shows the total amount of money the store received for the fabric from the bolt.

   Numerical Expression: _____.

Directions: Choose the <u>best answer</u> to each item.

1. Ernesto is paid $125 a week plus a $5 commission on each item that he sells in 28 days. Which numerical expression below determines the number of items he sold?

   (1) $125 + \frac{\$160}{\$5}$
   (2) $125 + $5(28)
   (3) $\frac{\$125}{(28)(\$5)}$
   (4) $125 − $5(28)
   (5) Not enough information is given.

2. Last year, the weekly cost of food for a family of four was $100. This year, the weekly cost is $110. Which of the following expressions shows the difference in the average cost per year for one family member?

   (1) $110 ÷ 4
   (2) ($110 − $100) ÷ 4
   (3) ($110 ÷ 4) + ($100 ÷ 4)
   (4) ($110 ÷ 4) + $100
   (5) 52($110 − $100) ÷ 4

<u>Item 3</u> refers to the following diagram.

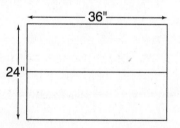

3. Which expression determines the number of books, each 2" thick, that will be needed to fill the two shelves of the bookcase in the diagram above?

   (1) 2 + (36 ÷ 2)
   (2) (36 ÷ 2) − 2
   (3) 2(36 ÷ 2)
   (4) (2 × 2) + 36
   (5) (2 × 2) ÷ 36

4. Which expression below determines the amount of each of Marcy's 24 monthly car payments if the total amount of her car loan is $6,096?

   (1) 24 + $6,096
   (2) $6,096 − 24
   (3) 24($6,096)
   (4) $\frac{\$6,096}{24}$
   (5) $12 \times \frac{\$6,096}{24}$

5. A postal carrier had three packages that had weights of 40 lb., 31 lb., and 51 lb. Which of the following expressions determines the average weight of the packages?

   (1) (40 + 31 + 51) ÷ 3
   (2) (40 + 31) + 51 ÷ 3
   (3) 40 + 31 ÷ 51 + 3
   (4) 3(40 + 31) + 51
   (5) 40 + 31 + 51(3)

6. Calvin drives 657 miles per week going to and from work. His car averages 18 miles per gallon of gas. Which expression below determines the total distance that Calvin travels in 3 weeks?

   (1) 3(657)
   (2) 657 + 3
   (3) 657 − 3
   (4) 657 ÷ 3
   (5) 657 ÷ 18 × 1.09

Fractions: Computation Practice

Review the rules for addition, subtraction, multiplication, and division of fractions in *Steck-Vaughn GED Mathematics* or *Steck-Vaughn Complete GED Preparation*.

<u>Directions:</u> Enter the answers on the lines provided.

1. What is the quotient when $\frac{1}{3}$ is divided by $\frac{3}{4}$? _____

2. What is the product of $\frac{5}{8}$ times 16? _____

3. If you multiply 32 times $\frac{13}{16}$, what is the product? _____

4. What is the difference between $21\frac{3}{10}$ and $13\frac{1}{4}$? _____

5. What is the sum of $\frac{7}{10}$ and $\frac{11}{30}$? _____

6. What is the sum of $8\frac{2}{5}$, $14\frac{7}{10}$, and $9\frac{9}{10}$? _____

7. If you divide 6 by $1\frac{1}{2}$, what is the quotient? _____

8. Divide $4\frac{1}{4}$ by $2\frac{4}{5}$. _____

9. Find the product of $2\frac{1}{3}$ times $1\frac{1}{5}$. _____

10. What is the difference between 6 and $5\frac{5}{6}$? _____

11. Add $12\frac{1}{4}$, $5\frac{13}{16}$, $4\frac{5}{8}$, and $3\frac{1}{2}$. _____

12. What does $14\frac{1}{8}$ minus $13\frac{1}{2}$ equal? _____

13. Find the product of $1\frac{3}{4}$ times 3. _____

14. What is the quotient of $1\frac{2}{3}$ divided by $2\frac{2}{3}$? _____

15. If you divide $\frac{3}{5}$ by 8, what is the quotient? _____

16. What is the total of $7\frac{2}{3}$, $5\frac{1}{6}$, and $3\frac{1}{12}$? _____

17. Find the difference between $9\frac{3}{8}$ and $5\frac{9}{16}$. _____

18. What is the sum of $15\frac{3}{8}$ and 9? _____

19. What is the product of 6 times $1\frac{1}{2}$ times $3\frac{3}{4}$? _____

20. What is the difference between $11\frac{1}{2}$ and $2\frac{1}{3}$? _____

21. Add $25\frac{3}{4}$ and $21\frac{5}{8}$. _____

22. Subtract $17\frac{5}{32}$ from 35. _____

 See Also

Mathematics
Complete Preparation

Unit 1, Lessons 5–8 and 11
Unit 7, Fractions

 **Fractions I**

Directions: Choose the <u>best answer</u> to each item.

1. The American Cab Company charges its riders $1.05 for the first $\frac{1}{4}$ mile of a trip and 35 cents for each additional $\frac{1}{4}$ mile. How much will a rider pay for a 5-mile trip?

   (1) $5.60
   (2) $6.65
   (3) $7.70
   (4) $8.00
   (5) $9.20

2. A distance runner ran $5\frac{1}{2}$ miles in the first hour and $6\frac{3}{8}$ miles in the second hour. At the end of the third hour, the runner was 18 miles from the starting point. How many miles did she run in the third hour?

   (1) $5\frac{1}{2}$
   (2) $6\frac{1}{8}$
   (3) $6\frac{3}{8}$
   (4) $7\frac{1}{8}$
   (5) $11\frac{7}{8}$

3. If a regional bus is scheduled to go a distance of $87\frac{1}{2}$ miles in $2\frac{1}{2}$ hours, what average speed must the bus travel?

   (1) 20 mph
   (2) 25 mph
   (3) 30 mph
   (4) 35 mph
   (5) 40 mph

4. An automobile wheel goes $9\frac{1}{6}$ feet in one revolution. How many times does it revolve in 5,280 feet?

   (1) 576
   (2) 800
   (3) 1,056
   (4) 1,320
   (5) 2,640

5. A bolt of fabric contained 25 yards of fabric. Three pieces of fabric $3\frac{1}{2}$ yards long were cut from the bolt. Next, 5 pieces of fabric $1\frac{1}{4}$ yards long were cut. How many yards of fabric remained on the bolt?

   (1) $1\frac{1}{4}$
   (2) $3\frac{1}{2}$
   (3) $8\frac{1}{4}$
   (4) $17\frac{1}{2}$
   (5) $23\frac{3}{4}$

6. A stack of books is $21\frac{7}{8}$ inches high. If each book is $\frac{5}{8}$ inch thick, how many books are in the stack?

   (1) 35
   (2) 40
   (3) 64
   (4) 175
   (5) 1,400

7. An architect's drawing was drawn so the scale of $\frac{1}{2}$ inch represented 6 feet. What was the actual height of a wall marked $4\frac{1}{2}$ inches high?

   (1) 9 ft.
   (2) 18 ft.
   (3) 27 ft.
   (4) 36 ft.
   (5) 54 ft.

8. If it takes $4\frac{3}{4}$ ounces of tint to mix one gallon of paint to the desired color, how many ounces of tint will be needed for 5 gallons?

   (1) 19
   (2) 20
   (3) 23
   (4) $23\frac{3}{4}$
   (5) 95

 **Fractions II**

Directions: Choose the <u>best answer</u> to each item.

1. If Juan reads one page in $1\frac{1}{5}$ minutes, how many minutes will it take him to complete the last 125 pages?

   (1)   25
   (2)   50
   (3)   60
   (4)   100
   (5)   150

2. Poole Electronics makes seventy-five tape recorders per eight-hour shift. If the quality control inspectors rejected $\frac{1}{5}$ of the tape recorders made on one shift, how many tape recorders were acceptable?

   (1)   15
   (2)   25
   (3)   60
   (4)   65
   (5)   70

3. Mr. and Mrs. Woods needed 84 square feet of ceramic tile to remodel their home. If the average weight for each square foot of tile was $6\frac{1}{4}$ pounds, how much did the tile needed for the job weigh?

   (1)   525
   (2)   250
   (3)   87.5
   (4)   84
   (5)   25

4. Warren had $24. He gave $\frac{1}{3}$ of the money to his daughter and spent $\frac{1}{2}$ of the money on lunch for the two of them. Which expression shows how much he has left?

   (1) $\$24 - \frac{1}{3}(\$24)$
   (2) $\$24 - \frac{1}{2}(\$24)$
   (3) $\$24 - \left(\frac{1}{3} + \frac{1}{2}\right)(\$24)$
   (4) $\frac{1}{3}(\$24) + \frac{1}{2}(\$24)$
   (5) $\left(\frac{1}{3} + \frac{1}{2}\right)(\$24)$

Item 5 refers to the following diagram.

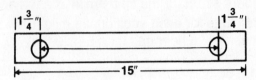

5. What is the distance between the center of the holes if 1 inch represents $4\frac{1}{2}$ feet?

   (1) $3\frac{1}{2}$ ft.
   (2)   11 ft.
   (3) $11\frac{1}{2}$ ft.
   (4) $13\frac{1}{4}$ ft.
   (5) $51\frac{3}{4}$ ft.

6. A dress designer must order the fabric to fill an order of 150 dresses of one style and one size. If one dress requires $3\frac{1}{2}$ yards of fabric, how many yards of fabric are needed to make the dresses?

   (1)   525
   (2)   475
   (3)   450
   (4)   425
   (5)   400

Item 7 refers to the following diagram.

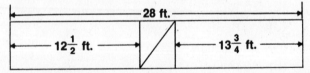

Note: Diagram is not drawn to scale.

7. Which statement determines the width of the gate in the diagram above?

   (1) $28 - 12\frac{1}{2}$
   (2) $28 - 13\frac{3}{4}$
   (3) $12\frac{1}{2} + 13\frac{3}{4}$
   (4) $28 - (12\frac{1}{2} + 13\frac{3}{4})$
   (5) $28 + (12\frac{1}{2} + 13\frac{3}{4})$

≣Decimals: Computation Practice

Review the rules for addition, subtraction, multiplication, and division of decimals in *Steck-Vaughn GED Mathematics* or *Steck-Vaughn Complete GED Preparation*.

Directions: Enter each answer on the lines provided.

1. What is the product of .04 and .09? _____

2. What is the sum of 1.9, 98, and 53? _____

3. Find the product of .368 times .62. _____

4. What is the quotient when 135.072 is divided by 1.44? _____

5. What is the difference between .7 and .35? _____

6. What is the sum of 1.853 and 8.1? _____

7. If you divide .8936 by 4, what is the quotient? _____

8. Add .1692, .3, and 15.8. _____

9. What is the difference between $50 and $25.25? _____

10. If you multiply 70.48 times .043, what is the product? _____

11. What is the difference between $700 and $446.58? _____

12. If you divide 265.2 by .39, what is the quotient? _____

13. What does $14.59 minus $7.00 equal? _____

14. What is the total of .80, 4, and .049? _____

15. What is the product of $14.25 times 11? _____

16. Find the difference between .8 and .007. _____

17. Find the product of .8 times .007. _____

18. What is the sum of $3.90 and $.98? _____

19. What is the quotient when 6.915 is divided by 15? _____

20. Divide 135.072 by .72. _____

21. Subtract .005 from .09. _____

22. Find the quotient of 375 ÷ 90 rounded to the nearest tenth. _____

See Also   Mathematics   Unit 1, Lessons 9–11
                Complete Preparation   Unit 7, Decimals

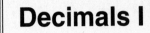

Directions: Use the steps for solving word problems. Choose the best answer to each item.

1. The Busy Bee Nursery sells 150 potted plants to the local grocery store at the wholesale price of $7.95 each. When the same plants are sold retail, each plant costs $10.95. What is the difference between the wholesale and retail prices for 150 plants?

   (1) $ 150.00
   (2) $ 450.00
   (3) $ 450.50
   (4) $1,192.00
   (5) $1,642.00

2. A loan of $1,500 will be repaid in 36 installment payments of $57.75 each. What is the finance charge for the loan?

   (1) $ 173.25
   (2) $ 346.50
   (3) $ 579.00
   (4) $1,500.00
   (5) $2,079.00

3. Best Builders charges $51.75 per square foot to build a two-car garage. What would be the total cost of a two-car garage that is 110 square feet in area?

   (1) $5,000.00
   (2) $5,175.00
   (3) $5,200.25
   (4) $5,692.50
   (5) $5,792.25

4. Mr. and Mrs. Montgomery sold 150 shares of stock at $37.75. If they originally paid $25.85 for each share, what was their profit on the sale of the stock?

   (1) $ 129.25
   (2) $ 188.75
   (3) $1,785.00
   (4) $3,877.50
   (5) $5,662.50

5. Mrs. Bertucci purchased a new sofa, paying $200 down. She agreed to pay $40.25 monthly for one year. What total amount will Mrs. Bertucci pay for the couch?

   (1) $402.50
   (2) $483.00
   (3) $683.00
   (4) $805.00
   (5) $966.00

6. Ernestine works at Brite Cleaners. She earns $70 a week, plus $.25 for each shirt she presses. If Ernestine earns $95 for one week, how many shirts did she press?

   (1)   50
   (2)   100
   (3)   150
   (4)   200
   (5)   250

7. Manuel wrote 4 checks for the following amounts: $43.21, $221.20, $32.50, and $150.59. The bank charged $.15 per check. How much was left in the account if his opening balance was $547.73?

   (1) $448.10
   (2) $447.50
   (3) $100.83
   (4) $100.23
   (5) $ 99.63

8. AutoParts store sells oil by the case, 12 quarts for $9.48. Which expression shows how much David will pay for 3 quarts of oil?

   (1) $\frac{\$9.48}{12}$
   (2) $\frac{\$9.48}{3}$
   (3) $\$9.48 \times \frac{12}{3}$
   (4) $\frac{\$9.48}{12} \times 3$
   (5) $\$9.48 \times 12 \times 3$

Directions: Choose the best answer to each item.

1. Leon bought the economy 15-pound package of flat head nails at Kissel's Hardware for $.98 a pound. Which of the following statements gives the best estimate of the amount he will spend on the nails?

   (1) $1.00(15)
   (2) $1.00 + 15
   (3) $1.00 − 15
   (4) $1.00 ÷ 15
   (5) 15 − $1.00

2. Maria drove 3,257.8 miles from Miami, Florida to Portland, Oregon. What was the odometer reading before the trip began if the reading after the trip was 27,329?

   (1) 30,586.8
   (2) 30,586.2
   (3) 24,072.2
   (4) 24,071.8
   (5) 24,071.2

3. A three-pound bag of apples can be purchased wholesale for $2.98. How many bags can a supermarket purchase for $149?

   (1) 100
   (2) 85
   (3) 75
   (4) 50
   (5) 25

4. A column weighs 15.7 pounds per linear foot. If this column is 35.4 feet long, how many pounds does the column weigh?

   (1) 555.78
   (2) 525
   (3) 247.8
   (4) 177
   (5) 157

5. An order for 52 legal size note pads costs $24.50. What is the cost per pad to the nearest cent?

   (1) $.47
   (2) $.48
   (3) $.49
   (4) $.50
   (5) $.60

6. The McCray Hobby Shop bought 550 model car kits to sell during the year. If each model kit costs $3.98, what was the total cost to the store?

   (1) $4,400
   (2) $3,980
   (3) $2,300
   (4) $2,200
   (5) $2,189

7. What is the total cost of six battery-operated screwdrivers for $19.98 each? Include the cost of 24 batteries that sell two for $1.79.

   (1) $ 25.06
   (2) $ 21.48
   (3) $ 42.96
   (4) $119.88
   (5) $141.36

8. As Mrs. Peterson puts grocery items in her cart, she estimates the total amount she is spending. The prices of six items she put in her cart were $3.99, $2.06, $0.87, $0.99, $2.85, and $7.56. The total cost of the items is between what two amounts?

   (1) $14 and $15
   (2) $15 and $16
   (3) $16 and $18
   (4) $18 and $20
   (5) $20 and $22

≡ Data Analysis
Mean, Median, and Number Series

Some problems on the GED Mathematics Test will test your ability to determine the <u>pattern</u> of a series, or the <u>mean</u> and <u>median</u> of a set of numbers. Each of these terms is defined below. Study the definitions and examples before completing the exercises.

The numbers 2, 4, 6, 8, and 10 form a <u>number series</u> or a special counting pattern. If you were asked to give the next two terms to this series, 12 and 14 would follow. The special counting pattern of this series is to increase each term by two. The numbers in the second number series increase by three.

Examples: 2, 4, 6, 8, 10, <u>12</u>, <u>14</u>
            3, 6, 9, 12, 15, <u>18</u>, <u>21</u>

To find the <u>mean</u> or <u>average</u> of a set of numbers, first determine the sum of the numbers. Then divide the sum by the number of numbers in the set.

Example: Find the mean of 5, 6, 7, 8, and 9

        5
        6
        7   Add 5 + 6 + 7 + 8 + 9 = 35.
        8
       +9   Divide 35 by the number of numbers you added (5).
       ---
       35   ÷ 5 = 7
The average of the numbers in this set is 7.

The <u>median</u> of a set of numbers is the middle value, so that the same number of values fall above the middle value as fall below the middle value. If there is an odd number of values in the set, the median is the middle value. In the number set 1, 2, 3, 4, and 5, the median is 3 because two of the numbers are above 3 and two are below. When there is an even number of values in the number set, the median lies between the two middle values and is computed to be the average of those two middle numbers. In the number set 2, 3, 4, and 5, the numbers 3 and 4 are the middle values. Three added to four, divided by two, is 3.5. Therefore, the median of the number set 2, 3, 4, and 5 is 3.5. Note that to find the median the numbers in the set must be arranged in order from smallest to largest or from largest to smallest.

Examples: 1, 2, <u>3</u>, 4, 5
            2, 3, <u>3.5</u>, 4, 5

Mathematics
Complete Preparation

Unit 1, Lesson 15
Unit 7, Ratio and Proportion

≡Mean, Median, and Number Series Practice

Directions: Enter the answers on the lines provided.

1. What is the average (mean) of 7.3, 8.4, 8.0, and 3.9? _____

2. What is the mean of the test scores? 97, 72, 89, 90, 90, and 87 _____

3. Determine the median of 185, 152, 165, and 163. _____

4. Determine the median of 53°, 56°, 57°, 58°, 59°, 61°, and 62°. _____

5. What is the next term in the series 48, 24, 12, 6? _____

6. What is the next term in the series 4, 8, 16, 32? _____

7. On the Police Officer Examination, 30 men scored an average of 80 points on the test. On the

   same examination, 20 women scored an average of 88 points. What was the mean score for both

   men and women? _____

8. During a five-month period, premium gas sold for the following prices: $1.35, $1.39, $1.43, $1.47,

   and $1.48 a gallon. What was the average price of gas during these months? Round to the

   nearest hundredth. _____

9. Find the median salary of those listed below. _____

   | $13,500 | $14,225 | $24,375 | $22,650 | $14,900 |
   | $68,000 | $20,750 | $41,175 | $24,500 | |

Items 10 and 11 refer to the following information.

Five houses on Elm Street cost $65,500, $56,000, $49,250, $32,750, and $43,600.

10. What is the mean (average) cost of a house on Elm Street? _____

11. What is the median cost of a house on Elm Street? _____

12. What is the next term is the series 1.5, 2.0, 2.5, 3.0? _____

13. What is the next term in the series $\frac{1}{4}$, $\frac{1}{2}$, $\frac{3}{4}$, 1, $1\frac{1}{4}$? _____

14. Nancy packs bundles of wrapping paper in boxes for a company. She recorded the number of

    boxes she packed each hour for five hours. She packed 27, 34, 29, 32, and 30 boxes. What was

    the mean (average) number of boxes she packed per hour? _____

15. In a bowling tournament, Ricardo bowled 192, 208, 186, 200, and 179 in his first five games. What

    is the median of Ricardo's scores? _____

≡Probability

Probability is defined as the chance a given event or action will occur. The probability that an event will occur is the ratio of the number of favorable outcomes to the number of all possible outcomes that could happen at the same time or in the same place. The probability of an event, $P(E)$, can be expressed as a fraction, such as $\frac{1}{2}$.

Example 1: Before a football game, the referee tosses a two-sided coin. The team that wins the toss chooses whether its team will start the game by kicking or receiving the ball. When the referee tossed the coin, one team captain called heads.

There are two possible outcomes—heads or tails. Each outcome is equally likely to occur. There is only one favorable outcome for the team captain who called heads. The probability that the coin will land heads up is 1 out of 2, or $\frac{1}{2}$. So,

$$\text{Probability of Heads} = \frac{1}{2} = \frac{\text{number of favorable outcomes}}{\text{number of possible outcomes}}$$

Example 2: A used car lot has 12 cars in 5 different colors as shown below. If you choose one car at random, what is the probability that the car is red?

| blue | black | red | red | yellow | green |
| black | blue | yellow | green | red | red |

The total number of cars on the lot is 12. This is the number of possible outcomes. There are 4 red cars on the lot. This is the number of favorable outcomes. So,

$$P(E) = \frac{4 \text{ red cars}}{12 \text{ possible outcomes}} = \frac{4}{12} = \frac{1}{3}$$

Example 3: What is the probability of spinning an even number when you spin this spinner? List all the possible outcomes for spinning the spinner once. There are 6 possible outcomes (1, 2, 3, 4, 5, 6).

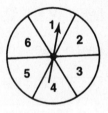

Find how many chances are possible of spinning an even number on one spin. There are three favorable outcomes (2, 4, 6). So,

$$P(E) = \frac{3 \text{ even outcomes}}{6 \text{ possible outcomes}} = \frac{3}{6} = \frac{1}{2}$$

The probability of spinning an even number is one out of every two spins.

 See Also

Mathematics
Complete Preparation

Unit 1, Lesson 15
Unit 7, Ratio and Proportion

 **Probability**

Directions: Choose the best answer to each item.

1. A flower vase of carnations contains 3 white, 4 blue, 2 yellow, and 6 red carnations. If one flower is randomly picked, what is the probability that it will be white?

   (1) $\frac{2}{15}$
   (2) $\frac{1}{5}$
   (3) $\frac{1}{3}$
   (4) $\frac{2}{5}$
   (5) $\frac{3}{5}$

2. Elena's shopping bag had 4 cans of soup, 3 cans of mixed vegetables, and 5 cans of corn. If she selects one can from the bag without looking, what is the probability that on the first pick Elena will choose a can of mixed vegetables?

   (1) $\frac{1}{5}$
   (2) $\frac{1}{4}$
   (3) $\frac{1}{3}$
   (4) $\frac{5}{12}$
   (5) $\frac{7}{12}$

3. Candy is packaged in a box that has 4 rows with 6 pieces per row. One row has nuts, another has creme fillings, another has jelly, and the last has cherries. When randomly selecting one candy, what is the probability of selecting a creme filled piece of candy?

   (1) $\frac{4}{5}$
   (2) $\frac{3}{5}$
   (3) $\frac{1}{2}$
   (4) $\frac{2}{5}$
   (5) $\frac{1}{4}$

4. Juan has $1.50 in change in a mason jar. There are 15 nickels, 5 dimes, and 25 pennies. If Juan randomly selects one coin, what is the probability of selecting a dime on the first try?

   (1) $\frac{1}{9}$
   (2) $\frac{1}{3}$
   (3) $\frac{1}{2}$
   (4) $\frac{5}{9}$
   (5) $\frac{2}{3}$

5. The queen of hearts, clubs, spades, and diamonds were placed face down on a table. What is the probability that the queen of spades will be picked on the first random draw of one card?

   (1) $\frac{1}{2}$
   (2) $\frac{1}{3}$
   (3) $\frac{1}{4}$
   (4) $\frac{1}{5}$
   (5) $\frac{1}{6}$

6. In a gumball machine, there is a mixture of 50 red gumballs and 50 yellow gumballs. What is the probability of getting a red gumball if you place a coin in the machine and receive one gumball?

   (1) $\frac{1}{2}$
   (2) $\frac{1}{3}$
   (3) $\frac{1}{4}$
   (4) $\frac{1}{5}$
   (5) $\frac{1}{6}$

≣Measurement: Computation Practice

Some problems on the GED Mathematics Test have mixed measures. Study the example below.

Example: Margaret had three packages of ground beef. The first weighed 5 pounds, the second weighed 32 ounces, and the third weighed 6 pounds. What was the total number of pounds of ground beef she purchased?

Since the answer is required in pounds, the 32 ounces must be changed to 2 pounds. The next step is to add the three like measures.

$$5 \text{ pounds} + 2 \text{ pounds} + 6 \text{ pounds} = 13 \text{ pounds}$$

The following exercise gives you practice in changing measures and solving measurement problems.

<u>Directions:</u> Enter your answers on the lines below.

1. 60 seconds = _____ minute

2. 12 months = _____ year

3. 52 weeks = _____ year

4. 4 quarts = _____ gallon

5. _____ hours = 1 day

6. _____ years = 1 decade

7. _____ inches = 1 foot

8. _____ ounces = 1 pound

9. _____ feet = 1 mile

10. 2,000 pounds = _____ ton

11. 3 feet = _____ yard

12. 2 pints = _____ quart

13. _____ inches = 1 yard

14. 4 gallons, 2 pints = _____ quarts

15. 6 pounds, $3\frac{1}{2}$ ounces = _____ ounces

16. 7 hours, 15 minutes = _____ minutes

17. 2 tons, 350 pounds = _____ pounds

18. 44 ounces = _____ pounds

19. 14 quarts = _____ gallons

20. 12 feet = _____ yards

21. Sue weighed 8 pounds 1 ounce at birth. Her brother weighed 17 ounces more than Sue. How much did Sue's brother weigh at birth? _____

22. Jan's truck can carry a 2-ton load of lumber. If the truck is loaded with 2,200 pounds at its first stop, how much can be added at the next stop? _____

23. If one gallon of milk costs $2, what is the cost per quart? _____

24. How many 10-inch pieces can be cut from a board that is 12 feet long? How much is left over?

_____

▶See Also   Mathematics Complete Preparation   Unit 1, Lesson 16 Unit 7, Measurement Systems

Directions: Choose the best answer to each item.

1. A train left Springfield at 9:30 A.M. and arrived at Union Station in Chicago at 2:15 P.M. If the train averaged 52 miles per hour, what is the distance between Springfield and Chicago?

   (1) 208 miles
   (2) 211 miles
   (3) 221 miles
   (4) 247 miles
   (5) 280 miles

2. It takes a train 5 hours and 12 minutes to travel from New York to Boston. A plane can travel the same distance in 1 hour and 15 minutes. How much time is saved by traveling by plane?

   (1) 4 hours 57 minutes
   (2) 4 hours 3 minutes
   (3) 3 hours 57 minutes
   (4) 3 hours 3 minutes
   (5) Not enough information is given.

3. The bottling plant supervisor has to monitor the maximum weight of cans of soda being stored before distribution. If one case weighs 288 ounces and contains 24 cans, what is the maximum number of cases that can be stored in an area with a weight capacity of 3,456 pounds?

   (1) 288
   (2) 192
   (3) 24
   (4) 12
   (5) 11

4. During the last week, Leonard spent the following time studying for the postal examination.
   Mon.:   2 hr. 15 min.
   Tues.:   3 hr.
   Wed.:   45 min.
   Thurs.:   1 hr. 40 min.
   Fri.:   2 hr. 20 min.
   What was the average amount of time spent studying per day?

   (1) 2 hours
   (2) 3 hours
   (3) 4 hours
   (4) 5 hours
   (5) 6 hours

Item 5 refers to the following chart.

TOTAL POUNDS DELIVERED	SHIPPING CHARGE PER TIRE
100–499	$1.01
500–999	.97
1,000–1,499	.93
1,500–2,999	.89
3,000 +	.85

5. Patterson Tire received a delivery of 8 dozen tires. Each tire weighed 21 lb. 8 oz. According to the chart, what was the shipping charge for the tires received by Patterson Tire?

   (1) $81.60
   (2) $85.44
   (3) $89.28
   (4) $93.12
   (5) $96.96

≡ Percents: Computation Practice

<u>Directions:</u> Complete the chart below of commonly used fractions, decimals, and percents. Enter each answer in the appropriate space in the chart.

	FRACTION	DECIMAL	PERCENT		FRACTION	DECIMAL	PERCENT
1.	$\frac{1}{8}$	.125	12.5%	7.	$\frac{5}{8}$	————	————
2.	————	————	25%	8.	————	————	$66\frac{2}{3}$%
3.	————	$.33\frac{1}{3}$	————	9.	————	.75	————
4.	————	————	37.5%	10.	$\frac{4}{5}$	————	————
5.	$\frac{1}{2}$	————	————	11.	————	.875	————
6.	————	.60	————	12.	$\frac{9}{10}$	————	————

The percent formula is **base × rate = part.** The triangle shows the relationship of these three elements. Use this formula to find the missing element in a percent problem.

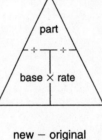

The percent increase or decrease is computed by subtracting the original amount from the new amount and dividing the difference by the original amount:

$$\frac{new - original}{original}$$

<u>Directions:</u> Enter your answers on the lines provided.

13. Find 125% of 90. _____

14. 3 is what percent of 5? _____

15. $\frac{1}{8}$% of 561 is what number? _____

16. 13 is what % of 25? _____

17. 34% of what number is 306?

_____

18. 45 is what percent of 90? _____

19. What number is 3% of 391? _____

20. 81 is 9% of what number? _____

21. 110% of what number is 22?

_____

22. 0.5% of 150 is what number?

_____

▶See Also   Mathematics   Unit 1, Lessons 11–14
Complete Preparation   Unit 7, Percents

Percents I

Directions: Use the steps for solving word problems. Choose the <u>best answer</u> to each item.

1. Yolanda earns $195 per week and pays 3% of her salary for health insurance. What does she pay <u>annually</u> for health insurance?

   (1) $195.00
   (2) $234.00
   (3) $304.20
   (4) $468.00
   (5) $585.00

2. Home Builder's Construction Company gave the Hendersons an estimate of "cost plus 40%" for a remodeling job. If the cost of materials is estimated at $5,770, how much would the total remodeling job cost?

   (1) $9,232.00
   (2) $8,078.00
   (3) $6,000.80
   (4) $5,770.00
   (5) $2,308.00

3. Shoes sold at the Shoe Express are discounted 25% off the original price. If a pair of shoes originally cost $46, calculate the sale price of the shoes.

   (1) $11.50
   (2) $23.00
   (3) $34.50
   (4) $46.00
   (5) $57.50

4. Mr. Garner is paid on a commission basis. His rate of commission is 20% of his total sales. How much did he sell this month if his commission was $240?

   (1) $ 240
   (2) $ 960
   (3) $1,200
   (4) $1,440
   (5) $4,800

5. As an apprentice carpenter, Grace earns $7.75 per hour. After her apprenticeship, her pay will increase to $11.75 per hour. By what percent of her current pay will her salary increase after she becomes a carpenter?

   (1) 40%
   (2) 45%
   (3) 51%
   (4) 52%
   (5) 60%

6. The cost of a haircut for senior citizens is lowered by 25% on Thursdays at the Style Center. If the original price is $7.00, what is the senior citizens' cost?

   (1) $1.75
   (2) $3.50
   (3) $4.00
   (4) $5.00
   (5) $5.25

7. Mr. Wilfred drove his cab 26,500 miles last year for the Island Taxi Company. This was 80% of the number of miles he drove the year before. How many miles did he drive the year before?

   (1) 21,200
   (2) 22,083
   (3) 31,800
   (4) 33,125
   (5) 47,700

8. Debra drove 120 miles on the first day and 80 miles on the second day of her vacation. She plans to drive 500 miles in all. Which expression represents the percent of the entire trip Debra drove in the first two days?

   (1) $80 + \frac{120}{500}$
   (2) $(80 + 120) \times 500$
   (3) $500 - (80 + 120)$
   (4) $\frac{(80 + 120)}{500}$
   (5) $\frac{500}{(80 + 120)}$

Directions: Choose the best answer to each item.

1. Lindsey earned $1,500 on her summer job. She spent $224 on school clothing and invested $750 in a savings certificate. What percent of her earnings was savings?

   (1) 10%
   (2) 20%
   (3) 30%
   (4) 40%
   (5) 50%

2. Melvin spends $6\frac{1}{4}$% of his monthly salary on transportation. If his salary is $1,600 a month, how much does he spend on transportation?

   (1) $ 96
   (2) $100
   (3) $200
   (4) $400
   (5) $450

3. The sales tax for a certain state is 7% on non-food items and 2.5% on food items. What would be the tax on a $25.25 purchase of non-food items?

   (1) $1.77
   (2) $1.65
   (3) $1.50
   (4) $ .63
   (5) $ .50

4. Ed Lee earned $200 a week plus a 15% commission on all sales greater than $1,000. If Mr. Lee's sales for one week were $2,500, what was his gross pay for that week?

   (1) $150
   (2) $325
   (3) $350
   (4) $425
   (5) $575

5. Value Village Lumber Company requires a minimum payment of 25% on all special order items. If Camella's order is $750, what is her minimum payment?

   (1) $125.25
   (2) $150.25
   (3) $175.25
   (4) $187.50
   (5) $562.50

6. Canfield Health Insurance Company pays 80% on all medical expenses over the $275 deductible. What will Canfield pay on medical expenses of $2,750?

   (1) $ 550
   (2) $ 770
   (3) $1,980
   (4) $2,200
   (5) $2,475

7. Rodriguez Office Supply has a job opening paying $15,000 a year. Wilson Office Supply has a similar position paying $1,025 per month. The higher paying position is what percent greater than the lower paying job?

   (1) 23%
   (2) 22%
   (3) 21%
   (4) 20%
   (5) 18%

8. Nita sells greeting cards for a commission of 40%. What are her total earnings on sales of $42.25, $34.20, and $35.45?

   (1) $13.68
   (2) $14.18
   (3) $16.90
   (4) $21.75
   (5) $44.76

Directions: Choose the best answer to each item.

Items 1–8 refer to the following pictograph.

Average Monthly Production of Paint for Great American Paint Company	
January	
February	
March	
April	
May	
June	
July	
August	
September	
October	
November	
December	

Key = 10,000 gallons

= 1,000 gallons

1. Which of the following represents the three lowest months of production of paint in ascending order?

   (1) August, January, and February
   (2) January, August, and February
   (3) January, February, and August
   (4) December, April, and October
   (5) January, August, and July

2. How many more gallons of paint were produced in April than in January?

   (1) 10,000
   (2) 20,000
   (3) 40,000
   (4) 60,000
   (5) 80,000

3. During which month was the production of paint the greatest?

   (1) April
   (2) May
   (3) September
   (4) October
   (5) December

4. Paint production in July and August represented what percent of the total in the production of paint? Round your answer to the nearest percent.

   (1) 89%
   (2) 25%
   (3) 11%
   (4) 10%
   (5) 5%

5. The total production of paint for January, July, and August exceeds which of the following pairs?

   (1) February and March
   (2) March and April
   (3) May and June
   (4) September and October
   (5) November and December

6. Which expression below determines the average monthly production of paint for March, June, and September?

   (1) $72,000 + 63,000 + 80,000$
   (2) $(72,000 + 63,000 + 80,000) \div 3$
   (3) $72,000 - 63,000 + (80,000) \div 3$
   (4) $(80,000 + 72,000) - (72,000) \div 3$
   (5) $(72,000 - 80,000) + (63,000) \div 3$

 **Circle Graphs**

Directions: Use the information from the following circle graph. Choose the <u>best answer</u> to each item.

<u>Items 1–4</u> refer to the following graph.

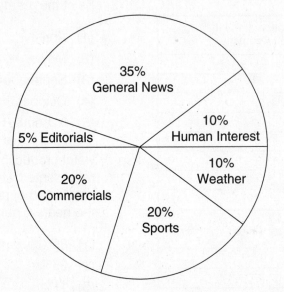

1. How many hours of human interest stories are scheduled daily?

    (1) 1.2
    (2) 2.4
    (3) 4.8
    (4) 8.4
    (5) 9.6

2. Which of the following represents 50% of the programming for the news network station?

    (1) editorials, commercials, and sports
    (2) commercials, sports, and weather
    (3) human interest, general news, and sports
    (4) general news, sports
    (5) human interest, weather, and editorials

3. Expressed as a fraction, what portion of the programming is devoted to editorials?

    (1) $\frac{1}{20}$
    (2) $\frac{1}{10}$
    (3) $\frac{1}{5}$
    (4) $\frac{1}{4}$
    (5) $\frac{7}{20}$

4. Which expression below determines the average number of hours spent on weather, human interest, and editorials?

    (1) $(2.4 + 2.4 + 1.2) \div 3$
    (2) $(8.4 + 4.8 + 1.2) \div 3$
    (3) $(1.2 + 8.4 + 4.8) \div 3$
    (4) $(4.8 + 4.8 + 2.4) \div 3$
    (5) $(1.2 + 4.8 + 4.8) \div 3$

Items 5–10 refer to the following graph.

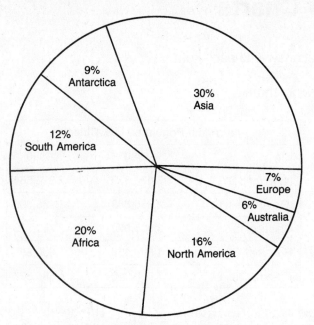

Approximately 58,000,000 square miles

5. Which continents have land masses greater than 9,000,000 square miles?

   (1) South America, Asia, and Australia
   (2) Europe, Africa, and Asia
   (3) North America, Asia, and Africa
   (4) Australia, Antarctica, and South America
   (5) Antarctica, Europe, and Africa

6. What is the approximate total square mileage of Antarctica and Australia?

   (1) 3,800,000
   (2) 5,300,000
   (3) 6,900,000
   (4) 8,700,000
   (5) 9,000,000

7. Which two continents together represent approximately 50% of Earth's land mass?

   (1) North America and Africa
   (2) North America and Asia
   (3) Africa and Asia
   (4) South America and North America
   (5) South America and Asia

8. Which continent represents approximately $\frac{1}{5}$ of Earth's land mass?

   (1) North America
   (2) Europe
   (3) Africa
   (4) Antarctica
   (5) Asia

9. Which expression can be used to approximate the difference in the total square miles between the largest and the smallest continents?

   (1) $30\% - 6\%$
   (2) $(.3 - .06) \times 58,000,000$
   (3) $.3(58,000,000) - .06$
   (4) $30\% + 6\% \times 58,000,000$
   (5) $\frac{58,000,000}{(.3 + .06)}$

10. What is the ratio of the land mass of Africa to the land mass of North America?

   (1) $\frac{4}{5}$
   (2) $\frac{3}{4}$
   (3) $\frac{5}{6}$
   (4) $\frac{6}{5}$
   (5) $\frac{5}{4}$

 **Charts**

Directions: Choose the best answer to each item.

Items 1–6 refer to the following chart.

Five Most Populated U.S. Cities		
City	1980	1990
New York, NY	7,071,639	7,322,564
Los Angeles, CA	2,966,850	3,485,398
Chicago, IL	3,005,072	2,783,726
Houston, TX	1,595,138	1,630,553
Philadelphia, PA	1,688,210	1,585,577

1. How many more people lived in New York, New York in 1990 than in 1980?

   (1)   35,415
   (2)   102,633
   (3)   221,346
   (4)   250,925
   (5)   518,548

2. What is the difference between the most populated city and the least populated city in 1980?

   (1)   45,310
   (2)   4,003,360
   (3)   4,104,789
   (4)   5,476,501
   (5)   5,619,800

3. The populations of which two cities decreased from 1980 to 1990?

   (1)   New York and Los Angeles
   (2)   Los Angeles and Chicago
   (3)   Chicago and Houston
   (4)   Houston and Philadelphia
   (5)   Philadelphia and Chicago

4. The greatest population increase between 1980 and 1990 occurred in which city?

   (1)   New York
   (2)   Los Angeles
   (3)   Chicago
   (4)   Houston
   (5)   Philadelphia

5. What was the average (mean) increase per year over the ten-year period for New York? (Round the answer to the nearest thousand.)

   (1)   25,000
   (2)   26,000
   (3)   30,000
   (4)   251,000
   (5)   300,000

6. What was the difference between the populations of the most populated city and the least populated city in 1990?

   (1)   429,367
   (2)   3,267,430
   (3)   5,736,987
   (4)   5,863,406
   (5)   6,327,456

Items 7–10 refer to the following chart.

Annual Health Care Spending per Person Listed by Age, 1993	
Age	Spending
0–5	$1,389
6–17	$ 730
18–44	$1,242
45–64	$2,402
65+	$4,840

Note: Table excludes older individuals living in nursing homes.

7. For which age category is annual health care spending the lowest?

(1) 0–5
(2) 6–17
(3) 18–44
(4) 45–64
(5) 65+

8. For which two age categories is annual health care spending about the same?

(1) 0–5 and 6–17
(2) 0–5 and 18–44
(3) 0–5 and 45–64
(4) 6–17 and 18–44
(5) 18–44 and 45–64

9. For which age category is annual health care spending more than two times the spending of the previous category?

(1) 6–17
(2) 18–44
(3) 45–64
(4) 65+
(5) Not enough information is given.

10. What is the average amount spent on annual health care for the age categories 18–44 and 45–64?

(1) $ 780.00
(2) $1,059.50
(3) $1,822.00
(4) $3,041.00
(5) $3,644.00

Items 11–14 refer to the following chart.

Number of Attempts to Climb Mt. McKinley in Alaska, 1988–1992		
Year	Attempts	Successes
1988	916	551
1989	1,009	517
1990	998	573
1991	935	553
1992	1,024	398

11. In which year was the ratio of attempts to successes about 2 to 1?

(1) 1988
(2) 1989
(3) 1990
(4) 1991
(5) 1992

12. In which year was the percent of successful climbs the greatest?

(1) 1988
(2) 1989
(3) 1990
(4) 1991
(5) 1992

13. What was the average number of successful climbs per year for the period 1988 through 1991?

(1) 438.8
(2) 518.4
(3) 547.0
(4) 548.0
(5) 548.5

14. Which of the following is the best estimate of the total number of attempts to climb Mt. McKinley from 1988 to 1992?

(1) 900
(2) 1,900
(3) 4,500
(4) 4,800
(5) 5,000

Items 1–6 refer to the following line graph.

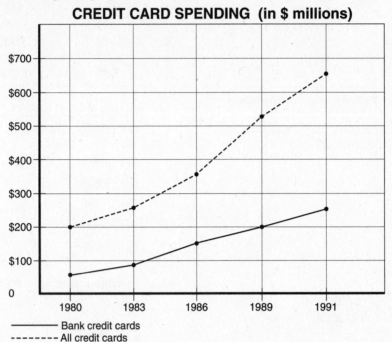

CREDIT CARD SPENDING (in $ millions)

——— Bank credit cards
- - - - - - All credit cards

1. How many dollars were spent using all credit cards in 1991?

   (1) $250 million
   (2) $550 million
   (3) $650 million
   (4) $800 million
   (5) $900 million

2. What percent of all credit card spending in 1980 was from bank credit cards?

   (1) 5%
   (2) 10%
   (3) 20%
   (4) 25%
   (5) 50%

3. The increase in all credit card spending from 1980 to 1991 is closest to what amount?

   (1) $200 million
   (2) $300 million
   (3) $350 million
   (4) $400 million
   (5) $450 million

4. What is the percent of increase in all credit card spending from 1983 to 1991?

   (1) 160%
   (2) 100%
   (3) 86%
   (4) 73%
   (5) 60%

5. During which time period was the increase in the dollars of bank credit card spending the greatest?

   (1) 1980–1983
   (2) 1983–1986
   (3) 1986–1989
   (4) 1989–1991
   (5) Not enough information is given.

6. Bank credit card spending represented what fraction of all credit card spending in 1991?

   (1) $\frac{1}{8}$
   (2) $\frac{1}{4}$
   (3) $\frac{2}{7}$
   (4) $\frac{5}{13}$
   (5) $\frac{7}{16}$

Directions: Choose the best answer to each item.

Items 1–6 refer to the following bar graph.

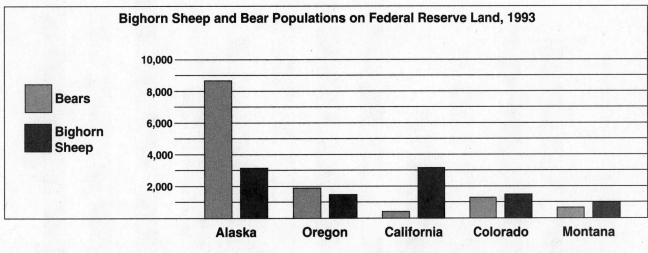

Bighorn Sheep and Bear Populations on Federal Reserve Land, 1993

1. Which two states had fewer than 1,000 bears on federal reserve lands in 1993?

   (1) Oregon and California
   (2) Oregon and Colorado
   (3) California and Colorado
   (4) California and Montana
   (5) Colorado and Montana

2. In which state were the most bears found on federal reserve lands?

   (1) Alaska
   (2) Oregon
   (3) California
   (4) Colorado
   (5) Montana

3. How many more bears were found on federal reserve lands in Oregon than in Colorado?

   (1)   250
   (2)   500
   (3)   750
   (4) 1,000
   (5) 1,500

4. In which two states were fewer bighorn sheep than bears found on federal reserve lands?

   (1) Alaska and California
   (2) Alaska and Oregon
   (3) California and Colorado
   (4) Colorado and Montana
   (5) Oregon and Colorado

5. How many bighorn sheep were found on federal reserve lands in California?

   (1)   500
   (2) 1,000
   (3) 1,500
   (4) 2,000
   (5) 3,000

6. How many more bears than bighorn sheep were on federal reserve lands in Alaska?

   (1) 3,500
   (2) 4,500
   (3) 5,500
   (4) 6,000
   (5) 8,500

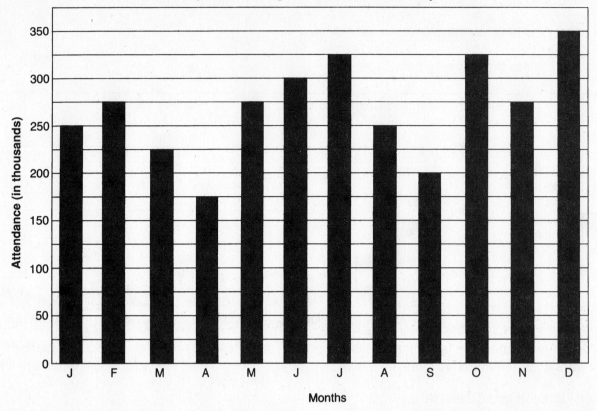

Raceway Indoor Racing Park Attendance Summary for 1994

7. Which of the following statements is <u>untrue</u>?

   (1) January and August were months with equal attendance.

   (2) February, May, and November were months with equal attendance.

   (3) July and October were months with equal attendance.

   (4) December was the month with the greatest attendance.

   (5) September was the month with the lowest attendance.

8. A semi-annual report presented the lowest attendance to the highest attendance by months. Which of the following expresses the order in which attendance was reported for the first half of the year?

   (1) January, February, March, April, May, and June

   (2) February, March, April, May, June, and January

   (3) March, April, May, June, January, and February

   (4) April, May, June, January, February, and March

   (5) April, March, January, February, May, and June

9. What was the mean attendance at Raceway Park during the months of January, June, August, and September?

(1) 125,000
(2) 150,000
(3) 175,000
(4) 200,000
(5) 250,000

10. What was the median number of people who attended Raceway Park during 1994?

(1) 175,000
(2) 200,000
(3) 262,500
(4) 275,000
(5) 300,000

11. To determine the total amount of proceeds (money taken in at the gate), what piece of information is needed?

(1) the cost of maintenance of the park
(2) the cost of the workers
(3) the price of the tickets for admission
(4) the cost of parking
(5) the cost of management

12. What was the average attendance for January, February, and March?

(1) 225,000
(2) 250,000
(3) 300,000
(4) 350,000
(5) 400,000

13. Which of the following expressions gives the average attendance for September, October, November, and December?

(1) $(200 + 325 + 275 + 350) \div 4$
(2) $(200 + 325 + 275 + 350)$
(3) $(250 + 275 + 225 + 175) \div 4$
(4) $(250 + 275 + 225 + 175)$
(5) $(400 + 325 + 250 + 200)$

14. If tickets cost $5 per person, what was the amount of money taken in by Raceway Park during June of 1994?

(1) $ 875,000
(2) $1,125,000
(3) $1,250,000
(4) $1,500,000
(5) $2,000,000

15. What is the difference between the highest and the lowest monthly attendance?

(1) 125,000
(2) 175,000
(3) 275,000
(4) 325,000
(5) 350,000

16. If $\frac{1}{3}$ of the tickets sold in June were senior citizens, about how many senior citizens attended the races in June?

(1) 900,000
(2) 600,000
(3) 300,000
(4) 200,000
(5) 100,000

17. About how many more people attended the park in the last three months than in the first three months?

(1) 100,000
(2) 175,000
(3) 200,000
(4) 225,000
(5) 300,000

18. About what percent of the total yearly attendance was the attendance in December?

(1) 8%
(2) 10%
(3) 11%
(4) 13%
(5) 18%

 **Mixed Practice**

Directions: Choose the best answer to each item.

Items 1–4 refer to the following pictograph.

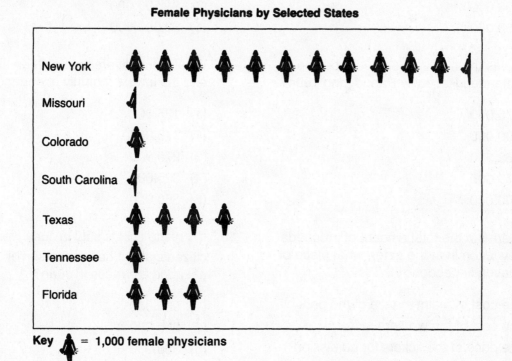

Female Physicians by Selected States

Key ♀ = 1,000 female physicians

1. Texas has how many more female physicians than South Carolina?

    (1)   500
    (2) 2,000
    (3) 2,500
    (4) 3,000
    (5) 3,500

2. Which of the following states have fewer than 1,000 female physicians?

    (1) Missouri and South Carolina
    (2) Tennessee and South Carolina
    (3) Colorado and Missouri
    (4) Tennessee and Missouri
    (5) Colorado and South Carolina

3. Calculate the average number of female physicians for the selected states shown. Round your answer to the nearest thousand.

    (1) 1,000
    (2) 2,000
    (3) 3,000
    (4) 4,000
    (5) 5,000

4. Which expression below determines the difference in the number of female physicians for Florida and Missouri?

    (1) $3(1,000) - 500$
    (2) $3(1,000) + 500$
    (3) $\frac{3(1,000)}{500}$
    (4) $4(1,000) - 500$
    (5) $4(1,000) + 500$

Items 5–7 refer to the following graph.

Sales of Cellular Phones

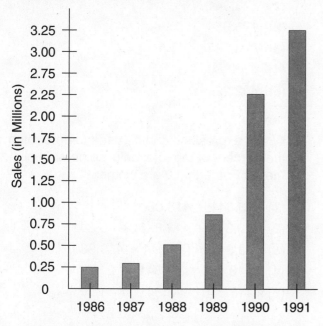

5. In which year was the greatest number of cellular phones sold?

   (1) 1986
   (2) 1988
   (3) 1989
   (4) 1990
   (5) 1991

6. Estimate the overall increase in sales from 1986 to 1991.

   (1) 2.0 million
   (2) 2.5 million
   (3) 2.8 million
   (4) 3.1 million
   (5) 3.4 million

7. Which expression below could be used to estimate the average sales per year for 1986, 1987, and 1988?

   (1) .25 + .3 + .5 ÷ 3
   (2) (.25 + .3 + .5) ÷ 3
   (3) (.25 + .3 + .5) × 3
   (4) (.25 + .3 + .5) − 3
   (5) .25 + .3 + .5 − 3

Items 8–10 refer to the following diagram.

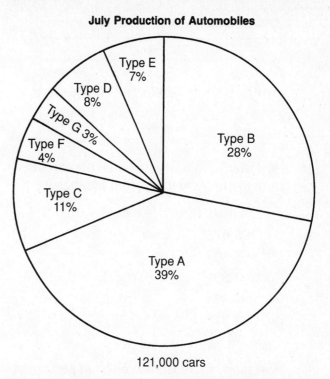

121,000 cars

8. During the month of July, how many Type E cars were produced by this auto company?

   (1) 3,630
   (2) 4,840
   (3) 8,470
   (4) 9,680
   (5) 13,310

9. Which type of car was the least-produced car by this company?

   (1) Type C
   (2) Type D
   (3) Type E
   (4) Type F
   (5) Type G

10. Express as a fraction the number of Type F cars produced during the month to the total number of cars produced?

   (1) $\frac{1}{2}$
   (2) $\frac{1}{5}$
   (3) $\frac{1}{16}$
   (4) $\frac{1}{20}$
   (5) $\frac{1}{25}$

Items 11–16 refer to the following chart.

1992 Enlisted Personnel in Armed Services

	Women	Men
Air Force	73,341	418,880
Army	83,681	656,859
Navy	56,970	524,356
Marines	9,300	184,549

11. How many more men enlisted personnel were in the Navy than in the Marines in 1992?

    (1) 105,476
    (2) 132,503
    (3) 234,331
    (4) 339,807
    (5) 472,310

12. How many more women enlisted personnel were in the Army than in the Air Force?

    (1) 10,000
    (2) 10,340
    (3) 16,371
    (4) 26,711
    (5) 74,376

13. What was the average number of women enlisted personnel in the Air Force, Army, and Navy in 1992? Round the answer to the nearest thousand.

    (1) 70,000
    (2) 71,000
    (3) 72,000
    (4) 73,000
    (5) 74,000

14. What was the total number of enlisted personnel in the Air Force in 1992?

    (1) 73,341
    (2) 193,854
    (3) 223,297
    (4) 418,880
    (5) 492,221

15. Which expression can be used to determine the percent of the total enlisted personnel in the Air Force that were women?

    (1) $73,341 \div 418,880$
    (2) $(73,341 + 418,880) \div 73,341$
    (3) $73,341 \div (73,341 + 418,880)$
    (4) $(418,880 - 73,341) \div 2$
    (5) $418,880 - 73,341$

16. Which branch of the Armed Services had the largest percent of women in 1992?

    (1) Air Force
    (2) Army
    (3) Navy
    (4) Marines
    (5) Not enough information is given.

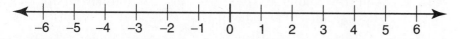# Properties of Numbers
Signed Numbers: Computation Practice

The number line below shows negative and positive numbers.

One way to determine the value of signed numbers is to use the number line. The numbers to the right of zero are positive numbers. The numbers to the left of zero are negative numbers. All numbers (both positive and negative) increase in value as you move to the right and decrease in value as you move to the left on the number line. Therefore, –7 is smaller in value than –3. Review the rules for addition, subtraction, multiplication, and division of signed numbers in *Steck-Vaughn GED Mathematics* or *Steck-Vaughn Complete GED Preparation* before solving the problems below.

<u>Directions:</u> Enter your answers on the lines below.

1. Express a temperature of 40° below 0. _____

2. Which is larger −3 or −5? _____

3. Which is larger −5 or 0? _____

4. Find the sum (−80) + (121). _____

5. Subtract (−2) from (+5). _____

6. What is the product of (−9)(−9)? _____

7. If you divide +1.25 by −.25, what is the quotient? _____

8. Find the difference of $\left(+2\frac{1}{2}\right)$ from $\left(-3\frac{1}{2}\right)$. _____

9. $\left(-4\frac{1}{4}\right) \div +2\frac{1}{2}$ equals what number? _____

10. Express a loss of 15 pounds. _____

11. Find the sum of (+93.118) + (−4.745). _____

12. Subtract (−2.009) from (−7.000). _____

13. Express a gain of 45 yards in a football game. _____

14. Express a $75 deposit in a checking account. _____

15. What is the sum of (−18.0164) + (+2.281) + (−35)? _____

16. Find the product of (+9)(−5)(0). _____

See Also   Mathematics   Unit 1, Lessons 19 and 21
Complete Preparation   Unit 7, Signed Numbers

Powers and Roots of Numbers

In your study of algebra, you will need to know how to find powers and roots of numbers.

Example 1: $2^4 = 2 \times 2 \times 2 \times 2 = 16$ You are asked to find 2 to the fourth power. The 2 is called the base and the raised 4 is called the exponent. The exponent tells you how many times to use the base as a factor; therefore 2^4 equals 16.

Example 2: $1^3 = 1 \times 1 \times 1 = 1$ One to any power is always one.

Example 3: $4^1 = 4$ A number raised to the first power is always the same number.

Example 4: $3^0 = 1$ Any number to the zero power (except 0) is always 1.

A <u>square root</u> is the opposite of a number to the second power. The sign for square root is $\sqrt{}$. When you see this symbol, ask yourself what number when multiplied by itself equals the number within the symbol.

Example 5: What is $\sqrt{16}$?   What number when multiplied by itself equals 16? That number is 4, because 4 times 4 equals 16.

Example 6: The square root of .25 is what number?   What number multiplied by itself equals .25? That number is .5 because $.5 \times .5 = .25$. Remember the rules for multiplying decimals.

<u>Scientific notation</u> is a way to write very large or very small numbers using powers of ten. Notice that the positive exponents for powers of ten equal the number of zeros in the large numbers and the negative powers of ten equal the zeros in the denominator of the fraction (or the number of decimal places).

$$10^0 = 1 \qquad\qquad 10^1 = 10 \qquad\qquad 10^2 = 100$$
$$10^3 = 1,000 \qquad 10^4 = 10,000 \qquad 10^5 = 100,000 \;\leftarrow\; 5 \text{ zeros}$$
$$10^{-1} = \tfrac{1}{10} = .1 \qquad 10^{-2} = \tfrac{1}{100} = .01$$
$$10^{-3} = \tfrac{1}{1,000} = .001 \qquad 10^{-4} = \tfrac{1}{10,000} \leftarrow 4 \text{ zeros} = .0001 \;\leftarrow\; 4 \text{ decimal places}$$

To write a number in scientific notation, move the decimal point until only one digit is to the left. This decimal is multiplied by the power of ten equal to the number of places moved. Movement to the left gives positive powers of ten and movement to the right gives negative powers of ten.

Example 7: Write 25,000 using scientific notation. $25,000 = 2.5 \times 10^4$
Move the decimal point until only the 2 remains to the left. Since you moved 4 places to the left, multiply by 10^4.

Example 8: Write 0.0056 in scientific notation. $0.0056 = 5.6 \times 10^{-3}$
Move the decimal point until only the 5 remains to the left. Since you moved 3 places to the right, multiply by 10^{-3}.

See Also

Mathematics Complete Preparation	Unit 2, Lessons 21 and 22 Unit 7, Exponents and Roots

≡Powers and Roots: Computation Practice

<u>Directions:</u> Use the examples on page 48 to help you evaluate the following expressions. Write your answers on the lines provided.

1. 8^2 _____

2. 1^5 _____

3. 2^3 _____

4. 6^2 _____

5. 9^3 _____

6. $\sqrt{16}$ _____

7. $\sqrt{25}$ _____

8. $\sqrt{100}$ _____

9. $\sqrt{.36}$ _____

10. $\sqrt{.81}$ _____

11. 3^4 _____

12. 12^2 _____

13. $\sqrt{169}$ _____

14. 11^3 _____

15. $\sqrt{121}$ _____

<u>Directions:</u> Write the following in scientific notation.

16. 3,500 _____

17. 29,000 _____

18. 85,700 _____

19. 126,000 _____

20. 3,000,000 _____

21. .005 _____

22. .0024 _____

23. .012 _____

24. .0001 _____

25. .0305 _____

<u>Directions:</u> Use the correct order of operations to evaluate the following expressions containing powers and roots.

Order of Operations

1. First, evaluate operations within parentheses.
2. Next, evaluate operations with powers and roots.
3. Perform multiplication and division operations from left to right.
4. Perform addition and subtraction operations from left to right.

---

26. $\sqrt{25} + (.05)^2$ _____

27. $3^2 - \sqrt{4} + 4^2$ _____

28. $\sqrt{144} - 2 \times 4$ _____

29. $\sqrt{100} + \sqrt{100} + \sqrt{121}$ _____

30. $\sqrt{169} \div (12 + 1)$ _____

31. $\sqrt{121} - 4^2$ _____

32. $15^2 + \sqrt{225}$ _____

33. $(5 + 3)^2$ _____

34. $7^2 - (4 + 2)$ _____

35. 9.3×10^3 _____

36. 2.73×10^{-2} _____

37. 4.0×10^2 _____

38. 1.9×10^{-3} _____

39. 8.26×10^4 _____

Directions: Choose the <u>best answer</u> to each item.

1. Which of the following pairs is <u>not</u> equal?

    (1) $\frac{1}{4}$ and .25
    (2) $\frac{4}{5}$ and .8
    (3) $\frac{7}{8}$ and .375
    (4) $1\frac{1}{7}$ and $\frac{8}{7}$
    (5) $\frac{15}{8}$ and $1\frac{7}{8}$

2. A bill for repairing the brakes on the Johnsons' car was $125.25. If 20% of the bill was for parts and the rest for labor, how much were the Johnsons charged for labor?

    (1) $ 25.25
    (2) $ 45.25
    (3) $ 80.00
    (4) $100.20
    (5) $105.25

3. Which of the following statements expresses a decrease?

    (1) a $50 deposit in a checking account
    (2) 12° above zero
    (3) 100 feet above sea level
    (4) 20 yard gain in football
    (5) a loss of 25 pounds

4. Which of the following equals $(9 - 3) \times 7$?

    (1) $9 - 3 \times 7$
    (2) $9 \times (7 - 3)$
    (3) $7 \times (9 - 3)$
    (4) $3 \times 7 - 9$
    (5) $(3 - 9) \times 7$

Items 5–7 refer to the following chart.

Television Set Ownership (1992)

Homes with	Number
Color TV sets	90,600,000
Black and white only	1,500,000
2 or more sets	60,000,000
1 set	32,100,000
Cable	56,200,000

Note: Numbers are based on 92,100,000 TV households, which is 98% of the total number of U.S. households.

5. How many more people own color sets than black and white only?

    (1) 1,500,000
    (2) 60,000,000
    (3) 89,100,000
    (4) 90,600,000
    (5) 92,100,000

6. What percent of all TV households has one TV? Round to the nearest tenth of a percent.

    (1) 2.9%
    (2) 3.5%
    (3) 32.1%
    (4) 34.9%
    (5) 65.2%

7. How many TV households do not have cable?

    (1) 1,500,000
    (2) 35,900,000
    (3) 56,200,000
    (4) 90,600,000
    (5) 92,100,000

8. The distance from Earth to the sun is about 92,900,000 miles. Which of the following expresses this number in scientific notation?

   (1) 9.29×10^7
   (2) 92.9×10^6
   (3) 929×10^5
   (4) 9.29×10^{-1}
   (5) 92.9×10^{-7}

9. Which are the next two numbers in the series 5, 13, 21, 29, 37?

   (1) 45 and 54
   (2) 45 and 53
   (3) 44 and 52
   (4) 43 and 49
   (5) 42 and 48

10. Ingall Hospital had 229 registered nurses on staff last year. Since then 15 nurses have retired, 3 nurses have been dismissed, and 16 new nurses have been hired. How many nurses are currently on staff at the hospital?

    (1) 244
    (2) 235
    (3) 232
    (4) 227
    (5) 220

11. A regular deck of 52 cards has 13 diamonds. If you select one card from the deck, what is the probability of drawing a diamond?

    (1) $\frac{1}{4}$
    (2) $\frac{4}{1}$
    (3) $\frac{3}{4}$
    (4) $\frac{4}{3}$
    (5) $\frac{2}{1}$

12. Which is an equal fraction, decimal, and percent?

    (1) $\frac{1}{2}$ .5 5%
    (2) $\frac{2}{5}$ .2 20%
    (3) $\frac{3}{4}$ .75 7.5%
    (4) $\frac{5}{8}$ .58 58%
    (5) $\frac{3}{10}$ .3 30%

Item 13 refers to the following diagram.

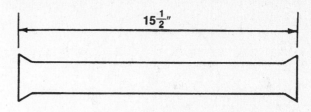

13. If you drill a line of holes $\frac{1}{8}$ inch apart (and $\frac{1}{8}$ inch from each end) in the metal plate, how many holes will you drill?

    (1) 248
    (2) 123
    (3) 62
    (4) $15\frac{5}{8}$
    (5) $15\frac{3}{8}$

14. Which number has the same value as $3^2 + 6(4 + 1)$?

    (1) 17
    (2) 20
    (3) 35
    (4) 36
    (5) 39

15. Jean's Bakery uses a special oven to bake large quantities of sweet rolls. If the cooking time is 17 minutes for a completely filled oven of 144 sweet rolls, about how many hours will it take to bake 7,776 sweet rolls?

    (1) 54 hours
    (2) 17 hours
    (3) 15 hours
    (4) 9 hours
    (5) 8 hours

16. Last year enrollment at Cedar Creek Day Care increased by 25%. If enrollment at the beginning of the year was 84, what was enrollment at the end of the year?

    (1) 21
    (2) 63
    (3) 105
    (4) 109
    (5) 111

Item 17 refers to the following diagram.

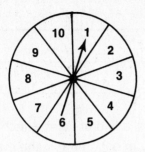

17. What is the probability of spinning an 8 on the first spin?

(1) $\frac{1}{10}$

(2) $\frac{1}{5}$

(3) $\frac{3}{10}$

(4) $\frac{5}{1}$

(5) $\frac{10}{1}$

18. Order the following values in ascending order: $\frac{5}{6}, \frac{1}{4}, \frac{3}{8}, .875,$ and .5.

(1) .875, $\frac{5}{6}$, .5, $\frac{3}{8}, \frac{1}{4}$

(2) $\frac{1}{4}, \frac{3}{8}$, .5, $\frac{5}{6}$, .875

(3) .5, $\frac{1}{4}, \frac{3}{8}, \frac{5}{6}$, .875

(4) $\frac{3}{8}, \frac{1}{4}$, .5, $\frac{5}{6}$, .875

(5) .5, $\frac{3}{8}, \frac{1}{4}$, .875, $\frac{5}{6}$

19. Express $\frac{(5.6)(-1.21)}{2}$ in simplified form.

(1) 13.552

(2) 6.776

(3) 3.388

(4) −6.776

(5) −3.388

20. A recipe for a party mix calls for $1\frac{1}{2}$ cups of peanuts, 3 cups of cereal, $4\frac{1}{2}$ cups each of pretzels and sesame sticks. How many cups of mix will this recipe make?

(1) 9

(2) $12\frac{1}{2}$

(3) $13\frac{1}{2}$

(4) 15

(5) $16\frac{1}{2}$

Items 21 and 22 refer to the following passage.

Ms. Ashley is manager for the Discount Center. She recorded total sales for six months: January, $4,270; February, $2,675; March, $2,751; April, $3,734; May, $2,683; June, $4,671.

21. What was the mean dollar of sales for the six months at the Discount Center?

(1) $2,683

(2) $3,464

(3) $3,734

(4) $4,270

(5) $4,671

22. What was the median dollar of sales figures for the Discount Center?

(1) $2,683.00

(2) $3,242.50

(3) $3,742.50

(4) $4,270.00

(5) $4,671.00

23. Dunn Rite Car Rental Company owns 225 cars which it rents. Twenty-five of these cars are in the auto repair shop for maintenance. About what percent of the cars are still available to be rented?

(1) 11%

(2) 25%

(3) 75%

(4) 80%

(5) 89%

24. Miranda made a dress which required 3 yards of fabric at $5.95 a yard. In addition to the fabric, she spent $5.19 for buttons and other notions. If she sold the dress for $45.00, how much did she profit from the sale? Round to the nearest dollar.

(1) $22

(2) $23

(3) $24

(4) $25

(5) $26

Item 25 refers to the following chart.

Miles Per Gallon of Gasoline

6 Cylinder Cars	mpg
Subcompact	25
Compact	23
Mid-size	20

25. If an owner of each of the cars listed above drove 20,000 miles last year and paid $1.25 per gallon of gasoline, how much less was spent on gas by the owner of the subcompact size car than by the owner of the mid-size car?

(1) $1,250
(2) $1,000
(3) $ 750
(4) $ 500
(5) $ 250

26. Leonard had 45 minutes to prepare for work. He spent $\frac{1}{3}$ of an hour bathing and dressing and $\frac{1}{5}$ of an hour eating breakfast. How many minutes did he have to spare?

(1) 12
(2) 13
(3) 20
(4) 32
(5) 45

27. Write the product of $1\frac{1}{2}$ and $\frac{2}{5}$ as a decimal.

(1) .4
(2) .5
(3) .6
(4) .7
(5) .8

28. Rochelle drove 50 miles per hour for the first five hours on an 8-hour driving trip. If she drove 430 miles, what was the average speed for the last 3 hours of her trip?

(1) 50 mph
(2) 55 mph
(3) 60 mph
(4) 65 mph
(5) 70 mph

29. Don monitored the daily high temperature on a Fahrenheit thermometer for 7 days during January. Those temperatures were: Monday, $-7°$; Tuesday, $+3°$; Wednesday, $-10°$; Thursday, $0°$; Friday, $+5°$; Saturday, $-15°$; Sunday, $+3°$. What was the difference between the highest and lowest temperatures?

(1) 5°
(2) 10°
(3) 13°
(4) 15°
(5) 20°

30. Simplify $12 - 2(8 + 2) + 5$.

(1) -12
(2) -3
(3) 0
(4) 3
(5) 5

31. Simplify $(\sqrt{81})(\sqrt{139})(0)$.

(1) 0
(2) 4
(3) 9
(4) 13
(5) 21

32. If the ratio of the number of boys to the number of girls in one school is 2 to 3, what percent of the students are boys?

(1) 20%
(2) 25%
(3) 30%
(4) 40%
(5) Not enough information is given.

33. Samantha put 20% down on a bedroom suite. If the suite costs a total of $865, what was the amount of her down payment?

(1) $173
(2) $200
(3) $329.50
(4) $432.50
(5) $692

Unit 2 Algebra

Introduction

In algebra you add, subtract, multiply, and divide according to the same rules and order of operations, but you use letters (variables) as place holders for unknown values.

The three math problems below are examples of algebraic and numerical equations.

Example 1:
$? + 5 = 7$

Example 2:
$5 + ? = 7$

Example 3:
$a + 5 = 7$

All three statements ask what number added to 5 equals 7. In Example 3, the letter a is used to represent the unknown number. The variable, a, serves as a place holder for the number 2. We know that when 2 is added to 5, the sum equals 7.

When you want to represent addition, you automatically use the addition $(+)$ sign. To subtract, you use the subtraction $(-)$ sign. For multiplication and division, you would usually use the $(\times)$ and $(\div)$ signs.

In algebra the same addition and subtraction signs are used to indicate addition and subtraction. However, the multiplication sign, $\times$, looks the same as the unknown or variable x. In algebra we indicate the multiplication operation by using different symbols. Study the five examples below. Each is a way of indicating multiplication.

Examples: $6(4) = 24$ $\quad$ $(6)(4) = 24$ $\quad$ $6 \cdot 4 = 24$ $\quad$ $6x$ $\quad$ xy

When letters or numbers and letters are written next to each other, you multiply.

The examples below indicate division.

Examples: $\quad \dfrac{y}{x} \quad\quad 1 \div \dfrac{2}{3} \quad\quad \dfrac{5xy}{5} \quad\quad \dfrac{aa}{ab} \quad\quad \dfrac{12}{2b}$

Algebraic expressions can be written to represent a mathematical expression written in words which includes an unknown number. Study the following table. The letter serves as a placeholder for an unknown value of the number in the expression.

Word expression	Algebraic expression
A number plus 4	$n + 4$
A number minus 17	$x - 17$
A number times 8	$8y$
A number divided by 22	$\dfrac{x}{22}$
42 minus a number	$42 - n$
26 divided by a number	$\dfrac{26}{z}$

See Also Mathematics Complete Preparation Unit 2, Lesson 19 Unit 7, Algebraic Expressions

Writing Algebraic Expressions

Directions: Write the following word expressions algebraically on the lines provided. Use *n* for the unknown. The first one has been done for you.

Word Expression	Algebraic Expression
1. A number divided by 5	$\frac{n}{5}$
2. The number 5 plus a number	_____
3. A number increased by ten	_____
4. The sum of a number and 12	_____
5. Twice a number	_____
6. A number divided by 2	_____
7. A number reduced by 3	_____
8. The product of 4 and a number	_____
9. One-third of a number is increased by 7.	_____
10. The number 10 reduced by a number	_____
11. The number *r* plus *t*	_____
12. The number *p* times *q*	_____
13. The number *x* divided by *a*	_____
14. If *b* and *h* represent two numbers, write the sum.	_____
15. If *b* and *h* represent two numbers, write the product.	_____
16. One half of *d*	_____
17. Twice a number is increased by one.	_____
18. Represent algebraically the number of inches in *y* yards.	_____
19. Represent algebraically the number of ounces in *p* pounds	_____
20. Represent algebraically the number of weeks in *d* days.	_____

 See Also | Mathematics Complete Preparation | Unit 2, Lesson 19 Unit 7, Algebraic Expressions

Simplifying Algebraic Expressions

To simplify algebraic expressions you may need to <u>combine terms</u> using addition, subtraction, multiplication, or division. Remember to use the rules of signed numbers. Review these rules in *Steck-Vaughn GED Mathematics* or *Steck-Vaughn Complete GED Preparation*.

Example 1: Simplify $5x + 6x$.

$5x + 6x = 11x$

$5x$ and $6x$ are <u>like terms</u> since both contain x. To simplify, add the value of the number coefficients, $5 + 6 = 11$.

Example 2: Simplify $3x^2 + 2 - 2x^2 - 1$.

$3x^2 - 2x^2 + 2 - 1 = x^2 + 1$

Rearrange the terms, that is, put like terms together, and subtract the like terms.

Example 3: Simplify $2(3x^2)$.

$2(3x^2) = 6x^2$

Multiply the whole numbers, $2(3) = 6$.

Example 4: Simplify $3(x - 4)$.

$3(x - 4) = 3x - 12$

Multiply each term in the parentheses by 3. This is called the <u>distributive property</u>.

Example 5: Simplify $\frac{(4x - 6)}{2}$.

$\frac{(4x - 6)}{2} = \frac{4x}{2} - \frac{6}{2} = 2x - 3$

Divide each term by 2.

Example 6: Simplify $4(2x + 6) - 5(x + 2)$.

$4(2x + 6) - 5(x + 2) =$

$8x + 24 - (5x + 10) =$

$8x + 24 - 5x - 10 =$

$8x - 5x + 24 - 10 = 3x + 14$

First multiply using the distributive property. Use parentheses to show that $5x + 10$ is being subtracted. Subtract the like terms.

 **See Also**

Mathematics
Complete Preparation

Unit 2, Lesson 19
Unit 7, Algebraic Expressions

56 Unit 2: Algebra

Directions: Simplify each expression using the correct order of operations and the rules for signed numbers. Write your answers on the lines provided.

1. $-4a + 5a$ _____

2. $5x^2 + 7 - 3x^2 - 8$ _____

3. $4(-3b^2)$ _____

4. $-2(y - 3)$ _____

5. $\dfrac{(5q - 10)}{5}$ _____

6. $3(4p + 1) - 3(p - 1)$ _____

7. $4d + 7d - 3d$ _____

8. $-2z^2 + 11 - 3z^2 - 6$ _____

9. $-7(1 - 5y^2)$ _____

10. $\dfrac{(-12r - 9)}{3}$ _____

11. $-9a^2 + 5a^2$ _____

12. $5(x^2 + 7) - 3x^2 - 8$ _____

13. $8(-2b^2) + 4(-6b^2)$ _____

14. $-(2y - 6) - 5(7 - y)$ _____

15. $\dfrac{3(-12r - 8)}{6}$ _____

16. $-3(3y)$ _____

17. $\dfrac{26m^2n^2}{-13}$ _____

18. $\dfrac{40st}{4}$ _____

19. $4(12xy^2) + 7$ _____

20. $\dfrac{(4 - 16a)}{4}$ _____

21. $(x^2 + 3x - 7) + (-3x^2 - 5x + 9)$ _____

22. $(22x - 12) - (-13x + 2)$ _____

23. $\dfrac{3(4x - 2)}{2}$ _____

24. $-2(-5p^2)$ _____

25. $(3x - 4) + (-5x - 7) + (x - 12)$ _____

26. $(5p^2 - pq - 3q^2) - (3p^2 - 4pq + 7q^2)$ _____

≡ Evaluating Algebraic Expressions Using Substitution

Substituting numerical values in algebraic expressions, and later in geometric formulas, is a very important skill that will help you on the GED Mathematics Test. The examples and exercise that follow require you to recall all the rules and skills that you have learned about positive and negative numbers, order of operations, and powers and roots. Study each example carefully.

Example 1: Find the value of $x + y$ if $x = 15$ and $y = 12$.
   1. Write the expression. $x + y$
   2. Substitute 15 for x and 12 for y. $15 + 12$
   3. Perform the operation of addition. $15 + 12 = 27$

Example 2: If $a = 3$ and $b = -5$, find the value of $a - b$.
   1. Write the expression. $a - b$
   2. Substitute 3 for a and -5 for b. $3 - (-5)$
   3. Perform the operation. $3 + 5 = 8$

Example 3: What does the value of $\frac{ab + c}{2}$ equal when $a = 2$, $b = 4$, and $c = 8$?
   1. Write the expression. $\frac{ab + c}{2}$

   2. Substitute 2 for a, 4 for b, and 8 for c. $\frac{(2)(6) + 8}{2}$

   3. Perform the operations. $\frac{12 + 8}{2} = \frac{20}{2} = 10$

In step two, parentheses are used to separate the 2 and 6 to indicate the operation to be performed.

Example 4: Find the value of $\frac{a}{b}$ if $a = 15$ and $b = 24$.
   1. Write the expression. $\frac{a}{b}$

   2. Substitute 15 for a, and 24 for b. $\frac{15}{24}$

   3. Perform the operation. $\frac{15}{24} = .625$
In this example, the answer is a decimal.

Directions: Evaluate each of the following expressions if $a = 3$, $b = 5$, $c = 6$, $d = 1$, $x = -1$, $y = 2$, and $z = -4$. Place your answers on the lines provided.

1. $bc - ad$ _____

2. $\frac{(xy - yz)}{xyz}$ _____

3. $\frac{b^3}{b^2}$ _____

4. $x^3 + (y - 2z)$ _____

5. $\frac{10cd}{abc}$ _____

6. $\frac{3(x + z)}{x}$ _____

7. $a^3 - b^3$ _____

8. $ay + by$ _____

9. $(5x - 5z) + ab$ _____

10. $3a^2b - 6$ _____

11. $3x(xy - b)$ _____

12. $\frac{y}{x} + yz$ _____

13. $a(7 - a)^2$ _____

14. $\frac{bc - 5a}{b}$ _____

15. $\frac{3(y + z)}{x}$ _____

16. $\frac{a}{b} + \frac{b}{c}$ _____

➤ See Also

Mathematics
Complete Preparation

Unit 2, Lesson 19
Unit 7, Algebraic Expressions

58   Unit 2: Algebra

Solving One-Step Equations

An <u>equation</u> can be defined as a mathematical sentence. Every equation has an equal sign to show the relationship between numbers and symbols. To solve an algebraic equation perform the operations necessary to place the variable on one side of the equation and the numbers on the other side. To retain the equality of the equation, you must perform the same operation to both sides. One-step equations can be solved by using the <u>inverse operation</u>, that is, the operation that is the opposite to the operation within the equation.

Example 1: In $6 + x = 10$, what number added to 6 equals 10?
You know that $6 + 4 = 10$, so you know that $x = 4$. If you solve the same equation algebraically, the solution looks like this.

$$6 + x = 10 \qquad \textbf{Check:} \quad 6 + x = 10$$
$$6 - 6 + x = 10 - 6 \qquad\qquad\quad 6 + 4 = 10$$
$$0 + x = 4$$
$$x = 4$$

The inverse operation for addition is subtraction. You balanced the equation by subtracting 6 from each side. In the solution to equations, the variable, or unknown side, is equal to the numerical side.

Example 2: Solve for x in $x - 10 = 15$. Think, $25 - 10 = 15$.
Algebraically, you will use addition to solve for x.

$$x - 10 = 15 \qquad \textbf{Check:} \quad x - 10 = 15$$
$$x - 10 + 10 = 15 + 10 \qquad\qquad 25 - 10 = 15$$
$$x + 0 = 25$$
$$x = 25$$

Example 3: Find x in the equation $2x = 14$
Mentally, you know that 2 times 7 equals 14.
Algebraically, you use division to solve for x.

$$2x = 14 \qquad\qquad \textbf{Check:} \qquad 2x = 14$$
$$\frac{2x}{2} = \frac{14}{2} \qquad\qquad\qquad\qquad 2 \cdot 7 = 14$$
$$x = 7$$

Example 4: Find the value of "x divided by 3 equals 7."
First, you must translate from words to an algebraic equation.
Then solve for x using multiplication.

$$\frac{x}{3} = 7 \qquad\qquad \textbf{Check:} \qquad \frac{x}{3} = 7$$
$$\frac{(3)x}{3} = (7)(3) \qquad\qquad\qquad \frac{21}{3} = 7$$
$$x = 21$$

Each example was checked by substituting the unknown value back into the equation. To solve some equations, a combination of these operations will be necessary. As you solve the problems on the next page, you will sharpen your skills for two-step equations.

▶See Also   Mathematics   Unit 2, Lesson 20
              Complete Preparation   Unit 7, Equations

≡One-Step Equations: Computation Practice

Directions: Solve the following one-step equations. Write your answers on the lines provided.

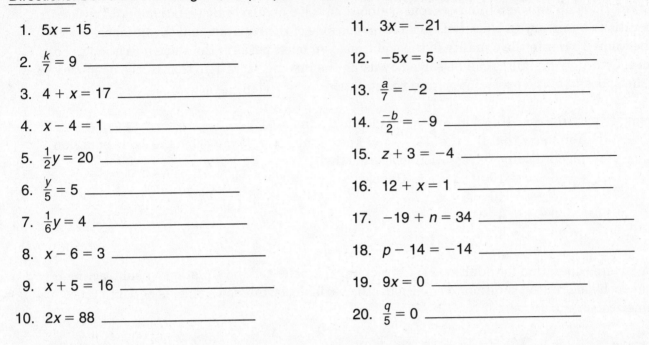

1. $5x = 15$ _____

2. $\frac{k}{7} = 9$ _____

3. $4 + x = 17$ _____

4. $x - 4 = 1$ _____

5. $\frac{1}{2}y = 20$ _____

6. $\frac{y}{5} = 5$ _____

7. $\frac{1}{6}y = 4$ _____

8. $x - 6 = 3$ _____

9. $x + 5 = 16$ _____

10. $2x = 88$ _____

11. $3x = -21$ _____

12. $-5x = 5$ _____

13. $\frac{a}{7} = -2$ _____

14. $\frac{-b}{2} = -9$ _____

15. $z + 3 = -4$ _____

16. $12 + x = 1$ _____

17. $-19 + n = 34$ _____

18. $p - 14 = -14$ _____

19. $9x = 0$ _____

20. $\frac{q}{5} = 0$ _____

Directions: Write and then solve the equations for the following items. Use *n* for each unknown number. Write your answers on the lines provided.

21. Twelve times a certain number is thirty-six. _____

22. A number added to ten equals eighty. _____

23. Six less than some number equals two. _____

24. Twenty-four more than some number is one hundred forty-four. _____

25. Twice a number is one hundred twenty-six. _____

26. A number increased by fourteen is equal to forty-two. _____

27. A number decreased by twelve is eighteen. _____

28. Four times a number is sixty. _____

29. A number plus forty is eighty-four. _____

30. A certain number decreased by 13 is equal to 39. _____

≡ Solving Two-Step Equations

Solving some equations requires two steps, that is, performing two different operations, each to both sides of the equation.

Example 1: Solve $2x + 5 = 9$.

$$2x + 5 = 9$$
$$2x + 5 - 5 = 9 - 5$$
$$2x = 4$$
$$\frac{2x}{2} = \frac{4}{2}$$
$$x = 2$$

Check: $2(2) + 5 = 9$
$$4 + 5 = 9$$
$$9 = 9$$

Subtract 5 from both sides of the equal sign. Divide both sides by 2. The solution is $x = 2$. To check the solution, substitute 2 for x in the original equation.

Example 2: Solve $-3x - 9 = 12$.

$$-3x - 9 = 12$$
$$-3x - 9 + 9 = 12 + 9$$
$$-3x = 21$$
$$\frac{-3x}{-3} = \frac{21}{-3}$$
$$x = -7$$

Check: $-3(-7) - 9 = 12$
$$21 - 9 = 12$$
$$12 = 12$$

Add 9 to both sides. Divide both sides by -3. The solution is $x = -7$. Check by substituting the solution into the original equation.

Example 3: Solve $\frac{x}{5} + 6 = 1$.

$$\frac{x}{5} + 6 = 1$$
$$\frac{x}{5} + 6 - 6 = 1 - 6$$
$$\frac{x}{5} = -5$$
$$5\left(\frac{x}{5}\right) = 5(-5)$$
$$x = -25$$

Check: $\frac{-25}{5} + 6 = 1$
$$-5 + 6 = 1$$
$$1 = 1$$

Subtract 6 from both sides. Multiply both sides by 5. The solution is $x = -25$. Check by substituting the solution into the original equation.

<u>Directions</u>: Solve the following two-step equations. Write your answers on the lines provided.

1. $4x + 7 = 11$ _____

2. $6x - 13 = 17$ _____

3. $\frac{x}{8} + 9 = 10$ _____

4. $\frac{x}{2} - 6 = 2$ _____

5. $-8x + 12 = 36$ _____

6. $\frac{-x}{9} - 7 = 3$ _____

7. $5 - 5x = -10$ _____

8. $14 + \frac{x}{4} = -2$ _____

9. $25 + 10x = 75$ _____

10. $-8 - 2x = -4$ _____

11. $-1 + \frac{x}{3} = 2$ _____

12. $17 - \frac{x}{10} = 5$ _____

Solving Multi-Step Equations

Use a combination of inverse operations to solve multi-step equations.

Example 1: Solve $2x - 9 = x + 10$.

To solve this equation, identify an unknown side of the equation. You want the unknowns on one side and the numbers on the other side.

Unknown Numerical	**Check:** $2x - 9 = x + 10$
$2x - 9 = x + 10$	$2(19) - 9 = 19 + 10$
$2x - x - 9 + 9 = x - x + 10 + 9$	$38 - 9 = 19 + 10$
$x = 19$	$29 = 29$

Move -9 from the unknown side to the numerical side by addition. The unknown x is moved from the numerical side by subtraction. The like terms are collected on both sides so that the unknown side is equal to the numerical side. Check your solution. Substitute into the original equation.

Example 2: Solve $7x - 2 = 11x - 1 + 15$.

Before any solution can be found, you must simplify the right-hand side of the equation by combining like terms, -1 and $+15$.

Numerical Unknown	**Check:** $7x - 2 = 11x - 1 + 15$
$7x - 2 = 11x - 1 + 15$	$7(-4) - 2 = 11(-4) - 1$
$7x - 2 = 11x + 14$	$-28 - 2 = -44 - 1 + 15$
$7x - 7x - 2 - 14 = 11x - 7x + 14 - 14$	$-30 = -30$
$-16 = 4x$	
$\frac{-16}{4} = \frac{4x}{4}$	
$-4 = x$	

Directions: Solve each equation, using inverse operations. Write your answers on the lines provided.

1. $100 + 7x = 250 - 18x$ _____

2. $5n - 6 = 4n + 2$ _____

3. $3(x - 4) - 2(x - 8) = 1$ _____

4. $14x - x + 1 = 14$ _____

5. $5x + 8 = 4x - 12$ _____

6. $5x - 75 = 3x + 7$ _____

7. $10(x - 3) - 7x = 0$ _____

8. $16 + 3x = x + 32$ _____

9. $3x + 1 = 25 - x$ _____

10. $36 = 18x - 12x + 6$ _____

Directions: Write and then solve an equation for each of the following. Use x as the unknown.

11. The sum of four times a number and four equals twenty.

12. Six is subtracted from nine times a number. The difference equals forty-eight.

13. The sum of two times a number and ten equals fourteen plus three times the same number.

14. Five times a number is decreased by four and equals four plus three times the same number.

15. Five times the sum of a number and three is equal to the sum of that number and fifteen.

See Also Mathematics
Complete Preparation

Unit 2, Lesson 20
Unit 7, Equations

≡Solving Word Problems

Use the rules that you learned in solving one-step, two-step, and multi-step equations to solve algebraic word problems. Study the format for organizing information in the examples that follow.

Example 1: The sum of three consecutive numbers is 48. Find the numbers.
  Step 1: Read the problem carefully. Be sure you understand the information you are given and what you are being asked to find.
  Step 2: Assign a variable to the unknown term or terms: Let x = 1st consecutive number; $x + 1$ = 2nd consecutive number; and $x + 2$ = 3rd consecutive number
  Step 3: Write the equation and solve for the unknown.

$$(x) + (x + 1) + (x + 2) = 48 \qquad\qquad 3x = 45$$
$$3x + 3 = 48 \qquad\qquad \frac{3x}{3} = \frac{45}{3}$$
$$3x + 3 - 3 = 48 - 3 \qquad\qquad x = 15$$

  Step 4: Substitute 15 as the value of x for each of the variables in Step 2.
    1st consecutive number = x = 15
    2nd consecutive number = $x + 1$ or $15 + 1 = 16$
    3rd consecutive number = $x + 2$ or $15 + 2 = 17$
    The three consecutive numbers are 15, 16, and 17: $15 + 16 + 17 = 48$.

Example 2: Claude's savings are two times Rene's savings. Together their savings total $6,000. How much has Claude saved?
  Step 1: Read the problem carefully. Note that you are being asked to find Claude's savings.
  Step 2: Assign a variable to the unknown term.
    Let x = Rene's savings and $2x$ = Claude's savings.
  Step 3: Write the equation and solve for the unknown.
    $2x + x = \$6,000$
    $\frac{3x}{3} = \frac{\$6,000}{3}$
    $x = \$2,000$
  Step 4: Substitute $2,000 as the value of x, the variable in Step 2: Rene's savings = x = $2,000 and Claude's savings = $2x$ = $2(\$2,000) = \$4,000$

<u>Directions:</u> Set up and solve the following word problems. Use *n* as the unknown.

1. The sum of two consecutive numbers is 111. Find the two numbers.

2. Marion is 4 years older than Pam. The sum of their ages is 32 years. How old are Marion and Pam?

3. One hundred eighty is divided into two parts so one part will be three times the other part. What is the larger part?

4. A blouse is sold for $26, $3 more than it cost. Find the original cost of the blouse.

5. The sum of two numbers is 98. If one number is six times the other, find the two numbers.

6. Evelyn and Eleanor worked a total of 36 hours. If Evelyn worked 10 hours longer than Eleanor, how many hours did each woman work?

Solving Word Problems

Directions: Set up and solve the following word problems. Choose the best answer to each item.

1. Twelve times the sum of a number and 2 is equal to 36. What is the number?

   (1) 24
   (2) 12
   (3) 6
   (4) 1
   (5) 0

2. Jerry swam twice as many laps as his younger brother Bill. If Jerry and Bill swam a total of 60 laps, how many laps did Jerry swim?

   (1) 50
   (2) 40
   (3) 30
   (4) 20
   (5) 10

3. The sum of three consecutive numbers is 24. What is the largest number?

   (1) 6
   (2) 7
   (3) 8
   (4) 9
   (5) 10

4. Mary works full time and earns 3 times as much as Sue who works part-time. Together they earn $560 per week. How much does Mary earn per week?

   (1) $140
   (2) $280
   (3) $420
   (4) $560
   (5) $700

5. A certain number is subtracted from 20. The result multiplied by 3 is equal to 45. What is the number?

   (1) 3
   (2) 5
   (3) 10
   (4) 15
   (5) 45

6. On the first day of their 600-mile vacation, the Jones family traveled three times as far as on the third day. On the second day, they traveled twice as far as on the third day. How far did they travel on the first day?

   (1) 100 miles
   (2) 200 miles
   (3) 300 miles
   (4) 400 miles
   (5) 500 miles

7. The sum of three consecutive even numbers is equal to two times the largest number. What is the largest number? (Let x, $x + 2$, and $x + 4$ represent the numbers.)

   (1) 2
   (2) 4
   (3) 6
   (4) 8
   (5) 10

8. Joan has 16 coins in her pocket. She has the same number of quarters as nickels and she has twice as many dimes as quarters. How many dimes does she have?

   (1) 4
   (2) 5
   (3) 6
   (4) 8
   (5) 12

≡ Ratio and Proportion

Fractions are sometimes referred to as ratios. A <u>ratio</u> is defined as a comparison of two objects or numbers. In the illustration below, 4 of the 5 people voted while one person did not vote. A comparison of the number of voters to non-voters is expressed in a ratio of 4 to 1. The order in which you write the numbers of a ratio is extremely important. Review ratio and proportion in *Steck-Vaughn GED Mathematics* or *Steck-Vaughn Complete GED Preparation*.

Ratios can be written in three different ways.

As a Fraction	In Words	With a Colon
$\dfrac{4 \text{ voters}}{1 \text{ non-voter}}$	4 to 1	4:1
	voters to non-voters	voters:non-voters

You have already used ratios with algebra to solve some types of problems as in Example 1.

Example 1: Each week, Janice gives a total of \$15 in allowances to her two children in the ratio of 3 to 2. How much does each child get?

Let $3x$ = amount for one child and $2x$ = amount for the other child

$3x + 2x = \$15$

$5x = \$15$

$x = \$3$ \qquad One child gets $3x$ or $3(\$3) = \$9$ and the other gets $2(\$3)$ or \$6.

A proportion is formed by putting an equal sign between two equal ratios.

$\dfrac{1}{2} = \dfrac{2}{4}$ \qquad $\dfrac{1}{2} \diagup\!\!\!\!\diagdown \dfrac{2}{4}$ \qquad Cross multiply: $\quad 1 \cdot 4 = 2 \cdot 2$

A proportion containing an unknown can be solved by using <u>cross multiplication.</u> You can solve many questions on the GED Mathematics Test by using the concepts of ratio and proportion.

Example 2: Solve for the unknown value in $\frac{x}{5} = \frac{80}{100}$.

$\dfrac{x}{5} = \dfrac{80}{100}$ \qquad The two ratios are equal and form a proportion.

$x \cdot 100 = 80 \cdot 5$ \qquad Cross multiply x times 100 and 80 times 5.

$100x = 400$

$\dfrac{100x}{100} = \dfrac{400}{100}$ \qquad Complete the process for solving for the unknown.

$x = 4$

To determine whether a word problem can be solved by using a proportion, look for two sets of related objects with three of the four elements given. The unknown is the missing element.

Example 3: Central Post Office processes 1,500 pieces of mail through the canceling machine in 3 hours. How many pieces of mail are processed during an eight-hour shift?

You have two sets of related objects: hours/pieces of mail = hours/pieces of mail
You have three elements: 3 hours, 1,500 pieces, and 8 hours.

$\dfrac{3}{1,500} = \dfrac{8}{x}$ \qquad The pieces of mail in 8 hours is the missing element.

$3x = 12,000$

$\dfrac{3x}{3} = \dfrac{12,000}{3}$

$x = 4,000$

Ratio and Proportion

Directions: Use ratio or proportion to solve the following problems. Choose the best answer to each item.

1. Tate Construction Company and a subcontractor split the income from a $1,525 remodeling job using a 1 to 3 ratio. How much money will Tate Construction make on the job?

   (1) $1,525.00
   (2) $1,143.75
   (3) $ 953.00
   (4) $ 762.25
   (5) $ 381.25

2. A cookie recipe required 3 ounces of margarine for every $3\frac{1}{2}$ cups of flour. If Bailey wanted to increase the recipe for a party, and he used 24 ounces of margarine, how many cups of flour will he need?

   (1) 8
   (2) $10\frac{1}{2}$
   (3) 28
   (4) 30
   (5) 84

3. Three students scored a total of 270 points on an arithmetic quiz in the ratio of 3:4:2. What was the highest score?

   (1) 60
   (2) 90
   (3) 120
   (4) 150
   (5) 180

4. Geraldine's rental car costs $35.95 for two days. How much will the car cost for 30 days?

   (1) $ 107.85
   (2) $ 539.25
   (3) $ 953.00
   (4) $ 976.25
   (5) $1,078.50

5. A cleaning liquid concentrate of 2 gallons requires 5 gallons of distilled water. If Bill has only 3 gallons of water, how many gallons of concentrate must he use?

   (1) 2
   (2) $1\frac{1}{5}$
   (3) $\frac{5}{6}$
   (4) $\frac{2}{3}$
   (5) $\frac{3}{5}$

6. Avalon's phone bill was $375 for the first three months of the year. Assuming that this amount remains fairly constant for a three-month period, project how much the company will spend in a year.

   (1) $ 250
   (2) $ 375
   (3) $ 750
   (4) $1,125
   (5) $1,500

7. Melinda earns $45.75 every 5 hours as a florist for Windmill Floral Shop. How much will Melinda earn in 40 hours?

   (1) $137.50
   (2) $228.75
   (3) $320.00
   (4) $366.00
   (5) $915.00

8. One of the life insurance policies at Kusay Insurance costs $.75 per month for each $1,000 of insurance. How much is the monthly premium for a $30,000 policy?

   (1) $18.75
   (2) $19.00
   (3) $19.75
   (4) $20.50
   (5) $22.50

9. A lottery prize of $4,500 was divided between two people in the ratio of 3:5. What was the value of the larger share?

   (1) $ 562.50
   (2) $1,681.50
   (3) $2,812.50
   (4) $2,250.00
   (5) one and three

10. Sales tax on a purchase of $8 is $.48. What is the sales tax on a purchase of $152?

   (1) $ 3.84
   (2) $ 9.12
   (3) $12.50
   (4) $16.75
   (5) $72.96

11. If an overseas telegram costs $2.95 for each 15 words, what is the cost of a telegram of 75 words?

   (1) $221.25
   (2) $111.25
   (3) $ 44.25
   (4) $ 14.75
   (5) $ 12.50

12. The ratio of teachers to students at Fernwood Elementary School is 2 to 35. What is the student population at Fernwood Elementary School if there are 26 teachers?

   (1) 70
   (2) 260
   (3) 350
   (4) 455
   (5) 910

13. Sue's car gets 25 miles to a gallon of gasoline. How many gallons of gasoline will she need for her 625-mile trip?

   (1) 10
   (2) 15
   (3) 20
   (4) 25
   (5) 30

14. The ratio of a mother's age to her daughter's age is 5:2. If the daughter's age is 12, how old is the mother?

   (1) 30
   (2) 32
   (3) 33
   (4) 34
   (5) 35

15. The ratio of Fern's monthly rent to her total monthly income is 1:5. If Fern's monthly rent is $225, what is her monthly income?

   (1) $1,150
   (2) $1,125
   (3) $1,100
   (4) $1,025
   (5) $ 950

16. Assuming that one serving, 8 ounces, would be adequate for each person, how many quarts of punch would be needed for 240 people? (Hint: 1 quart = 32 ounces)

   (1) 30
   (2) 60
   (3) 90
   (4) 150
   (5) 240

17. A bus traveled 90 miles in 1.5 hours. How many miles will the bus go, traveling at the same rate, in 10 hours?

   (1) 300
   (2) 600
   (3) 900
   (4) 1,200
   (5) 1,500

18. The scale on a map is .5 inches equals 200 miles. What is the distance, in miles, between two cities 2.5 inches apart on the map?

   (1) 400
   (2) 600
   (3) 800
   (4) 1,000
   (5) 1,200

Formula Problems: Interest, Distance, and Cost

Since you know how to substitute numerical values into algebraic expressions and how to solve equations, you can apply the same rules to solve problems involving formulas. The formulas that you will need on the GED Mathematics Test will be provided for you in your test booklet. Those same formulas are printed on the inside back cover of this book.

Directions: Select and use one of the formulas to solve each of the following items. Choose the best answer to each item.

Interest:	$i = prt$	$r = \frac{i}{pt}$	$t = \frac{i}{pr}$	$p = \frac{i}{rt}$
Distance:	$d = rt$	$r = \frac{d}{t}$	$t = \frac{d}{r}$	
Cost:	$c = nr$	$r = \frac{c}{n}$	$n = \frac{c}{r}$	

1. Jason entered the Windy City 40-kilometer race. His best race time in past races had been 6.5 kilometers per hour. At this same rate, about how long will it take Jason to complete the Windy City race?

   (1) 3 hours
   (2) 4 hours
   (3) 5 hours
   (4) 6 hours
   (5) 7 hours

2. The inventory at Leo's Hardware showed $1,500 worth of electrical circuit breakers priced at $2.50 each were in stock. How many circuit breakers were in stock?

   (1) 750
   (2) 700
   (3) 650
   (4) 600
   (5) 550

3. Marion deposited $800 in a savings account. One year later, the teller posted $56 in her savings book. At what rate of interest was she paid on her savings?

   (1) 5%
   (2) 6%
   (3) $6\frac{1}{2}$%
   (4) 7%
   (5) $7\frac{1}{2}$%

4. Mr. and Mrs. Kennedy borrowed $1,200 from their family for 9 months to invest in a small business venture. If they agreed to pay $8\frac{1}{2}$% interest annually, how much must they repay?

   (1) $ 72.00
   (2) $ 76.50
   (3) $1,176.50
   (4) $1,276.50
   (5) $1,806.00

5. The Frame Up picture framing store paid $8,000 to an independent distributor for a shipment of 1,000 picture frames each 11" X 16". What was the cost per frame?

   (1) $ 6
   (2) $ 8
   (3) $10
   (4) $12
   (5) $14

6. McCory's Bookstore received a shipment of novels costing $2.95 each. If there were 550 novels in the shipment, what was the total cost of the shipment?

   (1) $1,295.00
   (2) $1,375.00
   (3) $1,550.00
   (4) $1,622.50
   (5) $1,650.00

7. Midwestern Airway Airline's flight #403 from Springfield to Cincinnati takes $1\frac{3}{4}$ hours. If the rate of speed is 124 miles per hour, what is the distance from Springfield to Cincinnati?

   (1) 864 miles
   (2) 432 miles
   (3) 217 miles
   (4) 216 miles
   (5) 213 miles

8. Elinor borrowed money from the credit union to purchase a piece of property to build her own child care center. The loan was for 2 years and the annual interest rate was 8%. If Elinor paid $370 interest in the first year, what was the amount of money she borrowed?

   (1) $8,000
   (2) $7,000
   (3) $6,500
   (4) $5,500
   (5) $4,625

9. How long must Michael leave $2,750 in his savings account, which pays 7% simple interest, to earn $577? Round to the nearest whole year.

   (1) 2 years
   (2) 3 years
   (3) 4 years
   (4) 5 years
   (5) 6 years

10. An eighteen-wheeler truck traveled 390 miles in 6 hours. What was the average rate of speed for the eighteen wheeler?

    (1) 50 mph
    (2) 55 mph
    (3) 60 mph
    (4) 65 mph
    (5) Not enough information is given.

11. Mrs. Avers deposited $3,000 in her credit union savings account. What amount of interest will she receive on her deposit if she leaves the money in the account for one year at $8\frac{1}{2}$% interest?

    (1) $250
    (2) $255
    (3) $300
    (4) $350
    (5) $400

12. The total simple interest to be paid on a loan by the Walker Auto Service Center was $513. If the loan was borrowed at the rate of $4\frac{3}{4}$% for 2 years, what was the principal amount borrowed by Walker Auto?

    (1) $2,500
    (2) $3,000
    (3) $4,500
    (4) $5,000
    (5) $5,400

13. Wayne drove 160 miles to Stockton in 4 hours and another 146 miles beyond Stockton in 2 hours. What was Wayne's average speed for the total time that he drove?

    (1) 40 mph
    (2) 45 mph
    (3) 51 mph
    (4) 73 mph
    (5) 80 mph

14. A car and a truck left LaPointe at 1:15 P.M. traveling in opposite directions. If the driver of the car drove 55 miles per hour, and the truck averaged 50.5 miles per hour, how many miles apart will they be at 4:15 P.M.?

    (1) 151.5
    (2) 165
    (3) 316.5
    (4) 415
    (5) 540

15. Elaine's Style Shop received an order of 250 swimsuits from Swimsuits, Inc. If the owner of the shop paid $6.95 for each swimsuit, what was the total amount of money to be sent to Swimsuits, Inc.?

(1) $ 690.00
(2) $ 695.00
(3) $1,600.00
(4) $1,737.00
(5) $1,737.50

16. Herman purchased 20 different tropical fish, each of equal value, from Ryan's Pet Shop for $12.60. What was the cost per fish?

(1) $.75
(2) $.70
(3) $.65
(4) $.63
(5) $.60

17. A case of 32-ounce bottles of general purpose cleaner costs $25. If one bottle of cleaner costs $2.50, how many bottles of cleaner are in the case?

(1) 5
(2) 10
(3) 15
(4) 20
(5) 25

18. Mr. Tyler opened a savings account with his $1,000 income tax refund. His bank pays $6\frac{3}{4}\%$ interest annually. If he were to leave his deposit in the bank for an entire year, how much would he earn in interest?

(1) $ 6.75
(2) $ 33.75
(3) $ 67.50
(4) $ 75.00
(5) $135.00

19. Margaret O'Connor received $20 interest from First Home Bank on her savings account balance of $2,400 in one year. What was the simple annual rate of interest?

(1) 5%
(2) 10%
(3) 12%
(4) 15%
(5) 20%

20. Jerold traveled from New York City to Detroit by train. The train averaged 85 miles per hour for $7\frac{1}{2}$ hours. How many miles did he travel?

(1) 550
(2) 595
(3) 637.5
(4) 673.5
(5) 695

21. How long will it take Danette to travel 90 miles if she drives at an average speed of 50 mph for 25 miles and at an average speed of 65 mph the rest of the way?

(1) $\frac{1}{2}$ hour
(2) 1 hour
(3) $1\frac{1}{2}$ hours
(4) 2 hours
(5) $2\frac{1}{2}$ hours

22. Ron sells fresh pineapples at his fruit stand. How much should Ron charge for each pineapple if he pays $10.80 a dozen and wants to make a profit of $.75 each?

(1) $ .90
(2) $1.08
(3) $1.50
(4) $1.65
(5) $2.00

≡ Inequalities

An <u>inequality</u> is an algebraic statement used to show quantities that are <u>not</u> equal. For example, if you have more than \$2 in your pocket, you could algebraically represent that amount you have as $n > 2$. The symbols that are used in statements of inequality are:

> greater than   ≥ greater than or equal to
< less than   ≤ less than or equal to

The inequality $n > 2$ can be shown graphically on a number line.

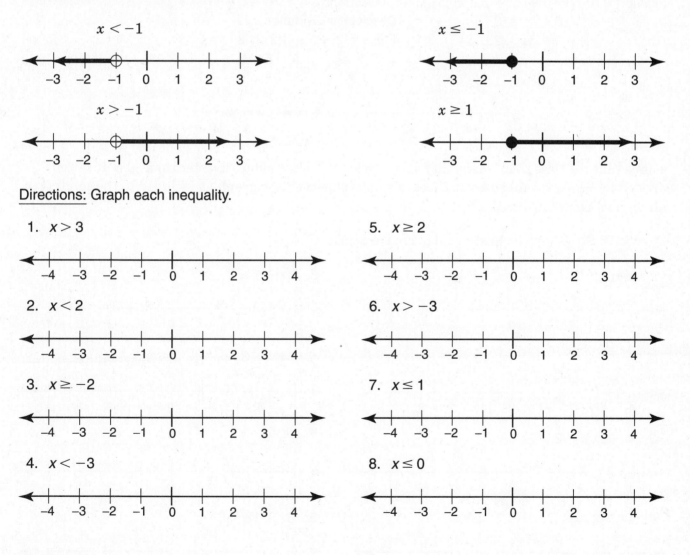

Since numbers get larger as we move to the right on the number line, any number n to the right of 2 will make the statement $n > 2$ true. Use the <u>open circle</u> to indicate that 2 is <u>not</u> included in the range of numbers satisfying the inequality (the solution set). Study the following inequalities and their graphs. (The closed circle indicates "or equal to.")

$x < -1$

$x \leq -1$

$x > -1$

$x \geq 1$

<u>Directions:</u> Graph each inequality.

1. $x > 3$

5. $x \geq 2$

2. $x < 2$

6. $x > -3$

3. $x \geq -2$

7. $x \leq 1$

4. $x < -3$

8. $x \leq 0$

Solving Inequalities

In an inequality one side of the statement has a greater value than the other side. It is <u>not</u> an equation because the sides are not equal. To solve an inequality, use the same steps as you would to solve an equation, with one exception. If you multiply or divide by a negative number, you must <u>reverse</u> the direction of the inequality symbol (see Example 2). When an inequality is solved, more than one number satisfies the inequality.

Example 1: Solve $2n + 6 > -8$.

$$2n + 6 > -8$$
$$2n + 6 - 6 > -8 - 6$$
$$2n > -14$$
$$n > -7$$

Check by substitution.

For $n = 0$: $\quad 2(0) + 6 > -8$
$$0 + 6 > -8$$
$$6 > -8$$

Subtract 6 from both sides. Divide both sides by 2. The solution is all numbers **greater than –7.** Check the answer by substituting a number greater than -7 into the original equation.

Example 2: Solve $5 - 3x < 2$ and graph the solution.

$$5 - 3x < 2$$
$$5 - 5 - 3x < 2 - 5$$
$$-3x < -3$$
$$x > 1$$

Check by substitution.

For $x = 2$: $\quad 5 - 3(2) < 2$
$$5 - 6 < 2$$
$$-1 < 2$$

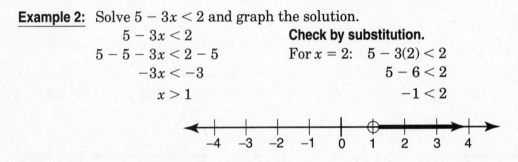

Notice that the "less than" inequality sign is reversed (changed to "greater than") because you divided by -3. The value used to check, $x = 2$, is shown on the graph as included in the solution of all numbers greater than 1.

<u>Directions:</u> Solve each inequality and graph the solution.

1. $x + 2 > 3$

5. $3x - 1 \geq 2$

2. $\frac{x}{2} + 1 \leq 1$

6. $3x > -3$

3. $4 - 2x \geq -2$

7. $\frac{x}{-3} \leq 1$

4. $5x - 2 < -17$

8. $6x + 12 < 0$

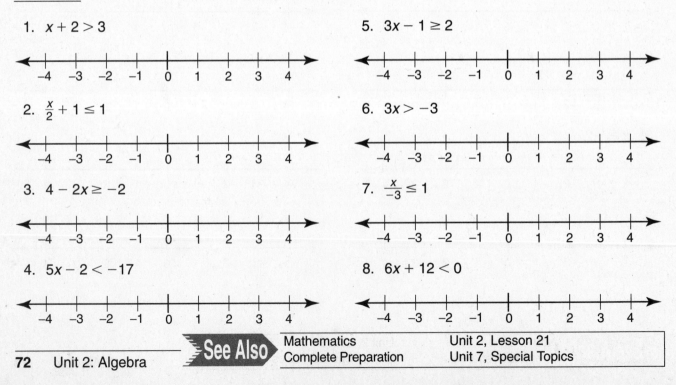

See Also

Mathematics
Complete Preparation

Unit 2, Lesson 21
Unit 7, Special Topics

Solving Quadratic Equations by Substitution

These statements, $x^2 - 16 = 0$ and $y^2 = 6y - 5$, are examples of quadratic equations. If you encounter an equation like this on the GED Mathematics Test, use substitution to help in selecting your answer choice.

Example: Which of the following is the solution for $x^2 - 16 = 0$?
- (1) 4 and -4
- (2) 4 and -2
- (3) 2 and -4
- (4) -4 and -2
- (5) -4 and -1

By substituting the answers listed from the options, you can solve the equation. Use the rules for positive and negative numbers, and remember the order of operations. Option 1 has the two numbers that will satisfy this equation.

Let $x = 4$	Let $x = -4$
$x^2 - 16 = 0$	$x^2 - 16 = 0$
$(4)^2 - 16 = 0$	$(-4)^2 - 16 = 0$
$(4)(4) - 16 = 0$	$(-4)(-4) - 16 = 0$
$16 - 16 = 0$	$+16 - 16 = 0$

Directions: Use substitution to determine the solution to each of the following problems. Choose the best answer to each item.

1. Which of the following pairs satisfies the equation $x^2 - 9x + 14 = 0$?

   - (1) -7 and -2
   - (2) 7 and 2
   - (3) 2 and -7
   - (4) -2 and 7
   - (5) Not enough information is given.

2. Which of the following pairs satisfies the equation $x^2 - 8x + 12 = 0$?

   - (1) -2 and -6
   - (2) -2 and 6
   - (3) 2 and -6
   - (4) 2 and 6
   - (5) Not enough information is given.

3. Which of the following pairs satisfies the equation $p^2 + 9p + 20 = 0$?

   - (1) -5 and 4
   - (2) 5 and -4
   - (3) 5 and 4
   - (4) -5 and -4
   - (5) Not enough information is given.

4. Which of the following pairs satisfies the equation $a^2 - 5a - 24 = 0$?

   - (1) 3 and 8
   - (2) 3 and -8
   - (3) -3 and 8
   - (4) -3 and -8
   - (5) Not enough information is given.

Directions: Choose the <u>best answer</u> to each item.

1. How long will it take Bryan Rodell to drive 615 miles averaging 60 miles per hour?

   (1) 10 hours
   (2) $10\frac{1}{4}$ hours
   (3) 11 hours
   (4) $11\frac{1}{4}$ hours
   (5) 12 hours

2. Solve for c in the inequality $3c - 8 \leq 7$.

   (1) $c \leq 15$
   (2) $c \leq 12$
   (3) $c \leq 8$
   (4) $c \leq 7$
   (5) $c \leq 5$

3. Where $m = 3$ and $n = 2$, evaluate $\frac{m - m^2 n}{3n}$.

   (1) $\frac{5}{2}$
   (2) 2
   (3) 1
   (4) $-\frac{3}{2}$
   (5) $-\frac{5}{2}$

4. If $3q = 6$, what does $\frac{1}{2}q$ equal?

   (1) 1
   (2) 2
   (3) 3
   (4) 4
   (5) 5

5. On a map, 1 inch equals 450 miles. How many inches equal 2,250 miles?

   (1) 3
   (2) 5
   (3) 7
   (4) 9
   (5) 10

6. Rhonda and Paul volunteered a total of 36 hours. If Rhonda volunteered 10 hours more than Paul, how many hours did Paul work?

   (1) 10
   (2) 13
   (3) 16
   (4) 18
   (5) 23

7. Last year a parcel of land was valued at $12,000. This year the value of the land rose to $15,000. What was the percent of increase for the land?

   (1) 20%
   (2) 25%
   (3) 50%
   (4) 75%
   (5) 80%

8. Which of the following means the same as $a + a + a + a + a$?

   (1) $a + 5$
   (2) $3a^2$
   (3) $5a^2$
   (4) $5a$
   (5) $5 - a$

9. Three typists are to share the typing of a 360-page manuscript in the ratio of 3:5:12. How many <u>more</u> pages will the typist who has the greatest number of pages type than the typist who types the least number of pages?

   (1) 18
   (2) 54
   (3) 90
   (4) 162
   (5) 216

10. If $3(x - 1) = 2(x + 1)$, what does x equal?

(1)   5
(2)   4
(3)   3
(4)   −4
(5)   −5

11. Sylvia is four times as old as Kim. If the difference between their ages is 24, how old is Sylvia?

(1) 24
(2) 28
(3) 32
(4) 36
(5) 40

12. In $(p - 3)(3p + 8)(2p + 5) = 0$, which factor must be equal to zero?

(1) $p - 3$
(2) $3p + 8$
(3) $2p + 5$
(4) all of the three factors
(5) any of the three factors

13. Express and then evaluate the following statement algebraically. A number increased by twenty-one is equal to that number times four.

(1)   3
(2)   4
(3)   7
(4) 21
(5) 24

14. Andrew deposited $800 into a savings account that pays $4\frac{1}{2}$% annual interest. How much will he have if he leaves the money in the account for 5 years?

(1) $ 36.00
(2) $ 90.00
(3) $ 180.00
(4) $ 980.00
(5) $1800.00

15. Which of the following expressions describes all values for y as solutions for the inequality $4y + 14 > 18$?

(1) $y > 8$
(2) $y < 8$
(3) $y > 1$
(4) $y < -8$
(5) $y < -1$

16. If $x = -1$ and $y = 4$, evaluate the expression $\frac{5}{y - x} + \frac{4}{2} + 6x$.

(1) $9\frac{1}{4}$
(2) -9
(3)   7
(4) $5\frac{1}{2}$
(5) -3

17. On a math test of fifty questions, there were 15 decimal problems. Which of the following expressions is the ratio of decimal problems to the total number of math problems?

(1)   2:10
(2)   3:10
(3)   10:3
(4)   1:5
(5)   4:5

18. If $a = -1$ and $b = 2$, what is the value of the expression $2a^3 - 3ab$?

(1)   8
(2)   4
(3) −1
(4) −4
(5) −8

19. One number exceeds another number by 5. If the sum of the two numbers is 39, what is the smaller number?

(1) 16
(2) 17
(3) 18
(4) 19
(5) 20

Unit 3 Geometry

Angles and Lines

Plane geometry is the study of shapes and figures that have length and width measurements only. These geometric figures are two-dimensional. Solid geometry is the study of shapes with three dimensions: length, width, and thickness. This unit reviews line segments, geometric shapes, triangles, and angle measurement to help you prepare for the GED Mathematics Test.

☰ Angles

When two rays or line segments meet at a point called a vertex, an angle (∠) is formed. Angles are measured in degrees. $\overline{XY}$ and $\overline{YZ}$ are the rays of the angle.

The angle is identified by using three letters, ∠XYZ or ∠ZYX. The middle letter is always the vertex. Sometimes angles are also referred to by the vertex letter alone, such as ∠Y.

Types of Angles

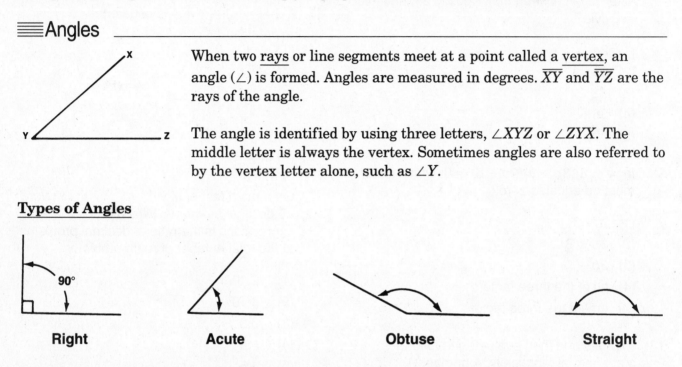

| **Right** | **Acute** | **Obtuse** | **Straight** |

A right angle measures 90°. A small square denotes that a right angle is formed.
An acute angle measures less than 90°.
An obtuse angle measures more than 90° and less than 180°.
A straight line forms a straight angle and measures 180°.

☰ Types of Pairs of Angles

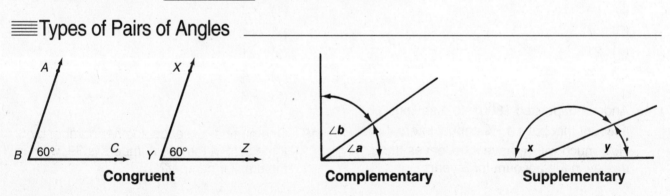

| **Congruent** | **Complementary** | **Supplementary** |

Equal angles are congruent.
Complementary angles are two angles whose sum is 90° like ∠a and ∠b above.
Supplementary angles are two angles whose sum is 180° like ∠x and ∠y above.
Angles next to each other (i.e., which share a common ray) are adjacent angles.

⮞ See Also Mathematics Complete Preparation — Unit 3, Lesson 24 / Unit 7, Angles

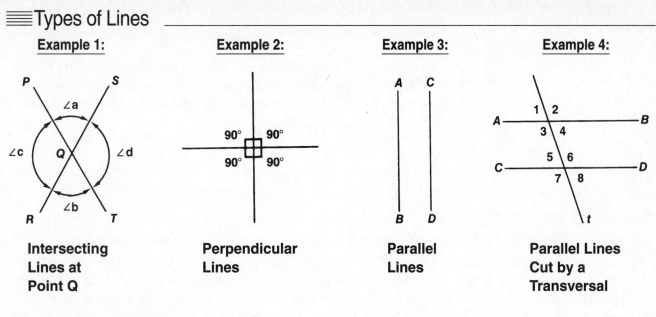

Example 1:

Intersecting
Lines at
Point Q

Example 2:

90°   90°
90°   90°

Perpendicular
Lines

Example 3:

Parallel
Lines

Example 4:

Parallel Lines
Cut by a
Transversal

≡ Lines and Angles

When two line segments cross at a point, pairs of angles are formed.

Intersecting (or crossing) lines, as in Example 1, form two pairs of vertical angles. Vertical angles are opposite each other and are congruent (equal). The $\angle a$ is equal to $\angle b$, and $\angle c$ is equal to $\angle d$.

Perpendicular lines form 4 right angles when the lines cross as in Example 2. The symbol used to show that lines are perpendicular is $\perp$. Four 90° angles are formed when lines are perpendicular.

Parallel lines, $\overline{AB}$ and $\overline{CD}$ in Example 3, are an equal distance apart at all points. The symbol used to show that lines are parallel is $\parallel$. Parallel lines by themselves do not form any angles. However, parallel lines crossed or cut by a line called a transversal, as in Example 4, form 8 angles. The 8 angles form 4 sets of different pairs:

> Four pairs are vertical angles (opposite equal angles). Two pairs of vertical angles are formed by each parallel line as if each line and the transversal were intersecting lines as in Example 1:
>
> | on line $\overline{AB}$ | on line $\overline{CD}$. |
> |---|---|
> | $\angle 1$ and $\angle 4$ | $\angle 5$ and $\angle 8$ |
> | $\angle 2$ and $\angle 3$ | $\angle 6$ and $\angle 7$ |

Four other pairs of angles formed in Example 4 are corresponding angles.

Corresponding angles are also congruent: $\angle 1$ on line $\overline{AB}$ corresponds with $\angle 5$ on line $\overline{CD}$. Likewise, $\angle 2$ and $\angle 6$, $\angle 3$ and $\angle 7$, $\angle 4$ and $\angle 8$.

The other sets of angle pairs formed in Example 4 are special pairs of congruent (equal) angles:
Alternate interior (inside) angles are $\angle 3$ and $\angle 6$, $\angle 4$ and $\angle 5$.
Alternate exterior (outside) angles are $\angle 1$ and $\angle 8$, $\angle 2$ and $\angle 7$.

Triangles

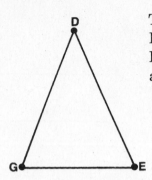

The <u>triangle</u> (△) is a plane (flat), closed, three-sided geometric figure. Each of the three points where an angle is formed is called a <u>vertex</u>. Each vertex of a triangle is formed when two sides meet to form an angle.

In triangle *GED* (△*GED*), the vertices (plural of vertex) are points *G*, *E*, and *D*. The sides of the triangle are $\overline{DG}$ and $\overline{ED}$. $\overline{GE}$ is the base of the triangle. The angles of △*GED* are ∠*G*, ∠*E*, and ∠*D*. Sometimes we use three letters to identify angles of a triangle: ∠*DGE,* ∠*GED,* and ∠*EDG* are the angles of the triangle above. When we use three letters, the middle letter is always the vertex of the angle being identified.

Triangles are classified by referring to their sides or their angles. When the three sides are equal, the triangle is called an <u>equilateral</u> triangle. When two sides of the triangle are equal, the triangle is called an <u>isosceles</u> triangle. If all three sides have different lengths, the triangle is called a <u>scalene</u> triangle.

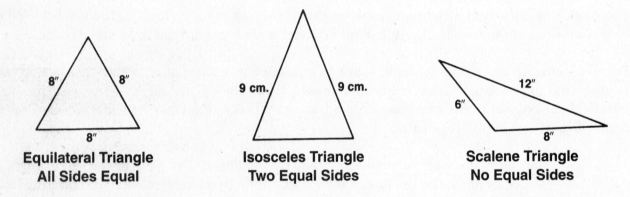

Equilateral Triangle
All Sides Equal

Isosceles Triangle
Two Equal Sides

Scalene Triangle
No Equal Sides

An <u>acute</u> triangle has three acute angles. The <u>obtuse</u> triangle has one obtuse angle. The <u>right</u> triangle has one right angle. An <u>equiangular</u> triangle has three equal angles and is also an equilateral triangle with all sides equal.

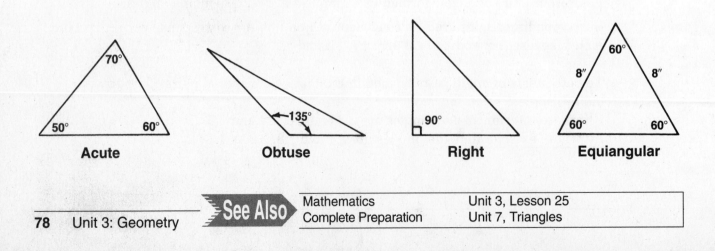

Acute   **Obtuse**   **Right**   **Equiangular**

> **See Also**   Mathematics   Unit 3, Lesson 25
>   Complete Preparation   Unit 7, Triangles

Triangle Rules

There are many basic principles or rules about triangles. The following rules will help you prepare for the GED Mathematics Test. If this is the first time you have studied basic geometry, your skills and knowledge will increase with practice.

Rule 1:   The base angles of the <u>isosceles</u> triangle are equal. In the isosceles triangle *BAE* (△*BAE*), $\overline{AB}$ and $\overline{AE}$ are the <u>sides</u> and $\overline{BE}$ is the <u>base</u>. The base angles are ∠*B* and ∠*E*. ∠*A* is called the <u>vertex angle</u>.

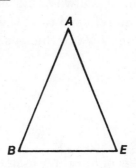

Rule 2:   The sum of the lengths of any two sides of a triangle must always be greater than the length of the third side. By adding the lengths of the two short sides, we can determine if the three given measurements can be sides of a triangle. Example A is a triangle because 4 + 6 is greater than 8. However, in Example B, 2 + 3 is less than 8. Therefore, we know Example B is not a triangle.

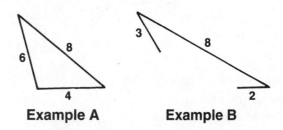

Example A   **Example B**

Rule 3:   The largest angle is opposite the longest side. In the right △*ESL*, the right angle *S* is the largest angle. The side opposite the right angle is called the <u>hypotenuse</u> ($\overline{EL}$). In △*XYZ*, ∠*Y* is opposite the longest side $\overline{XZ}$.

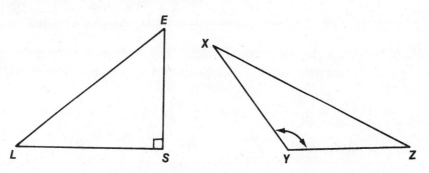

See Also

Mathematics
Complete Preparation

Unit 3, Lessons 25–27
Unit 7, Triangles

Unit 3: Geometry   **79**

Rule 4: The sum of the three angles of a triangle is always 180°. In the triangle *MNO* below, the sum of the values of three angles totals 180°. However, in the figure *RST*, the sum of the three angles exceeds 180°; therefore, *RST* is not a triangle.

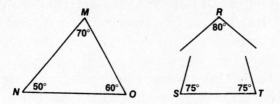

Rule 5: The right triangle's <u>hypotenuse</u> is always the longest side. The sides on the right triangle are often referred to as the <u>legs</u>. In $\triangle MLN$, $\overline{MN}$ is the hypotenuse, and $\overline{LM}$ and $\overline{LN}$ are the legs of the triangle.

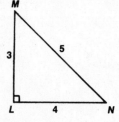

Rule 6: The <u>Pythagorean relationship</u> is used to find the hypotenuse of a right triangle. The sum of the squares of the legs of a right triangle (*a* and *b*) equals the square of the hypotenuse (*c*).

$$c^2 = a^2 + b^2$$
$$c^2 = 6^2 + 8^2$$
$$c^2 = 36 + 64$$
$$c^2 = 100$$
$$\sqrt{c^2} = \sqrt{100}$$
$$c = 10$$

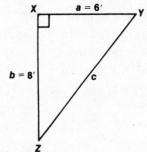

Rule 7: Two triangles are <u>congruent</u> when they have the same shape and size. Corresponding sides and corresponding angles are equal. Imagine lifting $\triangle ABC$ and placing it over the corresponding angles of $\triangle XYZ$.

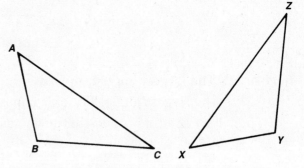

Rule 8: When two triangles have equal angles, the triangles are <u>similar</u> and have the same shape. A proportion can be made from corresponding sides of similar triangles.

$$\frac{4}{6} \diagup \!\!\!\!\! \times \frac{8}{\overline{EG}}$$
$$4\overline{EG} = 48$$
$$\frac{4\overline{EG}}{4} = \frac{48}{4}$$
$$\overline{EG} = 12$$

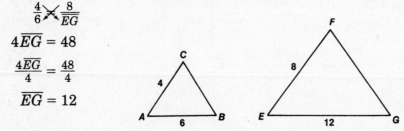

Solving Geometric Figure Problems

Directions: Use the information about angles, lines, and triangles to answer the following problems. Write the answers on the lines provided below the figures.

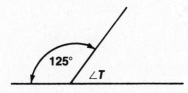

1. ∠T = _____

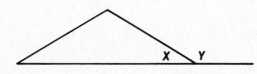

2. ∠X + ∠Y = _____

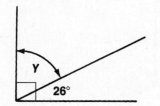

3. ∠Y = _____

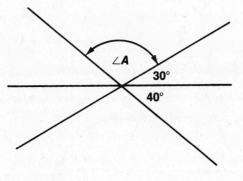

4. ∠A = _____

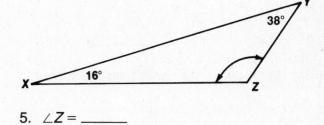

5. ∠Z = _____

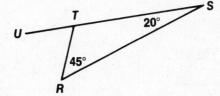

6. ∠RTU = _____

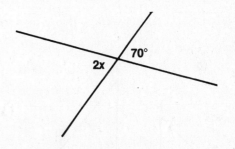

7. The value of x is _____

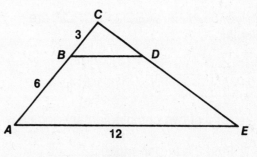

8. The length of $\overline{BD}$ is _____

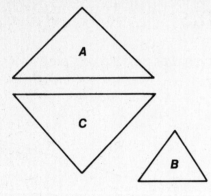

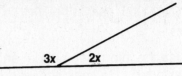

13. Find the value of *x*.

$x =$ _____

9. Which two of the above triangles appear to be congruent? _____

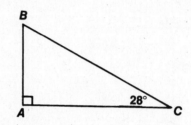

14. Find ∠*B*.

∠*B* = _____

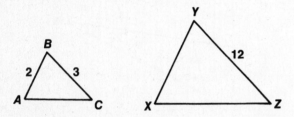

10. Find $\overline{XY}$ in △*XYZ* if △*ABC* and △*XYZ* are similar triangles.

$\overline{XY} =$ _____

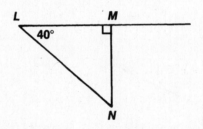

15. Find ∠*N*.

∠*N* = _____

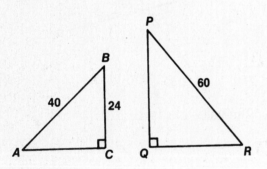

11. Solve for $\overline{PQ}$ if △*ABC* and △*PQR* are similar.

$\overline{PQ} =$ _____

12. The ratio of two complementary angles is 5:7. Find the larger angle. _____

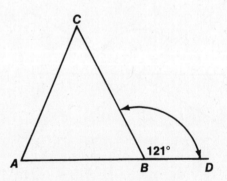

16. If $\overline{AC} = \overline{CB}$, find ∠*A*.

∠*A* = _____

Formula Problems: Perimeter, Circumference, Area, and Volume

By substituting the measurements of plane and solid geometric figures into formulas, you can solve a variety of problems. The measurements for the square and rectangle are referred to by the terms <u>length</u> and <u>width</u>. When referring to the triangle, the terms <u>base</u> and <u>height</u> are used. By adding the lengths and widths of the rectangle and square, you can find the distance around the objects, called the <u>perimeter</u>. The <u>area</u> of a figure is the surface that the figure covers. If you multiply the length and width by each other, you find the area of the rectangle or square. The <u>volume</u> of a three-dimensional figure is the space inside the figure. To find the volume you multiply the area of the base of the figure times the height of the figure. These formulas are given to you on the GED Mathematics Test.

Formulas for Perimeter, Circumference, Area, and Volume			
Rectangle $P = 2l + 2w$ $A = lw$	Square $P = 4s$ $A = s \times s = s^2$	Triangle $P = s + s + s$ $A = \frac{1}{2} bh$	Circle $C = (\pi)d \text{ or } 2(\pi)r$ $A = (\pi)r^2$
Rectangular solid $V = lwh$	Cube $V = s \times s \times s = s^3$	Pyramid $V = \frac{1}{2} bh \times h$	Cylinder $V = (\pi)r^2 \times h$

Rectangles, Squares, and Triangles

Example 1: Find the perimeter for each of the following.

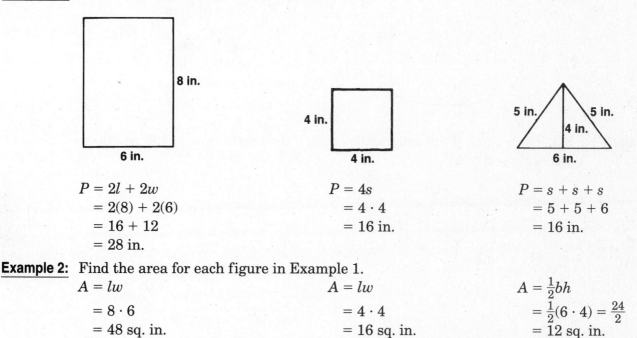

$$P = 2l + 2w$$
$$= 2(8) + 2(6)$$
$$= 16 + 12$$
$$= 28 \text{ in.}$$

$$P = 4s$$
$$= 4 \cdot 4$$
$$= 16 \text{ in.}$$

$$P = s + s + s$$
$$= 5 + 5 + 6$$
$$= 16 \text{ in.}$$

Example 2: Find the area for each figure in Example 1.

$$A = lw$$
$$= 8 \cdot 6$$
$$= 48 \text{ sq. in.}$$

$$A = lw$$
$$= 4 \cdot 4$$
$$= 16 \text{ sq. in.}$$

$$A = \frac{1}{2}bh$$
$$= \frac{1}{2}(6 \cdot 4) = \frac{24}{2}$$
$$= 12 \text{ sq. in.}$$

All of the answers are given in <u>squared</u> units because a measurement multiplied by the same measurement becomes squared.

See Also   Mathematics   Unit 1, Lesson 17 and Unit 3, Lessons 23, 28–29
Complete Preparation   Unit 7, Measurement and Volume

≡Circles

Circumference is the distance around a circle. Diameter is the widest distance across a circle. The diameter always goes through the center of the circle. Radius is the distance from the center of the circle to the edge and always equals $\frac{1}{2}$ the diameter. The symbol π (pi) is a constant used in each of the formulas for the circle. The value of this constant is rounded to 3.14 or $\frac{22}{7}$.

Example 3: Find the circumference and area of the circle shown below.

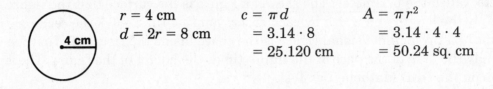

$$r = 4 \text{ cm}$$
$$d = 2r = 8 \text{ cm}$$

$$c = \pi d$$
$$= 3.14 \cdot 8$$
$$= 25.120 \text{ cm}$$

$$A = \pi r^2$$
$$= 3.14 \cdot 4 \cdot 4$$
$$= 50.24 \text{ sq. cm}$$

≡Volume of Geometric Solids

The volume of a three-dimensional figure is the area of the base of the figure times the height of the figure. When three like measurements are multiplied by each other, the answer is in cubic units.

Example 4: Find the volume of this cylinder.

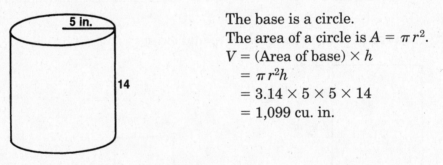

The base is a circle.
The area of a circle is $A = \pi r^2$.
$$V = (\text{Area of base}) \times h$$
$$= \pi r^2 h$$
$$= 3.14 \times 5 \times 5 \times 14$$
$$= 1{,}099 \text{ cu. in.}$$

Example 5: Find the volume of this rectangular solid if the length, width, and height are 7, 6, and 5 inches respectively.

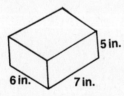

$$V = lwh$$
$$= 7 \times 6 \times 5$$
$$= 210 \text{ cu. in.}$$

Directions: Select and then use the appropriate formula to solve each of the following problems. Choose the best answer to each item.

Items 1 and 2 refer to the following diagram.

```
7 ft.
        Pool          18 ft.
        32 ft.
    7 ft.
```

Items 4 and 5 refer to the following figure.

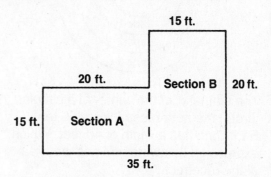

1. The measurements of a swimming pool are 32 feet by 18 feet. How much fencing is needed if the fence is to be built 7 feet from each side of the pool?

   (1) 100 ft.
   (2) 128 ft.
   (3) 134 ft.
   (4) 136 ft.
   (5) 156 ft.

2. Pool covers are sold in varying sizes. Which size cover would be the closest fit for the pool in the diagram above?

   (1) 400 sq. ft.
   (2) 500 sq. ft.
   (3) 600 sq. ft.
   (4) 700 sq. ft.
   (5) 800 sq. ft.

3. What is the area of a triangle whose base is 12 inches and height is 8 inches?

   (1) 100 sq. in.
   (2) 78 sq. in.
   (3) 50 sq. in.
   (4) 48 sq. in.
   (5) 15 sq. in.

4. Which expression below determines the total area of the figure above?

   (1) $(15 \times 20) + (15 \times 20)$
   (2) $(15 \times 20)(15 \times 20)$
   (3) $(15 \times 20) - (15 \times 20)$
   (4) $(15 \times 20) \div (15 \times 20)$
   (5) $(15 \times 20 \times 20 \times 15)$

5. The diagram above is a driveway. How much will it cost to blacktop the driveway if blacktopping costs $2.50 per square foot?

   (1) $ 500
   (2) $ 750
   (3) $1,250
   (4) $1,500
   (5) $1,750

6. The length of a rectangle is 28 inches and the perimeter is 84 inches. What is the area of the rectangle?

   (1)   392 sq. in.
   (2)   784 sq. in.
   (3)   920 sq. in.
   (4) 1,000 sq. in.
   (5) 1,568 sq. in.

Items 7 and 8 refer to the following diagram.

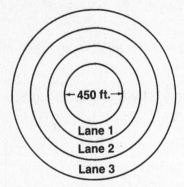

7. The diameter of the center of a circular three-lane auto racetrack is 450 feet. Each lane has a width of 40 feet. Which expression below determines the area of the racetrack?

(1) $3.14 \times 370 \times 370$
(2) $3.14 \times 345 \times 345$
(3) $3.14 \times 120 \times 120$
(4) 3.14×570
(5) 3.14×450

8. What is the approximate outer circumference of the racetrack?

(1) 2,166.6 ft.
(2) 1,789.8 ft.
(3) 1,413.0 ft.
(4) 1,161.8 ft.
(5) 753.6 ft.

9. Jackie needed to buy a piece of glass to cover the top of a circular lamp table with a diameter of 24 inches. How much glass is needed for the job?

(1) 37.68 sq. in.
(2) 75.36 sq. in.
(3) 225.25 sq. in.
(4) 452.16 sq. in.
(5) 1,808.64 sq. in.

10. A rectangle and a triangle have equal areas. The length and width of the rectangle are 24 cm and 8 cm respectively. If the base of the triangle is 16 cm, what is the height of the triangle?

(1) 24 cm
(2) 20 cm
(3) 16 cm
(4) 12 cm
(5) 8 cm

11. Al wants to build a concrete patio 9 inches thick. If the length of the patio is $14\frac{1}{2}$ feet and the width is $12\frac{3}{4}$ feet, about how many cubic feet of concrete will Al need?

(1) 3,672 cu. ft.
(2) 1,479 cu. ft.
(3) 184 cu. ft.
(4) 139 cu. ft.
(5) 26 cu. ft.

Item 12 refers to the following diagram.

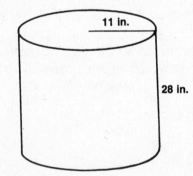

12. If one gallon contains 231 cubic inches, about how many gallons will the storage tank in the diagram hold?

(1) 11
(2) 46
(3) 90
(4) 121
(5) 10,638

Directions: Choose the best answer to each item.

1. Vincent Johnson wanted to reduce a picture from 12" × 16" so that the length would be 12". What will the width be?

   (1) 5 in.
   (2) 7 in.
   (3) 9 in.
   (4) 10 in.
   (5) 11 in.

Item 2 refers to the following diagram.

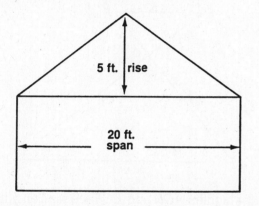

2. The pitch of a roof is the ratio of the vertical rise to the span. What is the pitch of a roof if the rise is 5 feet and the span is 20 feet?

   (1) 20:5
   (2) 5:1
   (3) 3:1
   (4) 1:4
   (5) 1:3

3. A 6-foot pole casts a 4-foot shadow. If the shadow of the tree is 25 feet, what is the height of the tree?

   (1) $25\frac{1}{2}$ ft.
   (2) $30\frac{1}{2}$ ft.
   (3) $37\frac{1}{2}$ ft.
   (4) $40\frac{1}{2}$ ft.
   (5) $45\frac{1}{2}$ ft.

4. A 3-foot seedling casts a 4-foot shadow at the same time a tree casts a 72-foot shadow. How tall is the tree?

   (1) 27 ft.
   (2) 54 ft.
   (3) 60 ft.
   (4) 72 ft.
   (5) 80 ft.

Item 5 refers to the following diagram.

5. The figure above shows a metal rod labeled AC in which AB:BC = 2:3. What is the length of the rod?

   (1) 20 ft.
   (2) 21 ft.
   (3) 24 ft.
   (4) 25 ft.
   (5) 30 ft.

Item 6 refers to the following diagram.

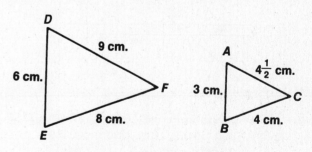

6. What kind of triangles are shown?

   (1) right
   (2) similar
   (3) congruent
   (4) equilateral
   (5) Not enough information is given.

Item 7 refers to the following diagram.

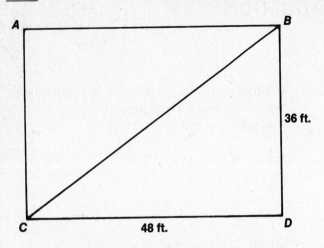

7. The rectangular flower bed in the center of a courtyard was planted with two colors of flowers. What is the length of $\overline{BC}$ in the diagram dividing the two colors of flowers?

(1) 50 ft.
(2) 60 ft.
(3) 65 ft.
(4) 70 ft.
(5) 75 ft.

Item 8 refers to the following diagram.

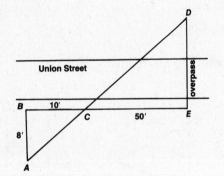

8. The engineers planned to build an overpass over Union Street. How long must the overpass $\overline{DE}$ be?

(1) 20 ft.
(2) 40 ft.
(3) 60 ft.
(4) 80 ft.
(5) 100 ft.

Item 9 refers to the following diagram.

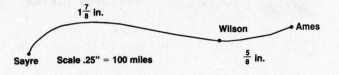

9. How many miles does Alfred travel if he starts at Sayre and ends at Ames?

(1) 100 miles
(2) 150 miles
(3) 200 miles
(4) 250 miles
(5) 1,000 miles

Item 10 refers to the following diagram.

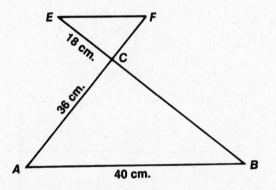

10. If triangles *ACB* and *ECF* are similar, what is the length of $\overline{EF}$ in the diagram above?

(1) 12 cm
(2) 18 cm
(3) 20 cm
(4) 24 cm
(5) 30 cm

Item 11 refers to the following diagram.

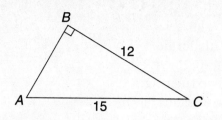

11. The triangle above is a right triangle. What is the length of $\overline{AB}$?

   (1)   3
   (2)   4
   (3)   9
   (4) 12
   (5) 15

Item 12 refers to the following diagram.

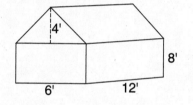

12. Stuart wants to put a new roof on his storage shed. He knows the roof is 12' long. Which expression should he use to find the width of the roof?

   (1) 6×12
   (2) $\frac{1}{2} \times 6 \times 4$
   (3) $\sqrt{3^2 + 4^2}$
   (4) $\sqrt{3^2 + 6^2}$
   (5) $2(6) + 2(12)$

13. In a right triangle the short leg is 11 and the hypotenuse is 15. Which expression below will give the length of the other leg?

   (1) $\sqrt{15 + 11}$
   (2) $\sqrt{15 - 11}$
   (3) $\sqrt{225 + 121}$
   (4) $\sqrt{225 - 121}$
   (5) Not enough information is given.

Item 14 refers to the following diagram.

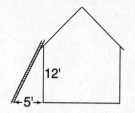

14. To repair her roof, Margie placed a ladder against the side of her house. The bottom of the ladder is 5 feet from the house and the top extends 2 feet above the roof. How long must the ladder be?

   (1) 12 ft.
   (2) 13 ft.
   (3) 14 ft.
   (4) 15 ft.
   (5) 16 ft.

Item 15 refers to the following diagram.

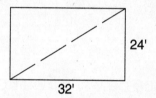

15. What is the length of the diagonal for the cement slab shown above?

   (1) 27 ft.
   (2) 30 ft.
   (3) 40 ft.
   (4) 45 ft.
   (5) 56 ft.

⣿Coordinates

A graph called a <u>coordinate system</u> can be used to describe algebraic relationships. Perpendicular lines x and y meet at an <u>origin</u>, (0,0). On this plane (a flat surface), the numbers to the right and above the origin are positive. The numbers to the left and below the origin are negative. The horizontal line is the x-axis and the vertical line is the y-axis. Each axis resembles the number line you studied earlier.

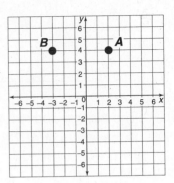

Each <u>point</u> on the plane is named by two numbers, an <u>x-coordinate</u> and a <u>y-coordinate</u>. The coordinates of point A are (2, 4), and the <u>coordinates</u> of point B are (−3, 4). The coordinates are called <u>ordered pairs</u> because the x-axis coordinate is always given first, and the y-axis coordinate is always given second (x, y).

Directions: Plot the following points.

1. $(-1, 3)$
2. $(2, -2)$
3. $(-3, 0)$
4. $(-4, -4)$
5. $(0, 2)$

Directions: Give the coordinates of the following points.

6. A _____
7. B _____
8. C _____
9. D _____
10. E _____

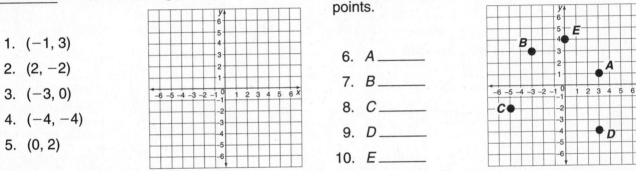

⣿Distance Between Two Points _____

To find the distance between two points on a graph when the points fall on a horizontal or vertical line, simply count the number of spaces between them. If, however, the points are <u>not</u> on a horizontal or vertical line, use the <u>distance formula</u>. Note that this formula is derived from the Pythagorean relationship.

$$d = \sqrt{(x_2 - x_1)^2 + (y_2 - y_1)^2}$$

To use the distance formula, you need the coordinates of two points, (x_1, y_1) and (x_2, y_2). Substitute the x and y values into the formula and solve for d.

Example 1: Find the distance between $(-3, 0)$ and $(5, 6)$.

$d = \sqrt{(x_2 - x_1)^2 + (y_2 - y_1)^2}$ $d = \sqrt{64 + 36}$
$d = \sqrt{(5 - (-3))^2 + (6 - 0)^2}$ $d = \sqrt{100}$
$d = \sqrt{(8)^2 + (6)^2}$ $d = 10$

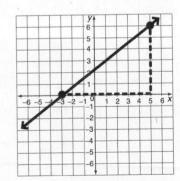

Directions: Find the distance between the following points.

11. $(-6, -7)$ and $(6, -2)$ _____
12. $(-7, 7)$ and $(-7, -9)$ _____
13. $(-8, -4)$ and $(4, 5)$ _____
14. $(-5, 4)$ and $(7, 4)$ _____
15. $(10, 9)$ and $(-10, -6)$ _____

See Also⟩ Mathematics
Complete Preparation

Unit 3, Lesson 21
Unit 7, Special Topics and Pythagorean Relationships

Graphing Linear Equations

An equation with both x and y variables with exponents of 1 is called a <u>linear equation</u>. Linear equations can be graphed on a coordinate system by finding two points on the line, plotting those points, and then drawing a line through the points.

Example 1: Graph the linear equation $x + 2y = 6$.
  Step 1: Pick a value for x, say $x = 0$. Substitute 0 into the equation for x. Solve for y.

$$x + 2y = 6$$
$$0 + 2y = 6$$
$$2y = 6$$
$$y = 3$$

When $x = 0$, $y = 3$. Now we can plot the point $(0, 3)$ on the graph. Notice that the point $(0, 3)$ is on the y-axis. This point is called the <u>y-intercept</u>; the line intercepts or crosses the y-axis at this point.

Find the <u>x-intercept</u> by letting $y = 0$ and solving for x. (see Step 2) Although other points can be used, the x- and y- intercept are often the easiest points to find when graphing linear equations.

  Step 2: Substitute $y = 0$ to find the x-intercept.

$$x + 2y = 6$$
$$x + 2(0) = 6$$
$$x = 6$$

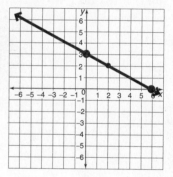

When $y = 0$, $x = 6$. Now plot the point $(6, 0)$ on the graph (remember that x is always given first) and draw a line through the points. Any point on this line is a solution to the linear equation $x + 2y = 6$. If you pick any point on the line, say $(2, 2)$ and substitute into the equation, you will get a true statement.

$$x + 2y = 6$$
$$2 + 2(2) = 6$$
$$2 + 4 = 6$$

Directions: Graph the following equations on the same graph.

1. Line 1 $x + y = 4$

2. Line 2 $x - y = -4$

3. Line 3 $x - y = 4$

4. Line 4 $x + y = -4$

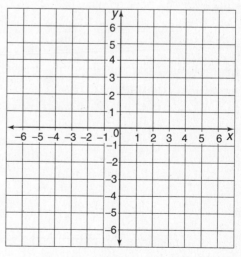

 Mathematics
Complete Preparation   Unit 2, Lesson 21
Unit 7, Special Topics

☰Slope of a Line

The <u>slope</u> of a line is the measure of the steepness of a line. Think of moving from point E to point F by first moving vertically ("rise"), then horizontally ("run"), as in Example 1. (This makes line $\overline{EF}$ the hypotenuse of a right triangle.)

Example 1:

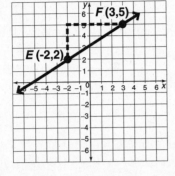

Example 2:

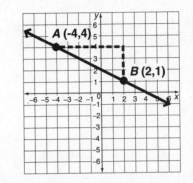

The slope of a line through points E and F is positive. Lines that slant upward toward the right have positive slopes. In Example 2, the slope of a line through points A and B is negative. Lines that point downward toward the right have negative slopes. Lines that are parallel to the x-axis (a horizontal line) have no slant and are said to have a slope of 0. Lines that are parallel to the y-axis (a vertical line) have no slant and are said to have an undefined slope. See Examples 3 and 4 below.

Example 3:

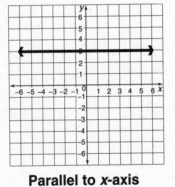

Parallel to *x*-axis

Example 4:

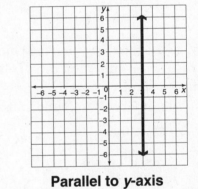

Parallel to *y*-axis

When given two points, the formula used to find the slope of a line (m) is the "rise" divided by the "run."

$$m = \frac{y_2 - y_1}{x_2 - x_1} = \frac{\text{rise}}{\text{run}}$$

Example 4: Find the slope of a line that passes through the points $(-2, 2)$ and $(4, 5)$.

Let $(-2, 2) =$ coordinate pair (x_1, y_1) and $(4, 5) = (x_2, y_2)$.

$$m = \frac{y_2 - y_1}{x_2 - x_1} = \frac{5 - 2}{4 - (-2)} = \frac{3}{6} = \frac{1}{2}$$

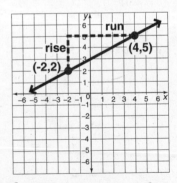

The graph shows the points and the line passing through them. Find the slope by substituting the x and y coordinates into the slope formula. The slope is $\frac{1}{2}$.

See Also | Mathematics Complete Preparation | Unit 2, Lesson 21 Unit 7, Special Topics

Directions: Plot the following points.

1. (4, 0)

2. (−2, −2)

3. (−3, 1)

4. (5, −2)

5. (0, 3)

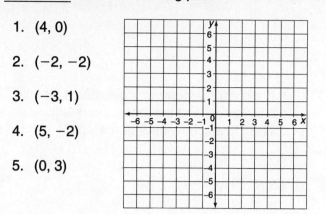

Directions: Give the coordinates of the following points.

6. A _____

7. B _____

8. C _____

9. D _____

10. E _____

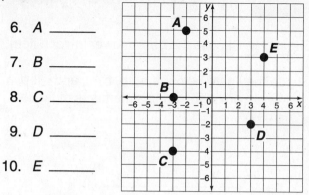

Directions: Find the distance between the following points.

11. (−3, 0) and (5, 6) _____

12. (−6, 6) and (3, −6) _____

13. (−4, −5) and (8, 0) _____

Directions: Choose the one best answer to each item.

14. Which ordered pair is a solution of $x + 2y = 7$?

   (1) (3, −2)
   (2) (−3, 1)
   (3) (2, 3)
   (4) (3, 2)
   (5) (1, −3)

15. Which of the following is the *y*-intercept for $2x − y = 9$?

   (1) (9, −2)
   (2) (5, 1)
   (3) (0, −9)
   (4) (0, −5)
   (5) (−9, 0)

16. Which of the following is the *x*-intercept for $3y − 4x = 8$?

   (1) (−4, 0)
   (2) (3, 4)
   (3) (0, 0)
   (4) (2, −5)
   (5) (−2, 0)

17. What is the slope of the line shown on the graph below.

   (1) $\frac{1}{2}$
   (2) 2
   (3) $\frac{2}{3}$
   (4) −3
   (5) $\frac{1}{3}$

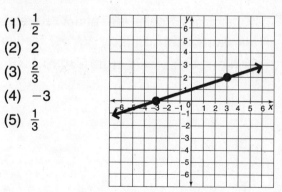

Directions: Choose the best answer to each item.

1. In the figure below, if a ∥ b, b ∥ c, and a⊥d, which of the following statements must be true?

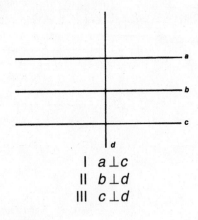

    I   a⊥c
   II b⊥d
  III c⊥d

(1) none
(2) I only
(3) I and II only
(4) II and III only
(5) I, II, and III

Item 2 refers to the following diagram.

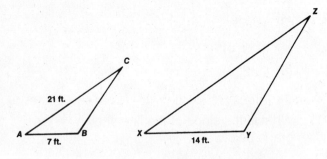

2. Triangular gardens *ABC* and *XYZ* are similar. If $\overline{AC}$ = 21 feet, $\overline{AB}$ = 7 feet, and $\overline{XY}$ = 14 feet, what is the length of $\overline{XZ}$?

(1)   7 ft.
(2)   21 ft.
(3)   42 ft.
(4)   84 ft.
(5) 294 ft.

3. If the outer diameter of a cylindrical tube is 27.14 inches and the inner diameter is 24.36 inches, how thick is the wall?

(1) 3.14 in.
(2) 2.79 in.
(3) 2.42 in.
(4) 2.29 in.
(5) 1.39 in.

4. The dimensions of a rectangular solid are 2, 3, and 4 inches. If the dimensions are doubled, what is the ratio between the volume of the original and the volume of the new rectangular solid?

(1) 1:2
(2) 1:8
(3) 2:1
(4) 2:5
(5) 3:4

5. The legs of a right triangle measure 18 inches and 24 inches. How long is the hypotenuse?

(1) 18 in.
(2) 20 in.
(3) 24 in.
(4) 26 in.
(5) 30 in.

6. Find the slope of the line that passes through the points (−2, 1) and (3, −4).

(1) −1
(2) 1
(3) 5
(4) −5
(5) 0

Items 7 and 8 refer to the following diagram.

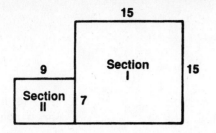

7. Which expression below expresses the difference in area between Section I and Section II?

   (1) $(7 \times 9) - (8 \times 9)$
   (2) $(7 + 9) - (15 + 15)$
   (3) $(15 \times 15) - (7 \times 9)$
   (4) $(15 + 24) - 2(7 + 9)$
   (5) $(15 \times 24) - (9 - 7)$

8. Which expression below expresses the difference in perimeter between Section I and Section II?

   (1) $2(7 + 9) - 2(15 + 24)$
   (2) $2(7 \times 9) - 2(15 \times 24)$
   (3) $2(15 + 15) - 2(7 + 9)$
   (4) $2(15 + 24) - (7 + 9)$
   (5) $2(15 + 24) - (7 \times 9)$

9. The perimeter of a rectangular garden is 84 feet. If the length is 24 feet, what is the width?

   (1) 30 ft.
   (2) 24 ft.
   (3) 20 ft.
   (4) 18 ft.
   (5) 16 ft.

10. The perimeter of a rectangle is 80 feet. If its length is 20 feet 6 inches, what is the width of the rectangle?

   (1) 29 ft.
   (2) $19\frac{1}{2}$ ft.
   (3) 18 ft. 6 in.
   (4) 18 ft.
   (5) 16 ft.

11. The area of one face of a cube is 25 sq. ft. What is the volume of the cube in cubic feet?

   (1)   5
   (2)   25
   (3)   125
   (4)   225
   (5)   250

Items 12 and 13 refer to the following diagram.

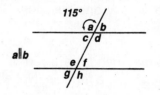

12. How many degrees are in $\angle b$?

   (1) 115°
   (2)   65°
   (3) $57\frac{1}{2}°$
   (4)   25°
   (5) none of these

13. Which angle corresponds to $\angle c$?

   (1) $\angle a$
   (2) $\angle b$
   (3) $\angle e$
   (4) $\angle f$
   (5) $\angle g$

Item 14 refers to the following diagram.

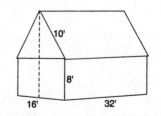

14. If the height of the barn walls is 8 feet, how high is the center of the roof from the ground?

   (1)   6 ft.
   (2)   8 ft.
   (3)   11 ft.
   (4)   14 ft.
   (5)   32 ft.

Simulated GED Test A

MATHEMATICS

Directions

The Mathematics Skills Simulated Test consists of multiple-choice questions intended to measure general mathematical skills and problem solving ability. The questions are based on short readings that often include a graph, chart, or figure.

You should spend no more than 90 minutes answering the questions. Work carefully, but do not spend too much time on any one question. Be sure you answer every question. You will not be penalized for incorrect answers.

Formulas you may need are given on the inside back cover of this book. Only some of the questions will require you to use a formula. Not all the formulas given will be needed.

Some questions contain more information than you will need to solve the problem. Other questions do not give enough information to solve the problem. If the question does not give enough information to solve the problem, the correct answer choice is "Not enough information is given."

The use of calculators is not allowed.

Record your answers on a copy of the answer sheet provided on page 156. Be sure all required information is properly recorded on the answer sheet. You may make extra copies of page 156.

To record your answers, mark the numbered space on the answer sheet beside the number that corresponds to the answer on the test.

Example:
If a grocery bill totaling $15.75 is paid with a $20.00 bill, how much change should be returned?

(1) $5.26

(2) $4.75

(3) $4.25

(4) $3.75

(5) $3.25   ① ② ● ④ ⑤

The correct answer is $4.25; therefore, answer space 3 would be marked on the answer sheet.

Do not rest the point of your pencil on the answer sheet while you are considering your answer. Make no stray or unnecessary marks. If you change an answer, erase your first mark completely. Mark only one answer space for each question; multiple answers will be scored as incorrect. Do not fold or crease your answer sheet.

Adapted with permission of the American Council on Education.

Directions: Choose the best answer for each item.

1. Guido purchased a coat on sale from a menswear store for 40% off the original price of $144. If the sales tax was 5%, what amount of change did Guido receive from a $100 bill?

   (1) $ 9.28
   (2) $13.60
   (3) $44.00
   (4) $52.40
   (5) $57.60

2. There are 20 cookies in a cookie jar. Some are raisin and some are sugar. Which of the following could not be a ratio of raisin cookies to sugar cookies?

   (1) 1:1
   (2) 3:2
   (3) 4:1
   (4) 5:1
   (5) 9:1

3. Harriet had 18 bus tokens. She gave $\frac{1}{3}$ of the tokens to her sister and $\frac{1}{3}$ of the remaining tokens to her brother. How many tokens did Harriet have left?

   (1)   4
   (2)   6
   (3)   8
   (4) 10
   (5) 12

4. Which expression has the same value as $3(4k + 2) + k$?

   (1) $8k + 8$
   (2) $12k + 6$
   (3) $12k + 8$
   (4) $13k + 6$
   (5) $15k + 6$

5. A swimmer competed in a diving meet and received the following scores for three events: 9.5 for the swan dive, 8.7 for the jackknife, and 8.8 for the cannonball dive. Which of the following statements expresses the arithmetic mean for the three dives?

   (1) $\frac{9.5 + 8.7 + 8.8}{3}$
   (2) $\frac{9.5 + 8.7}{8.8}$
   (3) $\frac{9.5 + 8.8 + 3}{8.7}$
   (4) $9.5 + 8.7 + 8.8$
   (5) 8.7

Items 6 and 7 refer to the following diagram.

SIGHT AND SOUND CD SALES

EACH O REPRESENTS 600 CDS	
COUNTRY AND WESTERN	O O O O O O O O O
RHYTHM AND BLUES	O O O O O O
CLASSICAL	O O O
JAZZ	O O O O

6. How many more rhythm-and-blues CDs were sold than jazz CDs?

   (1) 1,200
   (2) 1,800
   (3) 2,400
   (4) 3,600
   (5) 5,400

7. Which of the following expressions determines how many times greater the country-and-western CD sales were than classical CD sales?

   (1) $9(600) = 3(600)$
   (2) $\frac{9(600)}{3(600)}$
   (3) $\frac{3(600)}{9(600)}$
   (4) $9(600) + 3(600)$
   (5) $9(600) - 3(600)$

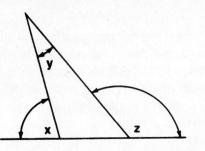

8. If ∠z equals 120°, what is the measurement of ∠y?

    (1) 80°

    (2) 60°

    (3) 40°

    (4) 20°

    (5) Not enough information is given.

9. If all sides of the polygon in the diagram below are equal in length, and its perimeter is 56 cm, what is the length of one side?

    (1) 4

    (2) 6

    (3) 8

    (4) 12

    (5) 14

10. The product of .49 × 97 is closest to which of the following expressions?

    (1) $\frac{1}{2}$ of 90

    (2) $\frac{1}{2}$ of 100

    (3) $\frac{1}{4}$ of 90

    (4) $\frac{1}{4}$ of 100

    (5) 4 times 100

11. Kenneth Wilburn traveled 121 miles on his way to a camping vacation. If the distance represented .2 of the entire trip, how many miles did he travel on his vacation?

    (1) 24.2

    (2) 96.8

    (3) 242

    (4) 484

    (5) 605

Item 12 refers to the following diagram.

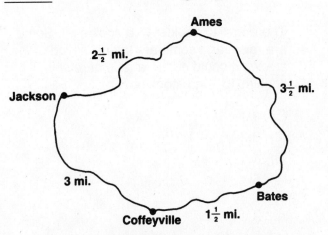

12. The Outfitters Backpacking Association planned its hiking outing to begin at Jackson and to end at Jackson. Which expression below states the average number of miles that the Outfitters planned to cover per hour if the hike was planned for 10 hours?

    (1) $\left(2\frac{1}{2} + 3 + 1\frac{1}{2} + 3\frac{1}{2}\right)$

    (2) $\left(2\frac{1}{2} + 3\frac{1}{2}\right)\left(3 + 1\frac{1}{2}\right) \div 4$

    (3) $\left(2\frac{1}{2} + 3\frac{1}{2}\right) - \left(3 + 1\frac{1}{2}\right) \div 10$

    (4) $\left(2\frac{1}{2} + 3\frac{1}{2} + 1\frac{1}{2} + 3\right) \div 10$

    (5) $\left(2\frac{1}{2} + 3\frac{1}{2}\right) \div \left(3 + 1\frac{1}{2}\right)$

13. Martha received an advertisement in the mail announcing a sale at Breyer's Fabric Store. The advertisement stated that all purchases of fabric and notions would be discounted by 20%. Martha has a preferred customer card which automatically gives an additional 10% discount on all purchases. If the piece of fabric that Martha wants to buy costs $12.90 per yard, what would be the cost of 4 yards?

(1) $15.20
(2) $15.48
(3) $36.12
(4) $41.68
(5) $46.44

14. Brent received a loan to purchase a car for $8,590. Which of the following expressions can be used to determine the amount of monthly payments (x) if the car was financed for 24 months?

(1) $24 - x = \$8,590$
(2) $x = \frac{\$8,590}{24} - 24$
(3) $\frac{\$8,590}{24} = x$
(4) $24 + x = \$8,590$
(5) $x = \$8,590(24)$

15. What is the value of y if $y - 14 = 10 - y$?

(1) −12
(2) −2
(3) 2
(4) 12
(5) 24

Item 16 refers to the following chart.

Candidate	A	B	C	D	E
Number of Votes Received	40	90	204	?	10

16. In a town of 600 voters, 5 candidates ran for the office of mayor. If every voter voted for exactly one candidate, as illustrated in the chart above, what is the maximum possible votes Candidate D can receive?

(1) 120
(2) 256
(3) 334
(4) 466
(5) 500

17. Telephone rates for Mendota to Oswego cost $4.50 for the first 20 minutes and $.75 for each 5 minutes thereafter. How long was a call from Mendota to Oswego if the total bill was $15.00?

(1) 30 min.
(2) 60 min.
(3) 90 min.
(4) 120 min.
(5) Not enough information is given.

18. Water glasses at Lippert Restaurant Supply House are priced at 10 glasses for $8.50. These same water glasses at Mary's Discount Dollar Store are reduced to $.55 per glass. What is the difference in price between the supply house and the discount store for 10 dozen glasses?

(1) $ 36
(2) $ 66
(3) $ 85
(4) $102
(5) $120

19. The Danish Baker Deli sold 356 roast beef sandwiches during one week. If each sandwich contains $\frac{1}{4}$ pound of roast beef, which expression below determines the number of pounds of roast beef served during that week?

(1) $356\left(\frac{1}{4}\right)$

(2) $356 - \frac{1}{4}$

(3) $\frac{1}{4} \div 356$

(4) $356 \div \frac{1}{4}$

(5) Not enough information is given.

Item 20 refers to the following diagram.

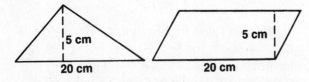

20. Which expression below determines the difference between the area of the triangle and the area of the parallelogram? (Hint: See formulas on inside back cover.)

(1) $5(20) - \frac{20 \times 5}{2}$

(2) $\frac{5 \times 20}{2} - 5(2)$

(3) $\frac{5 \times 20}{2} + 5(2)$

(4) $5(20) \div \frac{20 \times 5}{2}$

(5) $5(20) \div \frac{20 \times 2}{5}$

21. Evaluate $(5x - 5z) + ab$ if $a = 3$, $b = 5$, $x = 1$, and $z = -4$.

(1) 50

(2) 40

(3) 10

(4) −10

(5) −50

22. Martin purchased three fish at the Seafarer Fish Market. The total weight of the fish was $12\frac{3}{4}$ pounds. If the price per pound of the fish was $1.69, which expression below determines the amount Martin will pay for the fish?

(1) $\left(12\frac{3}{4}\right)(\$1.69)$

(2) $\left(12\frac{3}{4}\right)\$1.69 + 3$

(3) $\left(12\frac{3}{4} \times \$1.69\right) \div 3$

(4) $(\$1.69 \times 3) + 12\frac{3}{4}$

(5) $3\left(\$1.69 + 12\frac{3}{4}\right)$

23. The expression $-4(3x - 1)$ is equal to which expression below?

(1) $-12x - 4$

(2) $-12x + 4$

(3) $-12x - 1$

(4) $12x - 4$

(5) $12x + 1$

Items 24 and 25 refer to the following chart.

Selected Public Libraries

Location	Number of Branches	Volumes
Anaheim, CA	4	383,000
Baton Rouge, LA	10	493,509
Des Moines, IA	5	548,244
Louisville, KY	14	903,084
Philadelphia, PA	53	3,164,632
Syracuse, NY	8	509,386

24. What is the median number of bound volumes of books for the selected libraries in the chart above?

(1) 383,000

(2) 493,507

(3) 509,386

(4) 528,815

(5) 548,244

25. How many more bound volumes of books do the Philadelphia libraries have than the Anaheim libraries?

    (1) 2,261,548
    (2) 2,616,388
    (3) 2,655,246
    (4) 2,671,123
    (5) 2,781,632

26. Which of the following shows the correct order from smallest to largest value?

    (1) $\frac{2}{20}, \frac{28}{32}, \frac{15}{18}, \frac{32}{36}, \frac{32}{64}$

    (2) $\frac{28}{32}, \frac{15}{18}, \frac{32}{36}, \frac{32}{64}, \frac{2}{20}$

    (3) $\frac{15}{18}, \frac{32}{36}, \frac{32}{64}, \frac{2}{20}, \frac{28}{32}$

    (4) $\frac{2}{20}, \frac{32}{64}, \frac{15}{18}, \frac{28}{32}, \frac{32}{36}$

    (5) $\frac{32}{64}, \frac{15}{18}, \frac{28}{32}, \frac{2}{20}, \frac{32}{36}$

Item 27 refers to the following diagram.

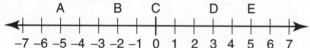

27. Which value on the number line above is equivalent to $-7.8 + 1.6 + 1.2$?

    (1) A
    (2) B
    (3) C
    (4) D
    (5) E

28. Four reading volunteers for the Lakeside Community Center share 354 hours of tutoring service. If the ratio of the number of hours tutored is 1:2:3:6, what is the greatest number of volunteer hours worked by any one volunteer?

    (1) 29.5
    (2) 59
    (3) 88.5
    (4) 147.5
    (5) 177

Item 29 refers to the following diagram.

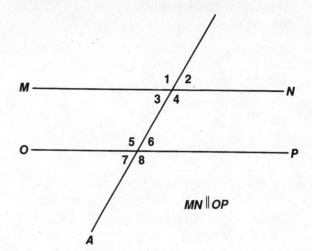

$MN \parallel OP$

29. Which statement is true about the diagram above?

    (1) $\angle 1$ is equal to $\angle 3$
    (2) $\angle 2$ and $\angle 8$ are alternate interior angles
    (3) $\angle 2$ and $\angle 6$ equal $180°$
    (4) $\angle 2$ and $\angle 7$ equal $180°$
    (5) $\angle 4$ and $\angle 5$ are alternate interior angles

30. Evaluate $(-2)^3 - 2(-2)$.

    (1) 4
    (2) -2
    (3) -4
    (4) -10
    (5) -12

31. The perimeter of a rectangular flower bed is 160 feet. Which of the following could be the length of one of its sides?

    I   60 feet
    II   80 feet
    III 100 feet

    (1) I only
    (2) II only
    (3) III only
    (4) I and II
    (5) II and III

32. Which of the following equations shows the sum of six times a number and four equals twenty-two?

    (1) $6 + 4n = 22$
    (2) $6x = 22$
    (3) $6x + 4 = 22$
    (4) $\frac{6x}{4} = 22$
    (5) $6(x + 4) = 22$

33. Of the 3,000 students enrolled at Thornton Consolidated High School, 53% are girls. Which expression below determines the number of boys?

    (1) $(1.00 - .53)(3,000)$
    (2) $(1.00 - .53) \div 3,000$
    (3) $1.00 + .53(3,000)$
    (4) $\frac{3,000}{1.00 - .53}$
    (5) $.53(3,000)$

34. The mileage scale on an interstate map shows that $\frac{1}{4}$ inch represents 140 miles. Using the same scale, what is the distance between two cities 2.5 inches apart?

    (1)   230
    (2)   500
    (3)   700
    (4) 1,000
    (5) 1,400

35. Which of the following equations means the same as "6 less than 5 times some number is 49"?

    (1) $5n + 6 = 49$
    (2) $5n - 6 = 49$
    (3) $5n = 49$
    (4) $5n + 6 = 43$
    (5) $5n - 6 = 6 + 49$

36. If the angles of triangle *EFG* are in the ratio of 2:3:4, what type of triangle is triangle *EFG*?

    (1) acute
    (2) equilateral
    (3) right
    (4) obtuse
    (5) Not enough information is given.

37. Which of the following expressions determines the distance of an automobile traveling at an average speed of 30 miles in *h* hours?

    (1) $d = 30h$
    (2) $d = \frac{30}{h}$
    (3) $h = \frac{d}{30}$
    (4) $h = \frac{30}{d}$
    (5) $30 = \frac{d}{h}$

Items 38 and 39 refer the following diagram.

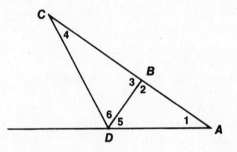

38. If $\angle BCD$ is another name for $\angle 4$, what is another name for $\angle 1$?

    (1) $\angle ACD$
    (2) $\angle BDA$
    (3) $\angle DAB$
    (4) $\angle CBC$
    (5) $\angle CDB$

39. Angles 2 and 3 are what type of angles?

    (1) complementary
    (2) supplementary
    (3) vertical
    (4) obtuse
    (5) acute

40. Due to financial problems at the Schurz Manufacturing Company, Darryl was asked to take a 10% annual cut in pay. How much will Darryl earn annually if his monthly salary is reduced to $1,665?

(1) $17,982
(2) $19,000
(3) $19,980
(4) $21,900
(5) $21,970

41. Find the value of $x^2 + y^2 + z^2$ if $x = -3$, $y = 2$ and $z = -1$.

(1) −15
(2)   −6
(3)   0
(4)   6
(5)   14

Item 42 refers to the following diagram.

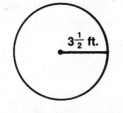

$3\frac{1}{2}$ ft.

42. The circular cover of a trampoline is pictured above. Which of the following is the approximate area of the trampoline cover? Round to the nearest whole square foot.

(1)   9
(2) 13
(3) 21
(4) 38
(5) 54

43. Find the value of x in the equation $3x - 6 = x + 4$.

(1) 2
(2) 3
(3) 4
(4) 5
(5) 6

Item 44 refers to the following diagram.

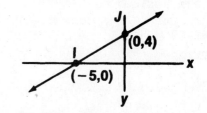

44. If the slope of a line indicates how much a line slants, describe the slope of the line passing through points I and J in the diagram above.

(1) zero
(2) positive
(3) negative
(4) not defined
(5) Not enough information is given.

Items 45 and 46 refer to the following information.

At the beginning of a trip, Mr. Clark's gas tank was filled with 19.8 gallons of gasoline and his odometer read 14,138.2 miles. During the trip, he stopped to refill his tank with 15.4 gallons of gas and his odometer reading was 14,446 miles.

45. How many miles per gallon did Mr. Clark average on his trip? Round your answer to the nearest gallon.

   (1) 19
   (2) 20
   (3) 21
   (4) 22
   (5) 23

46. What additional piece of information is necessary to determine the average cost per mile?

   (1) the cost of car insurance
   (2) the total cost of the car
   (3) the cost of a gallon of gas
   (4) the cost of finance charges
   (5) the monthly car note

47. The Dexter family budgeted $450 for food last month. Assuming that the cost of living rose 1.5% this month, how much more will the Dexter family spend for food this month?

   (1) $ 4.00
   (2) $ 4.50
   (3) $ 6.75
   (4) $45.00
   (5) $67.50

48. Which is the next value in the series $\sqrt{1}$, $\sqrt{4}$, $\sqrt{9}$, $\sqrt{16}$, $\sqrt{25}$?

   (1) $\sqrt{30}$
   (2) $\sqrt{36}$
   (3) $\sqrt{44}$
   (4) $\sqrt{49}$
   (5) $\sqrt{64}$

49. Amanda's shadow was 4 feet long when the shadow of a 16-foot statue was 12 feet long. How tall is Amanda?

   (1) 5 ft.
   (2) 5 ft. 1 in.
   (3) 5 ft. 2 in.
   (4) 5 ft. 3 in.
   (5) 5 ft. 4 in.

50. It takes 15 minutes to drain a pool containing 45 gallons of water. If a similar pool takes 35 minutes to drain at the same rate, how many gallons of water are in the similar pool?

   (1) 1,575
   (2) 1,500
   (3)   675
   (4)   525
   (5)   105

51. Which of the following formulas would be used to determine the simple interest rate received on a savings account of $800 if $126 is received for $3\frac{1}{2}$ years?

   (1) $r = \frac{pt}{i}$
   (2) $r = \frac{i}{pt}$
   (3) $r = \frac{t}{p}$
   (4) $r = \frac{ip}{r}$
   (5) $i = \frac{pt}{r}$

52. The Pattersons plan to lay a concrete block patio. The area that they want to cover is 15 feet by 18 feet. Each concrete block measures 3 feet by 3 feet. Three blocks sell for $15 or a single block sells for $7.50. Which expression below will provide the Pattersons with the number of blocks needed?

   (1) $(15 \times 18) - (3 \times 3)$
   (2) $3(3) \div (15 \times 18)$
   (3) $(18 \times 3) - (15 \times 3)$
   (4) $(15 \times 18) \div (3 \times 3)$
   (5) Not enough information is given.

Items 53 and 54 refer to the following diagram.

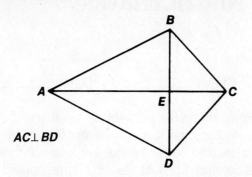

$AC \perp BD$

53. Which of the following angles is <u>not</u> a right angle?

   (1) $\angle BEA$
   (2) $\angle AED$
   (3) $\angle DEC$
   (4) $\angle BCE$
   (5) $\angle CED$

54. What is the measurement of $\angle ABE$?

   (1) 20°
   (2) 40°
   (3) 60°
   (4) 70°
   (5) Not enough information is given.

55. What does n equal if $111{,}111 + n = 191{,}111$?

   (1) 7×10^3
   (2) 8×10^4
   (3) 7×10^5
   (4) 8×10^5
   (5) 9×10^4

56. Which expression below determines the simple interest of $5\frac{1}{2}\%$ earned on $1,140 for 3 years?

   (1) $1,140 × 3 × 5.5
   (2) $1,140 × 3 × .055
   (3) $1,140 × .055
   (4) ($1,140 × .055) ÷ 3
   (5) ($1,140 × 3) ÷ 5.5

Analysis of Performance: Mathematics Simulated Test A

Name: _____   Class: _____   Date: _____

This chart can help you determine your strengths and weaknesses on the content and skill areas of the Mathematics GED Test. Use the Answer Key on pages 149–152 to check your answers to the test. Then circle on the chart the numbers of the test items you answered correctly. Put the total number correct for each content area and skill area in each row and column. Look at the total items correct in each column and row and decide which areas are difficult for you. Use the page references to study those areas.

Item Types	Set-Up	Solution	Total Correct
Arithmetic (pp. 3–53)			
Measurement	19, 20, 22, 31, 51, 56	1, 3, 11, 13, 18, 34, 40, 42, 45, 46, 47	_____ out of 17
Data Analysis	5, 7, 12, 33	6, 16, 24, 25	_____ out of 8
Number Relationships	10	2, 26, 48	_____ out of 4
Algebra (pp. 54–75)	14, 32, 35, 37	4, 15, 17, 21, 23, 27, 28, 30, 41, 43, 49, 50, 55	_____ out of 17
Geometry (pp. 76–95)	52	8, 9, 29, 36, 38, 39, 44, 53, 54	_____ out of 10
Total Correct	_____ out of 16	_____ out of 40	_____ out of 56 1–42 → You need more review. 43–56 → Congratulations! You are ready for the GED Test!

For additional help, see *Steck-Vaughn GED Mathematics.*

Simulated GED Test B

MATHEMATICS

Directions

The Mathematics Skills Simulated Test consists of multiple-choice questions intended to measure general mathematical skills and problem-solving ability. The questions are based on short readings that often include a graph, chart, or figure.

You should spend no more than 90 minutes answering the questions. Work carefully, but do not spend too much time on any one question. Be sure you answer every question. You will not be penalized for incorrect answers.

Formulas you may need are given on the inside back cover of this book. Only some of the questions will require you to use a formula. Not all the formulas given will be needed.

Some questions contain more information than you will need to solve the problem. Other questions do not give enough information to solve the problem. If the question does not give enough information to solve the problem, the correct answer choice is "Not enough information is given."

The use of calculators is not allowed.

Record your answers on a copy of the answer sheet provided on page 156. Be sure all required information is properly recorded on the answer sheet. You may make extra copies of page 156.

To record your answers, mark the numbered space on the answer sheet beside the number that corresponds to the answer on the test.

Example:
If a grocery bill totaling $15.75 is paid with a $20.00 bill, how much change should be returned?

(1) $5.26

(2) $4.75

(3) $4.25

(4) $3.75

(5) $3.25   ① ② ● ④ ⑤

The correct answer is $4.25; therefore, answer space 3 would be marked on the answer sheet.

Do not rest the point of your pencil on the answer sheet while you are considering your answer. Make no stray or unnecessary marks. If you change an answer, erase your first mark completely. Mark only one answer space for each question; multiple answers will be scored as incorrect. Do not fold or crease your answer sheet.

Adapted with permission of the American Council on Education.

Directions: Choose the best answer for each item.

1. The Smithson Building in the downtown area was resurfaced with 1,200 granite sections each 4' X 4'. Last year 30 sections needed to be repaired. What percent of the granite squares needed repair?

  (1)   2%

  (2) $2\frac{1}{2}$%

  (3) 20%

  (4) $20\frac{1}{2}$%

  (5) 25%

Item 2 refers to the following diagram.

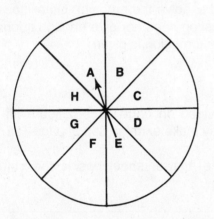

2. What is the probability of the spinner landing either on E or F on one spin?

  (1) $\frac{6}{8}$

  (2) $\frac{8}{6}$

  (3) $\frac{3}{4}$

  (4) $\frac{1}{4}$

  (5) $\frac{4}{1}$

3. Which of the following is not a true proportion?

  (1) $\frac{1}{2} = \frac{5}{10}$

  (2) $\frac{15}{3} = \frac{30}{10}$

  (3) $\frac{4}{6} = \frac{8}{12}$

  (4) $\frac{5}{8} = \frac{15}{24}$

  (5) $\frac{3}{15} = \frac{6}{30}$

Item 4 refers to the following diagram.

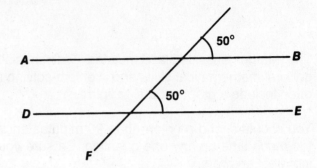

4. What type of line segments are $\overline{AB}$ and $\overline{DE}$ in the diagram above?

  (1) curved

  (2) perpendicular

  (3) vertical

  (4) intersecting

  (5) parallel

Items 5–10 refer to the table below.

World's Five Largest Cities Population Projections (in thousands)

City	1991	2000	Area (sq. mi.)
Tokyo-Yokohama, Japan	27,245	19,971	1,089
Mexico City, Mexico	20,899	27,872	522
Sao Paulo, Brazil	18,701	25,354	451
Seoul, Korea	16,792	21,976	342
New York, New York	14,625	14,648	1,274

5. Which city is expected to have the smallest population increase?

  (1) Tokyo-Yokohama

  (2) Mexico City

  (3) Sao Paulo

  (4) Seoul

  (5) New York

6. Which city is expected to have the largest population growth?

   (1) Tokyo-Yokohama
   (2) Mexico City
   (3) Sao Paulo
   (4) Seoul
   (5) New York

7. Which city has the largest area?

   (1) Tokyo-Yokohama
   (2) Mexico City
   (3) Sao Paulo
   (4) Seoul
   (5) New York

8. What was the population density (the ratio of people to area) of Seoul in 1991? Round to the nearest whole number.

   (1) 11 thousand per square mile
   (2) 25 thousand per square mile
   (3) 40 thousand per square mile
   (4) 49 thousand per square mile
   (5) 52 thousand per square mile

9. What will the population density for New York be in the year 2000?

   (1) 11 thousand per square mile
   (2) 18 thousand per square mile
   (3) 53 thousand per square mile
   (4) 56 thousand per square mile
   (5) 64 thousand per square mile

10. What will the percent of increase in population be for Mexico City for 1991 to 2000? Round to the nearest whole percent.

    (1) 1%
    (2) 10%
    (3) 31%
    (4) 33%
    (5) 36%

11. Which of the following statements is the smallest in value?

    (1) $6\frac{3}{4}$% of 50
    (2) 8% of 90
    (3) 50% of 100
    (4) $\frac{3}{10}$% of 70
    (5) $\frac{3}{4}$% of 240

12. Center City Gazette can print 125 Sunday newspapers in $1\frac{1}{4}$ hours. How many hours will it take to print the circulation quota of 2,000 newspapers?

    (1) 6
    (2) 8
    (3) 12
    (4) 18
    (5) 20

13. A fringe benefit package at Ace Novelty Corporation includes hospitalization, life insurance, dental care, and vision coverage. If the package is 15% of a worker's salary, what is the salary plus fringe benefits for a worker earning $21,600 annually?

    (1) $21,615
    (2) $22,695
    (3) $23,760
    (4) $24,040
    (5) $24,840

14. Mr. Perry bought three pieces of plastic tubing for three different projects. One project needed 1 foot 3 inches; the second project needed one piece 12 inches long. The third project needs 4.5 feet of tubing. If tubing costs $1.69 per foot, which of the following expressions below determines the cost of the tubing?

    (1) $\left(1\frac{1}{4} + 1 + 4\frac{1}{2}\right)(\$1.69)$
    (2) $\left(1\frac{1}{3} + 1 + 4\frac{1}{2}\right)(\$1.69)$
    (3) $\left(1\frac{1}{4} + 1 + 4\frac{1}{2}\right) + \$1.69$
    (4) $\left(1\frac{1}{3} + 1 + 4\frac{1}{2}\right) - \$1.69$
    (5) $\left(1\frac{1}{3} + 1 + 4\frac{1}{2}\right) \div \$1.69$

15. The cholesterol in one egg is 275 milligrams. How many milligrams are there in a half-dozen eggs?

    (1)   350
    (2)   412.5
    (3)   550
    (4) 1,650
    (5) 3,330

16. The expression $4.6 \times 10^3 + 125$ is equivalent to which expression below?

    (1) $4(100) + 6(10) + 125$
    (2) $4(1,000) + 6(100) + 25$
    (3) $4(1,000) + 6(1,000) + 125$
    (4) $4(1,000) + 7(100) + 25$
    (5) $4(1,000) + 7(100) + 125$

Item 17 refers to the following diagram.

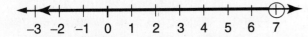

17. Which of the following solution sets is shown on the number line above?

    (1) $x > 7$
    (2) $x < 7$
    (3) $x < -7$
    (4) $x > -7$
    (5) $x = -7$

18. The Regal Book Store has 100 overstocked books to sell. The manager is going to mark some of the books $2 each and the remaining books $3 each. How many books must be priced at each price to receive $245?

    (1) 25 $2 books and 75 $3 books
    (2) 35 $2 books and 65 $3 books
    (3) 50 $2 books and 50 $3 books
    (4) 55 $2 books and 45 $3 books
    (5) 65 $2 books and 35 $3 books

19. In tossing a coin, what is the probability of landing on tails?

    (1) $\frac{1}{2}$
    (2) $\frac{1}{3}$
    (3) $\frac{1}{4}$
    (4) $\frac{1}{5}$
    (5) $\frac{1}{6}$

20. Twenty GED graduates are awarded a monetary scholarship to further their education. If the number of scholarship students represents 10% of the number of GED graduates, how many GED graduates are there in this class?

    (1)   90
    (2) 135
    (3) 150
    (4) 200
    (5) 250

21. The length of a rectangle is two less than twice the width. If the perimeter of the rectangle is 56 inches, what is the length?

    (1) 12 in.
    (2) 14 in.
    (3) 16 in.
    (4) 18 in.
    (5) 20 in.

Item 22 refers to the following diagram.

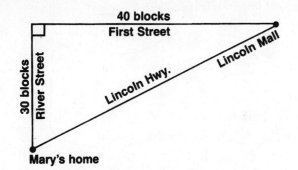

22. The diagram above shows two ways of going from Mary's home to Lincoln Mall. If First Street runs perpendicular to River Street, what is the distance in blocks if the trip is made on the Lincoln Highway?

   (1) 20
   (2) 30
   (3) 40
   (4) 50
   (5) 60

23. The difference between $\frac{1}{4}$ of a number and $\frac{1}{6}$ of the same number is 18. Which equation shows the correct relationship?

   (1) $\frac{1}{4}x - \frac{1}{6}x = 18$
   (2) $\frac{1}{4}x + \frac{1}{6}x = 18$
   (3) $\frac{1}{4} + 18 = \frac{1}{6}x$
   (4) $\frac{1}{6}x - \frac{1}{4}x = 18$
   (5) $\frac{1}{6}x + 18 = \frac{1}{4}x$

24. Of the 500 questionnaires sent out by Auto Review Magazine, the publisher received 225 questionnaires. Which of the following values represents the ratio of the responses to the number of questionnaires sent?

   (1) $\frac{1}{2}$
   (2) $\frac{1}{4}$
   (3) $\frac{1}{5}$
   (4) $\frac{1}{20}$
   (5) $\frac{9}{20}$

25. If $a = -1$ and $y = 2$, what is the value of the expression $2a^3 - 3ay$?

   (1) 8
   (2) 4
   (3) −1
   (4) −4
   (5) −8

26. Which of the following is greatest in value?

   (1) .0015
   (2) .005
   (3) .015
   (4) .05
   (5) .15

27. Five college students formed the Collegiate Cleaning Service to earn money during the summer months. The student leader was to receive $640 more than each of the other four students. If the students earned a total of $5,640 for the summer, what were the earnings of the student leader?

   (1) $4,000
   (2) $2,100
   (3) $1,640
   (4) $1,040
   (5) $ 640

Items 28 and 29 refer to the following diagram.

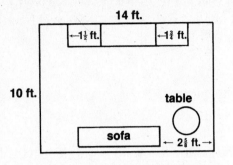

28. Scott purchased a three-section bookcase wall unit for one of the walls of his apartment. If Scott centers the unit on the wall, which expression below determines the amount of open space on each side of his wall unit?

(1) $1\frac{3}{4}$ ft. $+ 1\frac{1}{2}$ ft. $+ 2\frac{5}{8}$ ft.

(2) 14 ft $- \left(1\frac{3}{4}$ ft. $+ 1\frac{1}{2}$ ft. $+ 2\frac{5}{8}$ ft.$\right)$

(3) 14 ft $- \left(1\frac{3}{4}$ ft. $\times 1\frac{1}{2}$ ft. $\times 2\frac{5}{8}$ ft.$\right)$

(4) $1\frac{3}{4}$ ft. $+ 1\frac{1}{2}$ ft. $+ 2\frac{5}{8}$ ft. $- 10$ ft.

(5) Not enough information is given.

29. If Scott wants to carpet the living room with carpeting which costs $8.95 per square yard, how much money does he need? Round up to the nearest whole square yard.

(1) $143.20

(2) $134.25

(3) $116.35

(4) $107.40

(5) Not enough information is given.

30. Mr. and Mrs. LaMarr budgeted $3,250 to remodel their family room. The couple spent $1,250 on a few new furnishings. About what percent of money remained from the total remodeling budget? Round to the nearest whole percent.

(1) 21%

(2) 41%

(3) 62%

(4) 81%

(5) 85%

Item 31 refers to the following diagram.

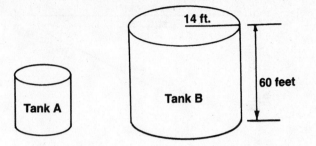

31. Grain awaiting transport by train is stored in cylindrical tanks. If both the radius and the height of Tank B are twice the size of Tank A, which expression below determines the approximate total number of cubic feet for both containers?

(1) $3.14 \times 14 \times 14 \times 60$

(2) $(3.14 \times 14 \times 14 \times 60) +$ $(3.14 \times 7 \times 7 \times 30)$

(3) $(3.14 \times 14 \times 14 \times 60) -$ $(3.14 \times 7 \times 7 \times 30)$

(4) $(3.14 \times 7 \times 7 \times 60)$

(5) Not enough information is given.

32. What is the value of x in the equation $10x + 7 - 8x = 13$?

(1) 2

(2) 3

(3) -1

(4) -2

(5) -3

33. The Concordia Apartment Complex was scheduled for renovation. One floor had 26,424 square feet of living space. If the renovation plans called for $\frac{1}{4}$ of the space for storage, how many square feet would be allowed for storage on that floor?

(1)   3,303

(2)   4,404

(3)   6,606

(4)   8,800

(5) 13,212

34. The Veterans' Club raises money for a local charity by selling all-occasion cards for a profit of $2 on each box. How many boxes must they sell to make a profit of $380?

(1) 100
(2) 105
(3) 155
(4) 190
(5) 210

35. The Metrovision Cable Company has four spools of electrical cable for the wiring of a section of town. The spools have 125 yards, 50 yards, 105 yards, and 100 yards of electrical wiring. If the section to be wired requires 600 yards, which expression below determines the additional wiring needed?

(1) $600 - (125 + 50 + 105 + 100)$
(2) $600(125 + 50 + 105 + 100)$
(3) $125 + 50 + 105 + 100 \div 600$
(4) $(50 + 105) \div (125 + 100)$
(5) $(50 + 105)600$

36. Mrs. Post flew from Cleveland to Memphis, a distance of 630 miles by air. If her return trip was made by car, and she drove 50 mph for $15\frac{1}{2}$ hours, what is the difference in miles between the distance of the flight and the distance by car?

(1) 55
(2) 75
(3) 85
(4) 95
(5) 145

37. Together Diane and Judy have $14.40. Diane has $\frac{1}{5}$ as much as Judy. Which equation could be used to find out how much money Judy has?

(1) $5n - 5 = \$14.40$
(2) $5n - n = \$14.40$
(3) $\frac{1}{5}n + n = \$14.40$
(4) $\frac{1}{5}n - \$14.50 = n$
(5) $\$14.50 + n = \frac{1}{5}n$

Item 38 refers to the following diagram.

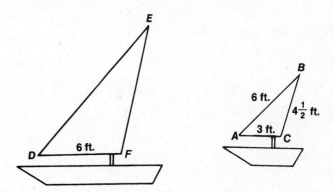

38. Assuming that the above triangular sails are similar, what is the length of $\overline{DE}$ in the larger triangle?

(1) 9 ft.
(2) 12 ft.
(3) 15 ft.
(4) 18 ft.
(5) 21 ft.

39. In an interest-paying account at Mutual State Bank, the interest on Mr. Wilson's account totaled $54 for the year. If the rate was 6% per year, which of the following expressions would determine the principle amount in the account?

(1) $\frac{\$54}{(.06)}$
(2) $.06(\$54)$
(3) $.06 \div \$54$
(4) $\frac{1}{.06} \times \$54$
(5) Not enough information is given.

Item 40 refers to the following diagram.

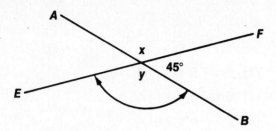

40. What is the value of ∠y in the diagram above?

   (1)   35°
   (2)   45°
   (3)   95°
   (4) 115°
   (5) 135°

41. If $n = -3$ and $x = (n + 5)(n - 5)$, what is the value of x?

   (1)   64
   (2)   16
   (3)   9
   (4)   -9
   (5) -16

42. William purchased a shirt and tie from the Men's Store. The two items were on sale and cost $20.00. The regular price of the two items was $25. What percent did he save by buying on sale instead of paying the regular price?

   (1) 10%
   (2) 20%
   (3) 25%
   (4) 30%
   (5) 35%

43. Write an equation for the following statement: Five times a number added to 9 is equal to the number decreased by 25.

   (1) $5x + 9 = x - 25$
   (2) $5x + x - 25 = 9$
   (3) $5 + x + x - 25 = 9$
   (4) $9 + 5x = -x - 25$
   (5) $9 + 5 + x = x - 25$

Items 44 and 45 refer to the following diagram.

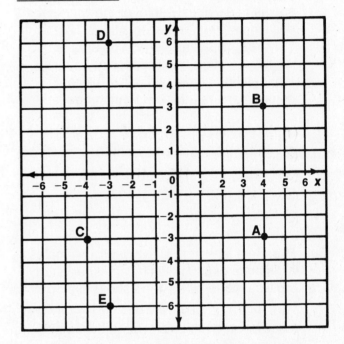

44. Which of the following points is not on this graph?

   (1) (4, 3)
   (2) (4, -3)
   (3) (-3, -6)
   (4) (-4, -3)
   (5) (-4, 4)

45. What is the distance between points A and B?

   (1) 2
   (2) 3
   (3) 4
   (4) 6
   (5) 8

Items 46 and 47 refer to the following diagram.

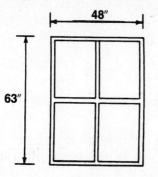

48. Donna bought an antique chest for $45 at a garage sale. She stripped and refinished the chest, and later sold it for 225% of what she had paid. What was the price of the refinished chest?

    (1) $ 50.00
    (2) $ 56.25
    (3) $ 59.85
    (4) $101.25
    (5) $112.50

46. Weather stripping is sold by the yard. If Regina has six windows with the measurements shown in her home that need to be weather stripped, which expression below determines the number of yards of weather stripping that will be needed? (Hint: 1 yard = 36 inches)

    (1) $6 \times 2(63 + 48) \div 12$
    (2) $6 \times 2(63 + 48) \div 6$
    (3) $6 \times 2(63 + 48) \div 36$
    (4) $6 \times 2(63 + 48) \div 4$
    (5) $6 \times 2(63 + 48) \div 16$

49. Lester measured the length of the street light's shadow to be 40 feet. Lester is 6 feet tall and his shadow's length was measured to be 4 feet long at the same time of day. How tall is the street light post?

    (1) 40 ft.
    (2) 60 ft.
    (3) 80 ft.
    (4) 100 ft.
    (5) 120 ft.

47. If one yard of weather stripping costs $.69, what is the total cost for the number of yards needed?

    (1) $76.59
    (2) $52.53
    (3) $35.25
    (4) $25.53
    (5) $24.84

50. The Riverside Drive Inn ran a coupon in the local newspaper for 50 cents off the hamburger deluxe meal that costs $4.50. If 250 customers used the cents-off coupons, which expression below determines the amount of money the restaurant took in for the hamburger deluxe meal?

    (1) 250 + $4.50 − $.50
    (2) 250($4.50 − $.50)
    (3) 250($4.50 + $.50)
    (4) 250($4.50)
    (5) $50(250) + $4.50

Items 51 and 52 refer to the following diagram.

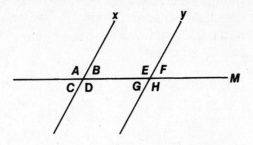

51. If lines x and y are parallel, which of the following angles is equal to ∠A?

   (1) ∠B
   (2) ∠F
   (3) ∠G
   (4) ∠C
   (5) ∠H

52. If ∠E is 20° greater than ∠G, what is the measure of ∠E?

   (1) 80°
   (2) 90°
   (3) 100°
   (4) 110°
   (5) 120°

Items 53 and 54 refer to the following diagram.

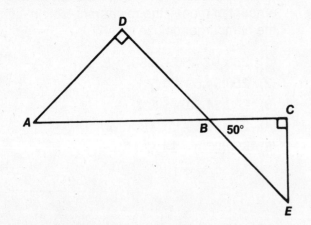

53. What is the measurement of ∠DAB?

   (1) 40°
   (2) 60°
   (3) 90°
   (4) 100°
   (5) 110°

54. What is the measurement of ∠DBC?

   (1) 100°
   (2) 110°
   (3) 120°
   (4) 130°
   (5) 140°

55. Which of the following cannot be the measures of the angles in a triangle?

   (1) 85°, 35°, and 90°
   (2) 70°, 55°, and 55°
   (3) 65°, $57\frac{1}{2}°$, and $57\frac{1}{2}°$
   (4) 60°, 60°, 60°
   (5) 45°, 45°, and 90°

56. If the vertex angle of an isosceles triangle measures 50°, what is the total sum of the base angles?

   (1) 134°
   (2) 130°
   (3) 75°
   (4) 68°
   (5) 65°

≣Analysis of Performance: Mathematics Simulated Test B

Name: _____ Class: _____ Date: _____

This chart can help you determine your strengths and weaknesses on the content and skill areas of the Mathematics GED Test. Use the Answer Key on pages 152–155 to check your answers to the test. Then circle on the chart the numbers of the test items you answered correctly. Put the total number correct for each content area and skill area in each row and column. Look at the total items correct in each column and row and decide which areas are difficult for you. Use the page references to study those areas.

Test B Analysis of Performance Chart

Item Types	Set-Up	Solution	Total Correct
Arithmetic (pp. 3–53)			
Measurement	14, 28, 35, 39, 46, 50	1, 15, 20, 29, 30, 33, 36, 42, 47, 48	_____ out of 16
Data Analysis		2, 7, 19	_____ out of 3
Number Relationships	16	3, 5, 6, 8, 9, 10, 11, 13, 24, 26	_____ out of 11
Algebra (pp. 54–75)	23, 37, 43	12, 17, 18, 21, 25, 27, 32, 34, 41, 49	_____ out of 13
Geometry (pp. 76–95)	31	4, 22, 38, 40, 44, 45, 51, 52, 53, 54, 55, 56	_____ out of 13
Total Correct	_____ out of 11	_____ out of 45	_____ out of 56 1–42 → You need more review. 43–56 → Congratulations! You are ready for the GED Test!

For additional help, see *Steck-Vaughn GED Mathematics.*

Answers and Explanations

UNIT 1: ARITHMETIC

Whole Number Concepts (page 3)

1. $324 < 432$

2. $973 = 973$

3. $1,036 > 1,008$

4. $560 < 5,600$

5. $2,779 > 2,769$

6. $400 < 430$

7. $6,325 < 6,394$

8. $12,992 > 12,991$

9. $180,000 > 18,000$

10. $85,063 < 85,630$

11. 293; 329; 392; 923; 932

12. 408; 480; 488; 804; 844

13. 5,316; 5,631; 6,153; 6,315; 6,531

14. 705; 750; 7,005; 7,050; 7,500

15. 8,914; 9,842; 18,429; 19,482; 98,421

16. 19 rounds to 20

17. 731 rounds to 730

18. 2,945 rounds to 2,950

19. 4,505 rounds to 4,500

20. 32,098 rounds to 32,100

21. 683,257 rounds to 683,300

22. 5,527 rounds to 6,000

23. 12,206 rounds to 12,000

24. 499,820 rounds to 500,000

25. 37,800 rounds to 40,000

26. 855,399 rounds to 860,000

27. 702,906 rounds to 700,000

28. 493,600 rounds to 500,000

29. 1,253,378 rounds to 1,300,000

30. 5,402,186 rounds to 5,400,000

31. 3,176,942 rounds to 3,000,000

32. 95,681,300 rounds to 96,000,000

33. 462,500,000 rounds to 463,000,000

Estimating with Whole Numbers (page 4)

1. **(3) $3,552** 592 rounds to 600
$600 \times \$6 = \$3,600$
$3,552 is closest to $3,600.

2. **(4) 2,046,000** Round 11 to 10 and 186,282 to 186,300.
$186,300 \times 10 = 1,863,000$
2,046,000 is the next <u>larger</u> answer. Note that option (3) 1,860,000 is not correct because 11 is greater than 10 and 186,282 is greater than 186,000, the numbers used to obtain this estimate.

3. **(2) 60** Round. 29,000 to 30,000
$\frac{30,000}{500} = 60$

4. **(5) 645** Round each number to the nearest hundred:
$3,500 - 2,800 = 700$.
In this problem estimating does not help. You must find the exact answer:
$3,452 - 2,807 = 645$

Whole Numbers: Computation Practice (page 5)

1.
$$
\begin{array}{r}
144 \\
\times\ 23 \\
\hline
432 \\
2\ 88 \\
\hline
3,312
\end{array}
$$

2.
$$
\begin{array}{r}
24,593 \\
-10,638 \\
\hline
13,955
\end{array}
$$

3.
```
  37,454
  41,345
  49,496
 +22,738
 151,033
```

4.
```
    28
32)896
  64
  256
  256
```

5.
```
   9,675
 ×   326
  58 050
  193 50
 2 902 5
 3,154,050
```

6.
```
  90,000
 −82,575
   7,425
```

7.
```
      6,400
36)230,400
   216
    14 4
    14 4
```

8.
```
  861
  495
 +827
 2,183
```

9.
```
    8,622
 ×   393
   25 866
   775 98
  2 586 6
  3,388,446
```

10.
```
    946
 30,306
 58,275
 +67,580
 157,107
```

11.
```
  658,235
 −621,791
   36,444
```

12.
```
  7,478
 +9,757
 17,235
```

13.
```
    5,763
 ×    472
   11 526
  403 41
 2 305 2
 2,720,136
```

14.
```
          708
502)355,416
   351 4
     4 016
     4 016
```

15.
```
      14
  11,000
 +     5
  11,019
```

16.
```
   8,311
  −7,059
   1,252
```

17.
```
    203
  ×111
    203
   2 03
  20 3
  22,533
```

18.
```
       30,677 R 6
24)736,254
   72
   16 2
   14 4
    1 85
    1 68
      174
      168
        6
```

GED Practice: Whole Numbers I (Page 6)

1. (3) 59
```
  753
 −694
   59
```

2. (4) $1,125
```
 225 groups of 3's
3)675
  6
   7
   6
  15
  15
```
```
    $5.00
 ×   225
   25 00
  100 0
 1 000
 $1,125.00
```

3. (4) 5,462
```
   356          1,307
 ×   8        ×     2
 2,848          2,614
```
```
   2,848
  +2,614
   5,462
```

4. (5) 65,658
```
  2,118
 ×   31
  2 118
 63 54
 65,658
```

5. (4) 5,241,799
```
  4,600,602
 +  641,197
  5,241,799
```

6. (4) 747
```
  3,121
 −2,374
    747
```

GED Practice: Whole Numbers II (pages 7–8)

1. (3) 2,000

	Exact	Rounded
Monday	531	500
Tuesday	116	100
Wednesday	285	300
Thursday	432	400
Friday	157	200
Saturday	480	+500
	2,001	2,000

2. (4) 258
```
   116          531
  +157         −273
   273          258
```

3. (4) $12
```
 200 shirts × $18 =  $3,600
 200 shirts × $14 = + 2,800
                     $6,400
```
```
  $7,000           $12
 − 6,400        50)$600
 $  600            50
                  100
                  100
```

4. (3) 15

$$\begin{array}{r} 108 \\ + 72 \\ \hline 180 \end{array}$$

$$\begin{array}{r} 15 \\ 12\overline{)180} \\ 12 \\ \hline 60 \\ 60 \end{array}$$

5. (1) 12 in.

$$\begin{array}{r} 36 \\ +24 \\ \hline 60 \end{array}$$

$$\begin{array}{r} 72 \\ -60 \\ \hline 12 \end{array}$$

6. (4) $2,304.20

$$\begin{array}{r} \$\ 258.45 \\ \times\quad 36 \\ \hline 1\ 550\ 70 \\ 7\ 753\ 5 \\ \hline \$9,304.20 \end{array}$$

$$\begin{array}{r} \$9,304.20 \\ -\ 7,000.00 \\ \hline \$2,304.20 \end{array}$$

7. (4) August

Month	Deposit	End-of-Month Balance
April	$75	$ 75
May	50	125
June	55	180
July	45	225
August	40	265
September	75	340

8. (1) $265

$50 + $55 + $45 + $40 + $75 = $265
or $340 − $75 = $265

9. (5) September

10. (4) $265

$340 − $135 = $205
$205 + $60 = $265

11. (3) 150 miles

$3 \times 50 = 150$

12. (4) 225

$450 \div 2 = 225$

13. (4) 9 hours

$90 \times 6 = 540$ 　　　$\dfrac{540}{60} = 9$

14. (2) Between 75 and 125 Round each number to the nearest 100. Add to find the number of pots used.

$$\begin{array}{r} 1,300 \\ 1,500 \\ +2,100 \\ \hline 4,900 \end{array}$$

Subtract the total from 5,000.

$$\begin{array}{r} 5,000 \\ -4,900 \\ \hline 100 \end{array}$$

GED Practice: Solving Word Problems I (Page 11)

1. (3) $2,000

$$\begin{array}{r} \$17,532 \\ +\ 6,468 \\ \hline \$24,000 \end{array}$$

$24,000 \div 12 =$
$2,000

2. (2) 148

$$\begin{array}{r} 15 \\ 36 \\ 20 \\ 5 \\ 24 \\ +48 \\ \hline 148 \end{array}$$

3. (3) $6,834

$$\begin{array}{r} \$169 \\ \times\quad 36 \\ \hline 1\ 014 \\ 5\ 07 \\ \hline \$6,084 \end{array}$$

$$\begin{array}{r} \$6,084 \\ +\quad 750 \\ \hline \$6,834 \end{array}$$

4. (3) 200

$$\begin{array}{r} 2\ 00. \\ 4.50\overline{)900.00} \\ 900 \end{array}$$

5. (5) $39

$$\begin{array}{r} \$259 \\ -\quad 25 \\ \hline \$234 \end{array}$$

$$\begin{array}{r} \$\ 39 \\ 6\overline{)\$234} \\ 18 \\ \hline 54 \\ 54 \end{array}$$

6. (3) $5,500

Exact	Rounded
$1,321	1,300
950	1,000
1,529	1,500
+ 1,734	1,700
	$5,500

7. (4) 25 min.

$$\begin{array}{r} \$2.25 \\ -\ .25 \\ \hline \$2.00 \end{array}$$

$$\begin{array}{r} 20. \\ .10\overline{)2.00} \\ 2\ 0 \end{array}$$

$$\begin{array}{r} 5 \\ +20 \\ \hline 25 \end{array}$$

GED Practice: Solving Word Problems II (page 12)

1. (3) $10,000

$$\begin{array}{r} \$10,000 \\ 15\overline{)\$150,000} \\ 15 \end{array}$$

2. (4) 2,635

$$\begin{array}{r} 15,810\ \text{bricks} \\ 4\overline{)63,240}\ \text{per layer} \\ 4 \\ \hline 23 \\ 20 \\ \hline 3\ 2 \\ 3\ 2 \\ \hline 4 \\ 4 \end{array}$$

$$\begin{array}{r} 2,635\ \text{bricks} \\ 6\overline{)15,810}\ \text{each day} \\ 12 \\ \hline 3\ 8 \\ 3\ 6 \\ \hline 21 \\ 18 \\ \hline 30 \\ 30 \end{array}$$

3. (4) 448

$$\begin{array}{r} 14 \\ \times\ 4 \\ \hline 56 \end{array} \qquad \begin{array}{r} 56 \\ \times\ 8 \\ \hline 448 \end{array}$$

4. (2) $515

$$\begin{array}{r} \$3,600 \\ 780 \\ +\ 1,800 \\ \hline \$6,180 \end{array} \qquad \frac{\$6,180}{12} = \$515$$

5. (5) $270

$$\begin{array}{r} 15 \\ \times 36 \\ \hline 90 \\ 45 \\ \hline 540 \end{array} \qquad \begin{array}{r} 5\ 40 \\ \times \$.50 \\ \hline \$270.00 \end{array}$$

6. (2) $150

$$\begin{array}{r} \$7.99 \\ \times\ \ 15 \\ \hline 39\ 95 \\ 79\ 9 \\ \hline \$119.85 \end{array} \qquad \begin{array}{r} \$270.00 \text{ from Item 5.} \\ -119.85 \\ \hline \$150.15 \end{array}$$

$150.15 rounds to $150

7. (4) 160

$$\begin{array}{r} 105 \\ \times\ \ 3 \\ \hline 315 \end{array} \qquad \begin{array}{r} 475 \\ -315 \\ \hline 160 \end{array}$$

Missing Information Practice (page 14)

1. the number of Republicans

2. the number of people in the Marble family

3. the number of bicycles sold

4. A. the number of miles to a gallon of gasoline for his car (to compute the number of gallons of gasoline used)
   B. the cost per gallon of gasoline

5. A. the original amount in the book account
   B. the amount spent on books for the first five months

6. A. the cost of each item purchased or the total bill
   B. the amount of money given to the clerk

Extraneous Information Practice (page 15)

1. Extra information: the interest amount of $1,578. The answer is ($1,055 + $325) ÷ 12 = $115.

2. Extra information: the driver was paid $5.00 per hour. The answer is $15.95 + $17.98 + $24.35 + $25.45 = $83.73

3. Extra information: union dues of $325. The answer is $18,750 − $15,750 = $3,000.

4. Extra information: the $1,675 cost of their appliances. The answer is $3,144 ÷ 24 = $131.

5. Extra information: the 1,574 papers sold by the Tribune and the daily amounts for all three papers. The answer is 2,631 − 587 = 2,044.

Order of Operations (page 16)

1. $3(7 + 4) - 18 \div 9 = 3(11) - 18 \div 9 = 33 - 2 = 31$

2. $\frac{5 \times 4 + 2}{17 - 2 \times 3} = \frac{20 + 2}{17 - 6} = \frac{22}{11} = 2$

3. $6(7 - 5) + 4 = 6(2) + 4 = 12 + 4 = 16$

4. $14 + 28 \div 7 = 14 + 4 = 18$

5. $\frac{5 \times 6 + 2}{12 - 4} = \frac{30 + 2}{8} = \frac{32}{8} = 4$

6. $8 + 4 \times 2 = 8 + 8 = 16$

7. $(5 + 3) \times (8 - 3) = 8 \times 5 = 40$

8. $25 \div 5 + (7 + 2) = 5 + 9 = 14$

9. $28 \div 4 + 28 \div 7 = 7 + 4 = 11$

10. $\frac{27}{9 - 2(3)} = \frac{27}{9 - 6} = \frac{27}{3} = 9$

11. $8(2 + 9) - 40 = 8(11) - 40 = 88 - 40 = 48$

12. $7 + (4 + 2) \times 3 = 7 + 6 \times 3 = 7 + 18 = 25$

13. $\frac{(6 - 2)}{(3 + 1)} = \frac{4}{4} = 1$

14. $5 + 2 \times 4 = 5 + 8 = 13$

15. $\frac{8}{2} + \frac{18}{6} = 4 + 3 = 7$

16. $6(3 + 7) - 4(4 - 2) = 6(10) - 4(2) = 60 - 8 = 52$

17. $\frac{21}{(5 - 2)} = \frac{21}{3} = 7$

18. $36 + \frac{12}{6} = 36 + 2 = 38$

19. $9 \times 9 + 3 \times 4 = 81 + 12 = 93$

20. $100 - 2 \times 50 = 100 - 100 = 0$

21. $(8 + 9) \times (4 + 3) = 17 \times 7 = 119$

22. $\frac{(3 + 7 + 10)}{(2 + 3)} = \frac{20}{5} = 4$

23. $\frac{63}{9} + 4 = 7 + 4 = 11$

24. $\frac{55}{11} \times \frac{81}{(3 + 6)} = 5 \times \frac{81}{9} = 5 \times 9 = 45$

Set-Up Problems Practice (page 18)

1. $\$110 \times 5 \div 40$ OR $\frac{\$110 \times 5}{40}$

2. $\$1,500 - (\$375 + \$700)$ OR $\$1,500 - \$375 - \$700$

3. $\$20 - (5 \times \$.59 + 4 \times \$1.69)$ OR $\$20 - (5 \times \$.59) - (4 \times \$1.69)$

4. $\$1.09 \div 12$ OR $\frac{\$1.09}{12}$

5. $\$19,500 - 12 \times \$1,100$

6. $\$150 \div \$12.50$ OR $\frac{\$150}{\$12.50}$

7. $60 - 5 \times 2$

8. $(27 \times \$3) + (30 - 27) \times \$1$ OR $27(\$3) + (30 - 27)(\$1)$

GED Practice: Set-Up Problems (page 19)

1. **(5) Not enough information is given.** You need to know the number of items Ernesto sold. (28 days is extraneous information.)

2. **(5) 52(\$110 − \$100) ÷ 4** You must change average cost per week for the family of four to average cost per year per family member.

3. **(3) 2(36 ÷ 2)**

4. **(4) $\frac{\$6,096}{24}$**

5. **(1) (40 + 31 + 51) ÷ 3**

6. **(1) 3(657)**

Fractions: Computation Practice (page 20)

1. $\frac{1}{3} \div \frac{3}{4} = \frac{1}{3} \times \frac{4}{3} = \frac{4}{9}$

2. $\frac{5}{8} \times 16 = \frac{5}{8} \times \frac{16}{1} = \frac{80}{8} = 10$

3. $32 \times \frac{13}{16} = \frac{32}{1} \times \frac{13}{16} = \frac{416}{16} = 26$

4. $\begin{aligned} 21\frac{3}{10} &= 21\frac{6}{20} \\ -13\frac{1}{4} &= 13\frac{5}{20} \\ \hline &\quad 8\frac{1}{20} \end{aligned}$

5. $\begin{aligned} \frac{7}{10} &= \frac{21}{30} \\ +\frac{11}{30} &= \frac{11}{30} \\ \hline \frac{32}{30} &= 1\frac{2}{30} = 1\frac{1}{15} \end{aligned}$

6. $\begin{aligned} 8\frac{2}{5} &= 8\frac{4}{10} \\ 14\frac{7}{10} &= 14\frac{7}{10} \\ + 9\frac{9}{10} &= 9\frac{9}{10} \\ \hline 31\frac{20}{10} &= 31 + 2 = 33 \end{aligned}$

7. $6 \div 1\frac{1}{2} = \frac{6}{1} \div \frac{3}{2} = \frac{6}{1} \times \frac{2}{3} = \frac{12}{3} = 4$

8. $4\frac{1}{4} \div 2\frac{4}{5} = \frac{17}{4} \div \frac{14}{5} = \frac{17}{4} \times \frac{5}{14} = \frac{85}{56} = 1\frac{29}{56}$

9. $2\frac{1}{3} \times 1\frac{1}{5} = \frac{7}{3} \times \frac{6}{5} = \frac{42}{15} = 2\frac{12}{15} = 2\frac{4}{5}$

10. $\begin{aligned} 6 &= 5\frac{6}{6} \\ -5\frac{5}{6} &= 5\frac{5}{6} \\ \hline &\quad \frac{1}{6} \end{aligned}$

11. $\begin{aligned} 12\frac{1}{4} &= 12\frac{4}{16} \\ 5\frac{13}{16} &= 5\frac{13}{16} \\ 4\frac{5}{8} &= 4\frac{10}{16} \\ +3\frac{1}{2} &= 3\frac{8}{16} \\ \hline 24\frac{35}{16} &= 26\frac{3}{16} \end{aligned}$

12. $\begin{aligned} 14\frac{1}{8} &= 14\frac{1}{8} = 13\frac{9}{8} \\ -13\frac{1}{2} &= 13\frac{4}{8} = 13\frac{4}{8} \\ \hline &\qquad\qquad \frac{5}{8} \end{aligned}$

13. $1\frac{3}{4} \times 3 = \frac{7}{4} \times \frac{3}{1} = \frac{21}{4} = 5\frac{1}{4}$

14. $1\frac{2}{3} \div 2\frac{2}{3} = \frac{5}{3} \div \frac{8}{3} = \frac{5}{3} \times \frac{3}{8} = \frac{15}{24} = \frac{5}{8}$

15. $\frac{3}{5} \div 8 = \frac{3}{5} \div \frac{8}{1} = \frac{3}{5} \times \frac{1}{8} = \frac{3}{40}$

16.
$$7\frac{2}{3} = 7\frac{8}{12}$$
$$5\frac{1}{6} = 5\frac{2}{12}$$
$$+3\frac{1}{12} = 3\frac{1}{12}$$
$$\overline{\phantom{+3\frac{1}{12} = }15\frac{11}{12}}$$

17.
$$9\frac{3}{8} = 9\frac{6}{16} = 8\frac{22}{16}$$
$$-5\frac{9}{16} = 5\frac{9}{16} = 5\frac{9}{16}$$
$$\overline{\phantom{-5\frac{9}{16} = 5\frac{9}{16} = }3\frac{13}{16}}$$

18. $15\frac{3}{8} + 9 = 24\frac{3}{8}$

19. $6 \times 1\frac{1}{2} \times 3\frac{3}{4} = \frac{6}{1} \times \frac{3}{2} \times \frac{15}{4} = \frac{270}{8} = 33\frac{3}{4}$

20.
$$11\frac{1}{2} = 11\frac{3}{6}$$
$$-2\frac{1}{3} = 2\frac{2}{6}$$
$$\overline{\phantom{-2\frac{1}{3} = }9\frac{1}{6}}$$

21.
$$25\frac{3}{4} = 25\frac{6}{8}$$
$$+21\frac{5}{8} = 21\frac{5}{8}$$
$$\overline{\phantom{+21\frac{5}{8} = }46\frac{11}{8} = 47\frac{3}{8}}$$

22.
$$35 = 34\frac{32}{32}$$
$$-17\frac{5}{32} = 17\frac{5}{32}$$
$$\overline{\phantom{-17\frac{5}{32} = }17\frac{27}{32}}$$

GED Practice: Fractions I (page 21)

1. (3) $7.70
$$5 = 4\frac{4}{4}$$
$$-\frac{1}{4} \text{ (the first } \frac{1}{4} \text{ mi. for \$1.05)}$$
$$\overline{\phantom{-\frac{1}{4}}4\frac{3}{4} \text{ (rest of trip)}}$$
$$4\frac{3}{4} \div \frac{1}{4} = \frac{19}{4} \times \frac{4}{1} = \frac{76}{4} = 19$$
$$19 \times \$.35 = \$6.65 \text{ (for rest of trip)}$$
$$\$6.65 + \$1.05 = \$7.70$$

2. (2) $6\frac{1}{8}$
$$5\frac{1}{2} = 5\frac{4}{8} \qquad\qquad 18 = 17\frac{8}{8}$$
$$+6\frac{3}{8} = 6\frac{3}{8} \qquad\qquad -11\frac{7}{8} = 11\frac{7}{8}$$
$$\overline{\phantom{+6\frac{3}{8} = }11\frac{7}{8}} \qquad\qquad \overline{\phantom{-11\frac{7}{8} = 11\frac{7}{8}}6\frac{1}{8}}$$

3. (4) 35 mph
$$87\frac{1}{2} \div 2\frac{1}{2} = \frac{175}{2} \div \frac{5}{2} = \frac{175}{2} \times \frac{2}{5} = \frac{350}{10} = 35$$

4. (1) 576
$$5,280 \div 9\frac{1}{6} = \frac{5,280}{1} \div \frac{55}{6} =$$
$$\frac{5,280}{1} \times \frac{6}{55} = \frac{31,680}{55} = 576$$

5. (3) $8\frac{1}{4}$
$$3\frac{1}{2} \times 3 = \frac{7}{2} \times \frac{3}{1} = \frac{21}{2} = 10\frac{1}{2} \text{ yd.}$$
$$1\frac{1}{4} \times 5 = \frac{5}{4} \times \frac{5}{1} = \frac{25}{4} = 6\frac{1}{4} \text{ yd.}$$
$$10\frac{1}{2} = 10\frac{2}{4} \qquad\qquad 25 = 24\frac{4}{4}$$
$$+6\frac{1}{4} = 6\frac{1}{4} \qquad\qquad -16\frac{3}{4} = 16\frac{3}{4}$$
$$\overline{\phantom{+6\frac{1}{4} = }16\frac{3}{4}} \qquad\qquad \overline{\phantom{-16\frac{3}{4} = 16\frac{3}{4}}8\frac{1}{4}}$$

6. (1) 35
$$21\frac{7}{8} \div \frac{5}{8} = \frac{175}{8} \times \frac{8}{5} = \frac{1,400}{40} = 35$$

7. (5) 54 ft.
$$4\frac{1}{2} \div \frac{1}{2} = \frac{9}{2} \times \frac{2}{1} = \frac{18}{2} = 9$$
$$9 \times 6 \text{ feet} = 54 \text{ feet}$$

8. (4) $23\frac{3}{4}$
$$4\frac{3}{4} \times 5 = \frac{19}{4} \times \frac{5}{1} = \frac{95}{4} = 23\frac{3}{4}$$

GED Practice: Fractions II (page 22)

1. (5) 150
$$1\frac{1}{5} \times 125 = \frac{6}{5} \times \frac{125}{1} = \frac{750}{5} = 150$$

2. (3) 60
$$75 \times \frac{1}{5} = \frac{75}{1} \times \frac{1}{5} = \frac{75}{5} = 15$$
$$75 - 15 = 60$$

3. (1) 525
$$84 \times 6\frac{1}{4} = \frac{84}{1} \times \frac{25}{4} = \frac{2,100}{4} = 525$$

4. (3) $24 - (\frac{1}{3} + \frac{1}{2})$ ($24)

5. (5) $51\frac{3}{4}$ ft.
$$2 \times 1\frac{3}{4} = \frac{2}{1} \times \frac{7}{4} = \frac{14}{4} = 3\frac{2}{4} = 3\frac{1}{2}$$
$$15 = 14\frac{2}{2}$$
$$-3\frac{1}{2} = 3\frac{1}{2}$$
$$\overline{\phantom{-3\frac{1}{2} = }11\frac{1}{2}}$$
$$11\frac{1}{2} \times 4\frac{1}{2} = \frac{23}{2} \times \frac{9}{2} = \frac{207}{4} = 51\frac{3}{4} \text{ ft.}$$

6. (1) 525
$$150 \times 3\frac{1}{2} = \frac{150}{1} \times \frac{7}{2} = \frac{1,050}{2} = 525$$

7. (4) $28 - (12\frac{1}{2} + 13\frac{3}{4})$

Decimals: Computation Practice (page 23)

1.
```
   .04
 ×.09
 .0036
```

2.
```
   1.9
  98.
 +53.
 152.9
```

3.
```
   .368
 × .62
   736
  2208
 .22816
```

4.
```
              93.8
 1.44) 135.07 2
       129 6
         5 47
         4 32
         1 15 2
         1 15 2
```

5.
```
    .7  = .70
 − .35  = .35
           .35
```

6.
```
   1.853
 +8.1
   9.953
```

7.
```
      .2234
 4) .8936
    8
     9
     8
     13
     12
     16
     16
```

8.
```
   .1692
   .3
 +15.8
  16.2692
```

9.
```
  $50    = $50.00
 − 25.25 =  25.25
            $24.75
```

10.
```
   70.48
 × .043
   21144
  2 8192
  3.03064
```

11.
```
  $700    = $700.00
 − 446.58 =  446.58
             $253.42
```

12.
```
             680.
 .39) 265.20
      234
       31 2
       31 2
```

13.
```
   $14.59
 −  7.00
  $ 7.59
```

14.
```
   .80  = 0.800
   4.   = 4.000
 + .049 = 0.049
           4.849
```

15.
```
   $14.25
 ×     11
    14 25
   142 5
  $156.75
```

16.
```
    .8   = .800
 − .007  = .007
            .793
```

17.
```
     .8
 × .007
   .0056
```

18.
```
   $3.90
 +  .98
  $4.88
```

19.
```
       .461
 15) 6.915
     6 0
       91
       90
        15
        15
```

20.
```
            1 87.6
 .72) 135.07 2
      72
      63 0
      57 6
       5 47
       5 04
         432
         432
```

21.
```
    .09  = .090
 − .005  = .005
            .085
```

22.
```
            4.16 rounds to 4.2
 90) 375.00
     360
      15 0
       9 0
       6 00
       5 40
         60
```

GED Practice: Decimals I (page 24)

1. **(2) $450.00**
$$150 \times (\$10.95 - \$7.95) = 150 \times \$3 = \$450$$

2. **(3) $579**
```
   $57.75          $2,079.00
 ×     36        −  1,500.00
   346 50           $579.00
 1 732 5
 $2,079.00
```

3. **(4) $5,692.50**
```
   $51.75
 ×   1 10
   517 50
  5 175
 $5,692.50
```

4. **(3) $1,785**
$$150 \times (\$37.75 - \$25.85) =$$
$$150 \times \$11.90 = \$1,785.00$$

5. **(3) $683**
```
 $ 40.25         $483.00
 ×    12       + 200.00
   80 50         $683.00
  402 5
 $483.00
```

6. **(2) 100**
```
  $95                       1 00
 − 70         $.25) $25.00
  $25                25
```

7. **(5) $99.63**
```
 $ 43.21          $.15
  221.20        ×    4
   32.50         $.60
 + 150.59
 $447.50

 $447.50          $547.73
 +   .60        − 448.10
 $448.10         $ 99.63
```

8. **(4)** $\dfrac{\$9.48}{12} \times 3$

GED Practice: Decimals II (page 25)

1. **(1) $1.00(15)**

2. **(5) 24,071.2**
   27,329
   − 3,257.8
   ‾‾‾‾‾‾‾‾
   24,071.2

3. **(4) 50**
   $$\begin{array}{r} 50. \\ 2.98{\overline{\smash{\big)}\,149.00}} \\ \underline{149\ 0} \end{array}$$

4. **(1) 555.78**
   35.4
   ×15.7
   ‾‾‾‾‾‾
   24 78
   177 0
   354
   ‾‾‾‾‾‾
   555.78

5. **(1) $.47**
   $.471 rounds to $.47
   $$\begin{array}{r} .471 \\ 52{\overline{\smash{\big)}\,\$24.500}} \\ \underline{20\ 8} \\ 3\ 70 \\ \underline{3\ 64} \\ 60 \\ \underline{52} \\ 8 \end{array}$$

6. **(5) $2,189**
   $3.98
   × 5 50
   ‾‾‾‾‾‾‾
   199 00
   1 990
   ‾‾‾‾‾‾‾
   $2,189.00

7. **(5) $141.36**
   $ 19.98
   × 6
   ‾‾‾‾‾‾‾
   $119.88 for screwdrivers
   24 ÷ 2 = 12 sets of two batteries
   12 × $1.79 = $21.48 for batteries
   $119.88 + $21.48 = $141.36

8. **(4) $18 and $20**
   $4 + $2 + $1 + $1 + $3 + $8 = $19

Data Analysis: Mean, Median, and Number Series Practice (page 27)

1. **6.9**
   7.3 + 8.4 + 8.0 + 3.9 = 27.6
   $$\begin{array}{r} 6.9 \\ 4{\overline{\smash{\big)}\,27.6}} \\ \underline{24} \\ 3\ 6 \\ \underline{3\ 6} \end{array}$$

2. **87.5** Add the test scores.
   97 + 72 + 89 + 90 + 90 + 87 = 525
   Divide by the number of test scores.
   $$\begin{array}{r} 87.5 \\ 6{\overline{\smash{\big)}\,525.0}} \\ \underline{48} \\ 45 \\ \underline{42} \\ 30 \\ \underline{30} \end{array}$$

3. **164** Arrange numbers in order from smallest to largest.
   152
   163 ⎫
   165 ⎬—middle values
   185
   Add middle values.
   165 + 163 = 328
   Find the average of the two middle values.
   $$\begin{array}{r} 164 = \text{median} \\ 2{\overline{\smash{\big)}\,328}} \\ \underline{2} \\ 12 \\ \underline{12} \\ 8 \\ \underline{8} \end{array}$$

4. **58°** Arrange numbers in order from smallest to largest.
   53°
   56°
   57°
   58° ← middle value = median
   59°
   61°
   62°

5. **3** Each term is divided in half: 6 ÷ 2 = 3

6. **64** Each number is two times the number before it: 32 × 2 = 64

7. **83.2**
   30 × 80 = 2,400
   20 × 88 = +1,760
   ‾‾‾‾‾‾‾‾
   4,160
   $$\begin{array}{r} 83.2 \\ 50{\overline{\smash{\big)}\,4,160.0}} \\ \underline{4\ 00} \\ 160 \\ \underline{150} \\ 100 \\ \underline{100} \end{array}$$

8. **$1.42**
   $1.35 + $1.39 + $1.43 + $1.47 + $1.48 = $7.12
   $1.424 rounds to $1.42 per gallon
   $$\begin{array}{r} 1.424 \\ 5{\overline{\smash{\big)}\,\$7.120}} \\ \underline{5} \\ 2\ 1 \\ \underline{2\ 0} \\ 12 \\ \underline{10} \\ 20 \\ \underline{20} \end{array}$$

9. **$22,650** Arrange in order from smallest to largest.

$13,500
14,225
14,900
20,750
22,650 ← median
24,375
24,500
41,175
68,000

10. **$74,420**

$ 65,500
56,000
49,250
32,750
+ 43,600
———————
$247,100

$$\frac{\$247,100}{5} = \$49,420$$

11. **$49,250** Arrange in order from smallest to largest.

$32,750
$43,600
$49,250 ← median
$56,000
$65,500

12. **3.5** Each term is increased by 0.5:
$3.0 + 0.5 = 3.5$

13. **$1\frac{1}{2}$** Each term is increased by $\frac{1}{4}$:
$1\frac{1}{4} + \frac{1}{4} = 1\frac{2}{4} = 1\frac{1}{2}$

14. **30.4** Add the numbers and divide by 5:
$27 + 34 + 29 + 32 + 30 = 152$
$152 \div 5 = 30.4$

15. **192** Arrange in order from smallest to largest.
179, 186, <u>192</u>, 200, 208: 192 is the median

GED Practice: Probability (page 29)

1. (2) $\frac{1}{5}$ $\frac{\text{white}}{\text{total}} = \frac{3}{3+4+2+6} = \frac{3}{15} = \frac{1}{5}$

2. (2) $\frac{1}{4}$ $\frac{\text{mixed}}{\text{total}} = \frac{3}{4+3+5} = \frac{3}{12} = \frac{1}{4}$

3. (5) $\frac{1}{4}$ $\frac{\text{creme}}{\text{total}} = \frac{6}{6 \times 4} = \frac{6}{24} = \frac{1}{4}$

4. (1) $\frac{1}{9}$ $\frac{\text{dimes}}{\text{total}} = \frac{5}{15+5+25} = \frac{5}{45} = \frac{1}{9}$

5. (3) $\frac{1}{4}$ $\frac{\text{1 card drawn}}{\text{4 total cards}} = \frac{1}{4}$

6. (1) $\frac{1}{2}$ $\frac{\text{red}}{\text{total}} = \frac{50}{50+50} = \frac{50}{100} = \frac{1}{2}$

Measurement: Computation Practice (page 30)

1. **1 minute**
2. **1 year**
3. **1 year**
4. **1 gallon**
5. **24 hours**
6. **10 years**
7. **12 inches**
8. **16 ounces**
9. **5,280 feet**
10. **1 ton**
11. **1 yard**
12. **1 quart**
13. **36 inches**
14. **17 quarts**
15. **$99\frac{1}{2}$ ounces**
16. **435 minutes**
17. **4,350 pounds**
18. **$2\frac{3}{4}$ pounds**
19. **$3\frac{1}{2}$ gallons**
20. **4 yards**

21. **9 pounds 2 ounces**

8 pounds 1 ounce
+   17 ounces
————————————————
8 pounds 18 ounces = 9 pounds 2 ounces

22. **1,800 pounds**

2 tons = 4,000 pounds
−2,200
————
1,800

23. **$.50**

1 gallon = 4 quarts
$$\frac{\$2.00}{4} = \$.50$$

24. **14 pieces, 4 in. piece left**

12 feet × 12 = 144 inches
$$\frac{144}{10} = 14 \text{ R } 4$$

GED Practice: Measurement (page 31)

1. **(4) 247 miles**

9:30 A.M. to 12 noon = 2 hr. 30 min. = $2\frac{1}{2}$ hrs.

12 noon to 2:15 P.M. = 2 hr. 15 min. = $+2\frac{1}{4}$ hrs.
————————
$4\frac{3}{4}$ hrs.

$$4\frac{3}{4} \times 52 = \frac{19}{4} \times \frac{52}{1} = \frac{988}{4} = 247$$

2. (3) 3 hr. 57 min.

$$5 \text{ hr. } 12 \text{ min.} = 4 \text{ hr. } 72 \text{ min.}$$
$$\underline{-1 \text{ hr. } 15 \text{ min.}} = \underline{1 \text{ hr. } 15 \text{ min.}}$$
$$3 \text{ hr. } 57 \text{ min.}$$

3. (2) 192 Change 288 ounces to 18 pounds (16 ounces = 1 pound).

```
      18                    192
 16)288              18)3,456
     16                   1 8
    128                   1 65
    128                   1 62
                            36
                            36
```

4. (1) 2 hours

```
 2 hr.  15 min.
 3 hr.
        45 min.
 1 hr.  40 min.
+2 hr.  20 min.
 8 hr. 120 min. = 10 hr.
```

$$\frac{10 \text{ hours}}{5 \text{ days}} = 2 \text{ hours}$$

5. (2) $85.44

8 dozen = 8 × 12 = 96 tires
21 lb. 8 oz. = 21.5 lb.

```
      × 96
      129 0
      1935
    2,064.0 lb.
```

Find 2,064 lb. on the chart (between 1,500–2,999). The shipping charge is $.89 per tire.

```
   $  .89
   ×   96
     5 34
    80 1
   $85.44
```

Percents: Computation Practice (page 32)

Example for $\frac{1}{8}$:

To find the decimal:

```
     .125
 8)1.000
    8
    20
    16
     40
     40
```

To find the percent:

```
    .125
  ×  100
  12.500 = 12.5%
```

	FRACTION	DECIMAL	PERCENT
1.	$\frac{1}{8}$	.125	12.5%
2.	$\frac{1}{4}$	.25	25%
3.	$\frac{1}{3}$	$.33\frac{1}{3}$	$33\frac{1}{3}\%$
4.	$\frac{3}{8}$	.375	37.5%
5.	$\frac{1}{2}$	.5	50%
6.	$\frac{3}{5}$	.6	60%
7.	$\frac{5}{8}$	.625	62.5%
8.	$\frac{2}{3}$	$.66\frac{2}{3}$	$66\frac{2}{3}\%$
9.	$\frac{3}{4}$	.75	75%
10.	$\frac{4}{5}$	.8	80%
11.	$\frac{7}{8}$	.875	87.5%
12.	$\frac{9}{10}$	.9	90%

13. $125\% \times 90 = 1.25 \times 90 = 112.5$

14. To find the percent, divide the part by the whole.

```
      .6 = 60%
  5)3.0
    3 0
```

15. $\frac{1}{8}\% = .125\%$

$$\frac{1}{8}\% \text{ of } 561 = \frac{1}{8} \times \frac{1}{100} \times 561 = .70125$$

OR $.125\% \text{ of } 561 = .00125 \times 561 = .70125$

16. To find the percent, divide the part by the whole.

```
        .52 = 52%
  25)13.00
     12 5
       50
       50
```

17. To find the number, divide 306 by .34. (.34 = 34%)

```
          9 00
  .34)306.00
       306
```

18. To find the percent, divide the part by the whole.

```
         .50 = 50%
  90)45.00
     45 0
```

19. 3% of 391 = .03 × 391 = 11.73

20. To find the base, divide part by the rate:
(.09 = 9%)

$$.09\overline{)81.00}$$
$$\underline{81}$$
$$900$$

21. To find the base, change the percent to a decimal and divide into the part:

110% = 1.1 $\frac{22}{1.1} = 20$

22. To find the part, change the percent to a decimal and multiply times the base:
0.5% = .005   .005 × 150 = .75

GED Practice: Percents I (page 33)

1. (3) $304.20

$1 95	$ 5.85
× .03	× 52
$5.85	11 70
52 weeks = 1 year	292 5
	$304.20

2. (2) $8,078.00
"Cost plus 40%" means
100% + 40% = 140% = 1.40

$ 5,770
× 1.40
2 308 00
5 770
$8,078.00

3. (3) $34.50

$ 46	$46.00
× .25	− 11.50
2 30	$34.50
9 2	
$11.50	

4. (3) $1,200 To find the total sales (the base), you divide $240 (the part) by 20% (the rate).

$$.20\overline{)\$240.00}$$
quotient $1,200
20
40
40

5. (4) 52%
$$\frac{New - Old}{Old} = \frac{\$11.75 - \$7.75}{\$7.75} = \frac{4.00}{7.75}$$

.516 rounds to 52%

$$7.75\overline{)\$4.00\,000}$$
3 87 5
12 50
7 75
4 750
4 650
100

6. (5) $5.25

$ 7.00	$7.00
× .25	− 1.75
35 00	$5.25
1 40 0	
$1.75 00	

7. (4) 33,125 miles To find the number of miles, change the percent to a decimal and divide.

$$.8\overline{)26,500.0}$$
quotient 33,12 5
24
2 5
2 4
10
8
20
16
4 0
4 0

8. (4) $\frac{(80 + 120)}{500}$

GED Practice: Percents II (page 34)

1. (5) 50% To find the percent, divide $750 by $1,500.

$$\$1,500\overline{)\$750.00}$$
quotient .50 = 50%
750 0

2. (2) $100 Change $6\frac{1}{4}\% = 6.25\% = .0625$

$ 1,600
× .0625
8000
3 200
96 00
$100.0000

3. (1) $1.77

$$\begin{array}{r} \$\ 25.25 \\ \times\quad .07 \\ \hline \$1.7675 \text{ rounds to } \$1.77 \end{array}$$

4. (4) $425

$$\begin{array}{r} \$2,500 \\ -\ 1,000 \\ \hline \$1,500 \end{array} \qquad \begin{array}{r} \$1,500 \\ \times\quad .15 \\ \hline 75\ 00 \\ 150\ 0 \\ \hline \$225.00 \end{array} \qquad \begin{array}{r} \$200 \\ +\ 225 \\ \hline \$425 \end{array}$$

5. (4) $187.50

$$\begin{array}{r} \$\ 750 \\ \times\quad .25 \\ \hline 37\ 50 \\ 150\ 0 \\ \hline \$187.50 \end{array}$$

6. (3) $1,980

$$\begin{array}{r} \$2,750 \\ -\ 275 \\ \hline \$2,475 \end{array} \qquad \begin{array}{r} \$\ 2,475 \\ \times\quad .80 \\ \hline \$1,980.00 \end{array}$$

7. (2) 22%

$1,025 \times 12 = \$12,300$

$\dfrac{\text{New} - \text{Old}}{\text{Old}} = \dfrac{\$15,000 - \$12,300}{\$12,300} = \dfrac{\$2,700}{\$12,300} = .219$

.219 rounds to 22%

8. (5) $44.76

$$\begin{array}{r} \$\ 42.25 \\ 34.20 \\ +\ 35.45 \\ \hline \$111.90 \end{array} \qquad \begin{array}{r} \$\ 111.90 \\ \times\quad .40 \\ \hline \$44.76\ 00 \end{array}$$

Graphs and Charts
GED Practice: Pictographs (pages 35)

1. (3) January, February, and August

January $= 3(10,000) + 1,000 = 31,000$
February $= 3(10,000) + 6(1,000) = 36,000$
August $= 4(10,000) + 2(1,000) = 42,000$

2. (4) 60,000

$$\begin{array}{r} 91,000 \\ -31,000 \\ \hline 60,000 \end{array}$$

3. (5) December 95,000 gallons is greater than all other months.

4. (3) 11% The total of the twelve months was 794,000 gallons of paint.
July and August totaled 85,000 gallons.
To find the percent, divide 85,000 gallons by 794,000 gallons.

$$\begin{array}{r} .107 \text{ rounds to } 11\% \\ 794,000\overline{)85,000.000} \\ 79\ 400\ 0 \\ \hline 5\ 600\ 000 \\ 5\ 558\ 000 \\ \hline 42\ 000 \end{array}$$

5. (1) February and March

January	31,000
July	43,000
August	+42,000
	116,000

(1) February	36,000
March	+72,000
	108,000

(2) March	72,000
April	+91,000
	163,000

(3) May	82,000
June	+63,000
	145,000

(4) September	80,000
October	+93,000
	173,000

(5) November	66,000
December	+95,000
	161,000

Total production for January, July and August was 116,000 gallons. This exceeds the 108,000 gallons produced in February and March.

6. (2) (72,000 + 63,000 + 80,000) ÷ 3
March + June + September

GED Practice: Circle Graphs (pages 36–37)

1. **(2) 2.4** Find 10% of 24 hrs.

    24
    $\times .10$
    $\overline{2.40}$

2. **(2) commercials, sports, and weather**
    20% + 20% + 10% = 50%

3. **(1) $\frac{1}{20}$**

    $\frac{editorials}{100} = \frac{5}{100} = \frac{1}{20}$

4. **(1) (2.4 + 2.4 + 1.2) ÷ 3**
    Compute hours spent on each type.
    Average = sum of items ÷ total of items
    weather and human interest each =
    $24 \times .10 = 2.40$
    editorials = $24 \times .05 = 1.20$
    Average = $\frac{2.4 + 2.4 + 1.2}{3}$

5. **(3) North America, Asia, and Africa** Since
    the continent land masses are given in
    percents, convert 9,000,000 to a percent:
    9,000,000 ÷ 58,000,000 = .155 = 15.5%. Then
    choose the continents with land masses
    greater than 15.5%

6. **(4) 8,700,000** Add the percents:
    Antarctica + Australia = 9% + 6% = 15%.
    Convert the total percentage to square miles:
    $58,000,000 \times .15 = 8,700,000$

7. **(3) Africa and Asia**
    20% + 30% = 50%

8. **(3) Africa** Convert the fraction to a percent:
    $\frac{1}{5} = \frac{20}{100} = .20 = 20\%$
    Only Africa is 20% of Earth's land mass.

9. **(2) (.3 − .06) × 58,000,000** Change each
    percent to a decimal. Subtract. Multiply the
    result by the total land mass.

10. **(5) $\frac{5}{4}$** The ratio of the percents is the same as
    the ratio of the land masses.

    $\frac{Africa}{N.\ America} = \frac{20\%}{16\%} = \frac{5}{4}$

    Note: The first item mentioned goes on top.
    The item to which the other is being compared
    goes on the bottom.

GED Practice: Charts (pages 38–39)

1. **(4) 250,925**

    7,322,564
    $\underline{-7,071,639}$
    250,925

2. **(4) 5,476,501**

    7,071,639
    $\underline{-1,595,138}$
    5,476,501

3. **(5) Philadelphia and Chicago**
    1,688,210 > 1,585,577
    3,005,072 > 2,783,726

4. **(2) Los Angeles**
    NY   7,322,564 − 7,071,639 = 250,925
    LA   3,485,398 − 2,966,850 = 518,548
    Hous.   1,630,553 − 1,595,138 = 35,415

5. **(1) 25,000**

    7,322,564 $\frac{250,925}{10} = 25,092.5$
    $\underline{-7,071,639}$
    250,925   25,092.5 rounds to 25,000

6. **(3) 5,736,987**

    7,322,564
    $\underline{-1,585,577}$
    5,736,987

7. **(2) 6–17**

8. **(2) 0–5 and 18–44**

9. **(4) 65+**
    $4,840 > 2 \times $2,402

10. **(3) $1822.00**

    $1,242
    $\underline{+\ 2,402}$
    $3,644 ÷ 2 = $1,822

11. **(2) 1989** 1,009: 517 is about 2:1

12. **(1) 1988** 1988: $\frac{551}{916} = .601$

13. **(5) 548.5**
    551 + 517 + 573 + 553 = 2,194
    2,194 ÷ 4 = 548.5

14. **(4) 4,800** Round each to the nearest thousand.

$$916 \rightarrow 900$$
$$1{,}009 \rightarrow 1{,}000$$
$$998 \rightarrow 1{,}000$$
$$935 \rightarrow 900$$
$$1{,}024 \rightarrow 1{,}000$$

Total $\overline{4{,}800}$

GED Practice: Line Graphs (pages 40)

1. **(3) $650 million**

2. **(4) 25%**
$$\frac{50}{200} = \frac{1}{4} = 25\%$$

3. **(5) $450 million**
$$\$650 - 200 = \$450$$

4. **(1) 160%**
$$\frac{\text{New} - \text{Old}}{\text{Old}} = \frac{(650 - 250)}{250} = \frac{400}{250} = 1.6 = 160\%$$

5. **(2) 1983–1986**

6. **(4) $\frac{5}{13}$**
$$\frac{250}{650} = \frac{5}{13}$$

GED Practice: Bar Graphs (pages 41–43)

1. **(4) California and Montana**

2. **(1) Alaska**

3. **(3) 750**
about $2{,}000 -$ about $1{,}250 = 750$

4. **(2) Alaska and Oregon**

5. **(5) 3,000**

6. **(3) 5,500**
about $8{,}750 - 3{,}200 = 5{,}500$

7. **(5) September was the month with the lowest attendance.**

8. **(5) April, March, January, February, May, and June**

April	175 (thousands)
March	225
January	250
February	275
May	275
June	300

9. **(5) 250,000**

250 January
300 June
250 August
+200 September
$\overline{1{,}000}$ (thousands)
$1{,}000{,}000 \div 4 = 250{,}000$

10. **(4) 275,000** Arrange numbers in order from smallest to largest. (Numbers are in thousands.)

April	175
September	200
March	225
January	250
August	250
February	275
May	275
November	275
June	300
July	325
October	325
December	350

February 275 and May 275 — middle values

Usually you would need to average the two values in the middle, but since they are the same, that value is the median.

11. **(3) the price of tickets for admission**

12. **(2) 250,000**

250 January
275 February
+225 March
$\overline{750}$ (thousands)
$750{,}000 \div 3 = 250{,}000$

13. **(1) $(200 + 325 + 275 + 350) \div 4$**

14. **(4) $1,500,000**
$300{,}000 \text{ people} \times \$5 = \$1{,}500{,}000$

15. **(2) 175,000**

350,000 December
−175,000 April
$\overline{175{,}000}$

16. **(5) 100,000**
$$\frac{1}{3} \times 300{,}000 = \frac{300{,}000}{3} = 100{,}000$$

17. **(3) 200,000**

Jan:	250,000	Oct:	325,000
Feb:	275,000	Nov:	275,000
Mar:	+225,000	Dec:	+350,000
	$\overline{750{,}000}$		$\overline{950{,}000}$

$950{,}000 - 750{,}000 = 200{,}000$

18. **(3) 11%**

$$3225 \overline{)350.000}$$
$$\underline{322\,5}$$
$$27\,500$$
$$\underline{25\,800}$$
$$1\,700$$

.108 rounds to .11 or 11%

GED Practice: Mixed Practice (pages 44–46)

1. **(5) 3,500**
$4,000 - 500 = 3,500$

2. **(1) Missouri and South Carolina**

3. **(3) 3,000** Round first, then divide:
$21,000 \div 7 = 3,000$

4. **(1) 3(1,000) − 500**

5. **(5) 1991**

6. **(4) 3.1 million**
about 3.35 million − about .25 million = 3.10 million

7. **(2) (.25 + .3 + .5) ÷ 3**

8. **(3) 8,470**
$121,000 \times .07 = 8,470.00$

9. **(5) Type G**

10. **(5) $\frac{1}{25}$**
Type F = 4%; 4% = $\frac{4}{100} = \frac{1}{25}$

11. **(4) 339,807**
$$524,356$$
$$\underline{-184,549}$$
$$339,807$$

12. **(2) 10,340**
$$83,681$$
$$\underline{-73,341}$$
$$10,340$$

13. **(2) 71,000**
$$73,341 \rightarrow 73,000$$
$$83,681 \rightarrow 84,000$$
$$\underline{+56,970 \rightarrow 57,000}$$
$$214,000$$
$214,000 \div 3$ rounds to 71,000

14. **(5) 492,221**
$$73,341$$
$$\underline{+418,880}$$
$$492,221$$

15. **(3) 73,341 ÷ (73,341 + 418,880)**

16. **(1) Air Force** Round and use fractions: $\frac{\text{women}}{\text{total}}$
The largest fraction is the largest percent.
AF: $\frac{70}{70 + 420} = \frac{70}{510}$ approx. = $\frac{1}{7}$
A: $\frac{90}{90 + 660} = \frac{90}{750}$ approx. = $\frac{1}{8}$
N: $\frac{60}{60 + 530} = \frac{60}{590}$ approx. = $\frac{1}{10}$
M: $\frac{10}{10 + 190} = \frac{10}{200} = \frac{1}{20}$

Signed Numbers Computation Practice (page 47)

1. **−40°**

2. **−3**

3. **0**

4. **+41**
$+121 + (-80) = +121 - 80 = +41$

5. **+7**
$+5 - (-2) = +5 + 2 = +7$

6. **+81**
$(-9)(-9) = +81$

7. **−5**
$\frac{1.25}{-.25} = -5$

8. **−6**
$-3\frac{1}{2} - (2\frac{1}{2}) = -3\frac{1}{2} - 2\frac{1}{2} = -6$

9. **$-1\frac{7}{10}$**
$-4\frac{1}{4} \div (+2\frac{1}{2}) = -\frac{17}{4} \div \frac{5}{2} = -\frac{17}{4} \times \frac{2}{5} = -\frac{34}{20} =$
$-1\frac{14}{20} = -1\frac{7}{10}$

10. **−15 pounds**

11. **+88.373**
$+93.118 + (-4.745) =$
$+93.118 - 4.745 = +88.373$

12. −4.991

$-7.000 - (-2.009) =$
$-7.000 + 2.009 = -4.991$

13. +45 yards

14. +$75

15. −50.7354

$$\begin{array}{r} -18.0164 \\ -35 \\ \hline -53.0164 \\ +\quad 2.281 \\ \hline -50.7354 \end{array}$$

16. 0

$(+9)(-5)(0) = (-45)(0) = 0$

Powers and Roots: Computation Practice (page 49)

1. $8 \times 8 = 64$

2. $1 \times 1 \times 1 \times 1 \times 1 = 1$

3. $2 \times 2 \times 2 = 8$

4. $6 \times 6 = 36$

5. $9 \times 9 \times 9 = 729$

6. $\sqrt{16} = 4$ because $4 \times 4 = 16$

7. $\sqrt{25} = 5$ because $5 \times 5 = 25$

8. $\sqrt{100} = 10$ because $10 \times 10 = 100$

9. $\sqrt{.36} = .6$ because $.6 \times .6 = .36$

10. $\sqrt{.81} = .9$ because $.9 \times .9 = .81$

11. $3 \times 3 \times 3 \times 3 = 81$

12. $12 \times 12 = 144$

13. $\sqrt{169} = 13$ because $13 \times 13 = 169$

14. $11 \times 11 \times 11 = 1,331$

15. $\sqrt{121} = 11$ because $11 \times 11 = 121$

16. $3,500 = 3.5 \times 10^3$

17. $29,000 = 2.9 \times 10^4$

18. $85,700 = 8.57 \times 10^4$

19. $126,000 = 1.26 \times 10^5$

20. $3,000,000 = 3.0 \times 10^6$

21. $.005 = 5.0 \times 10^{-3}$

22. $.0024 = 2.4 \times 10^{-3}$

23. $.012 = 1.2 \times 10^{-2}$

24. $.0001 = 1.0 \times 10^{-4}$

25. $.0305 = 3.05 \times 10^{-2}$

26. $5 + .0025 = 5.0025$

27. $9 - 2 + 16 = 23$

28. $12 - 8 = 4$

29. $10 + 10 + 11 = 31$

30. $\frac{13}{13} = 1$

31. $11 - 16 = -5$

32. $225 + 15 = 240$

33. $8^2 = 64$

34. $49 - 6 = 43$

35. 9,300

36. .0273

37. 400

38. .0019

39. 82,600

GED Review: Arithmetic (pages 50–53)

1. (3) $\frac{7}{8}$ and .375 (fractions and decimals)

$\frac{7}{8} = .875$

$.375 = \frac{3}{8}$

Therefore, $\frac{7}{8}$ and .375 are not equal.

2. **(4) \$100.20** (percents)

$$\begin{array}{r} \$\,125.25 \\ \times\quad .20 \\ \hline \$25.0500 \end{array} \qquad \begin{array}{r} \$125.25 \\ -\quad 25.05 \\ \hline \$100.20 \end{array}$$

3. **(5) a loss of 25 pounds** (positive and negative numbers)

4. **(3) $7 \times (9 - 3)$** (order of operations)

5. **(3) 89,100,000** (charts)

$$\begin{array}{r} 90,600,000 \\ -\ 1,500,000 \\ \hline 89,100,000 \end{array}$$

6. **(4) 34.9%** (charts and percents)

$\frac{32,100,000}{92,100,000} = .3485$

.3485 rounds to 34.9%

7. **(2) 35,900,000** (charts)

$$\begin{array}{r} 92,100,000 \\ -56,200,000 \\ \hline 35,900,000 \end{array}$$

8. **(1) 9.29×10^7** (scientific notation)

9. **(2) 45 and 53** (number series) Each term is increased by 8.

10. **(4) 227** (whole numbers)

$$\begin{array}{r} 229 \\ -\ 18 \\ \hline 211 \end{array} \qquad \begin{array}{r} 211 \\ +\ 16 \\ \hline 227 \end{array}$$

11. **(1) $\frac{1}{4}$** (probability)

$\frac{13 \text{ diamonds}}{52 \text{ cards}} = \frac{1}{4}$

12. **(5) $\frac{3}{10}$ .3 30%** (fractions, decimals, and percents)

13. **123** (fractions)

$15\frac{1}{2} \div \frac{1}{8} = \frac{31}{2} \div \frac{1}{8} = \frac{31}{2} \times \frac{8}{1} = \frac{248}{2} = 124$

However, the 124th hole would be drilled in the end of the plate, therefore, only 123 holes can be drilled.

14. **(5) 39** (exponents and order of operations)

$3^2 + 6(4 + 1) = 9 + 6(5) = 9 + 30 = 39$

15. **(3) 15 hours** (whole numbers)

$$\begin{array}{r} 54 \\ 144\overline{)7,776} \\ 7\ 20 \\ \hline 576 \\ 576 \\ \hline \end{array}$$

54 batches $\times$ 17 minutes = 918 minutes

$15\frac{18}{60} = 15\frac{3}{10}$ rounds to 15 hours

$$\begin{array}{r} 60\overline{)918} \\ 60 \\ \hline 318 \\ 300 \\ \hline 18 \end{array}$$

16. **(3) 105** (Percents)

$84 \times .25 = 21$

$84 + 21 = 105$

17. **(1) $\frac{1}{10}$** (probability)

There is only one 8 on the spinner. Therefore, the probability of landing on an 8 is $\frac{1}{10}$.

18. **(2) $\frac{1}{4}, \frac{3}{8}, .5, \frac{5}{6}, .875$** (fractions and decimals)

Change all fractions to decimals and then compare values. Since $\frac{1}{4} = .25$; $\frac{3}{8} = .375$; $\frac{5}{6} = .83\frac{1}{3}$; the decimal order is: .25, .375, .5, $.83\frac{1}{3}$, .875.

19. **(5) −3.388** (positive and negative numbers)

$\frac{(5.6)(-1.21)}{2} = \frac{-6.776}{2} = -3.388$

20. **(3) $13\frac{1}{2}$** (fractions)

$1\frac{1}{2} + 3 + 4\frac{1}{2} + 4\frac{1}{2} = 12 + \frac{3}{2} = 12 + 1\frac{1}{2} = 13\frac{1}{2}$

21. **(2) \$3,464** (whole number averages)

$$\begin{array}{r} \$\ 4,270 \\ 2,675 \\ 2,751 \\ 3,734 \\ 2,683 \\ +\ 4,671 \\ \hline \$20,784 \end{array} \qquad \$20,784 \div 6 = \$3,464$$

22. (2) $3,242.50 (median) Order the numbers from smallest to largest.

$2,683
$2,675
$2,751 ⎫
$3,734 ⎭—middle values
$4,270
$4,671

Add the middle values

$$
\begin{array}{r}
\$\ 2{,}751 \\
+\ \ 3{,}734 \\
\hline
\$\ 6{,}485
\end{array}
$$

median: $6,485 ÷ 2 = $3,242.50

23. (5) 89% (percents)

$$
\begin{array}{r}
225 \\
-\ 25 \\
\hline
200
\end{array}
$$

To find the percent, divide the total number of cars into the number that is available for rent.

$$
\begin{array}{r}
.888 \text{ rounds to } 89\% \\
225\overline{)200.000} \\
\underline{180\ 0} \\
20\ 00 \\
\underline{18\ 00} \\
2\ 000 \\
\underline{1\ 800} \\
200
\end{array}
$$

24. (1) $22 (decimals)

$$
\begin{array}{r}
\$\ 6 \\
\times\ \ 3 \\
\hline
\$18
\end{array}
\qquad
\begin{array}{r}
\$\ 18 \\
+\ \ \ 5 \\
\hline
\$\ 23
\end{array}
\qquad
\begin{array}{r}
\$\ 45 \\
-\ \ 23 \\
\hline
\$\ 22
\end{array}
$$

25. (5) $250 (decimals)

Mid-size:
$$\frac{20{,}000 \text{ miles}}{20 \text{ mpg}} = 1{,}000 \times \$1.25 = \$1{,}250.00$$

Subcompact:
$$\frac{20{,}000 \text{ miles}}{25 \text{ mpg}} = 800 \times \$1.25 = \$1{,}000.00$$

$$
\begin{array}{r}
\$1{,}250 \\
-\ 1{,}000 \\
\hline
\$\ \ 250
\end{array}
$$

26. (2) 13 (fractions and measurements)

dressing : 60 minutes $\times \frac{1}{3}$ hr. = 20 minutes

eating : 60 minutes $\times \frac{1}{5}$ hr. = 12 minutes

$$
\begin{array}{r}
20 \\
+12 \\
\hline
32
\end{array}
\qquad
\begin{array}{r}
45 \\
-32 \\
\hline
13
\end{array}
$$

27. (3) .6 (fractions and decimals) Change both fractions to decimals.

$1\frac{1}{2} = 1.5$ and $\frac{2}{5} = .4$

$1.5 \times .4 = .6$

28. (3) 60 mph (whole numbers averages)

$$
\begin{array}{r}
\text{total distance} =\ \ \ 430 \text{ mi.} \\
-50 \text{ mph.} \times 5 \text{ hr.} = \underline{-250 \text{ mi.}} \\
180 \text{ mi.} \div 3 \text{ hr.} = \\
60 \text{ mph.}
\end{array}
$$

29. (5) 20° (positive and negative numbers)

$(5°) - (-15°)$

$5° + 15° = +20°$

30. (2) −3 (order of operations)

$12 - 2(8 + 2) + 5 = 12 - 2(10) + 5 =$
$12 - 20 + 5 = -3$

31. (1) 0 (exponents and roots)

$(\sqrt{81})(\sqrt{139})(0) = (9)(13)(0) = 0$

32. (4) 40% (ratios and percents)

$\frac{2}{(2 + 3)} = \frac{2}{5} = .4 = 40\%$

33. (1) $173 (percents)

$865 \times .2 = $173

UNIT 2: ALGEBRA
Writing Algebraic Expressions
(page 55)

1. $\frac{n}{5}$

2. $5 + n$ or $n + 5$

3. $10 + n$ or $n + 10$

4. $12 + n$ or $n + 12$

5. $2n$

6. $\frac{n}{2}$

7. $n - 3$

8. $4n$

9. $\frac{1}{3}n + 7$ or $7 + \frac{1}{3}n$

10. $10 - n$

11. $r + t$

12. pq

13. $\frac{x}{a}$

14. $b + h$

15. bh

16. $\frac{1}{2}d$ or $\frac{d}{2}$

17. $2n + 1$

18. $36y$

19. $16p$

20. $\frac{d}{7}$ or $\frac{1}{7}d$

Simplifying Algebraic Expressions (page 57)

1. a
2. $2x^2 - 1$
3. $-12b^2$
4. $-2y + 6$
5. $q - 2$
6. $9p + 6$
7. $8d$
8. $-5z^2 + 5$
9. $-7 + 35y^2$
10. $-4r - 3$
11. $-4a^2$
12. $2x^2 + 27$
13. $-40b^2$

14. $+3y - 29$
15. $-6r - 4$
16. $-9y$
17. $-2m^2n^2$
18. $10st$
19. $48xy^2 + 7$
20. $1 - 4a$
21. $-2x^2 - 2x + 2$
22. $35x - 14$
23. $6x - 3$
24. $10p^2$
25. $-x - 23$
26. $2p^2 + 3pq - 10q^2$

Substitution (page 58)

1. $bc - ad = (5)(6) - 3(1) = 30 - 3 = 27$

2. $\frac{xy - yz}{xyz} = \frac{-1(2) - 2(-4)}{-1(2)(-4)} = \frac{-2 + 8}{8} = \frac{6}{8} = \frac{3}{4}$

3. $\frac{b^3}{b^2} = \frac{5^3}{5^2} = \frac{125}{25} = 5$

4. $x^3 + (y - 2z) = (-1)^3 + [2 - 2(-4)] = -1 + 2 + 8 = -1 + 10 = 9$

5. $\frac{10cd}{abc} = \frac{10(6)(1)}{3(5)(6)} = \frac{60}{90} = \frac{2}{3}$

6. $\frac{3(x + z)}{x} = \frac{3(-1 + -4)}{-1} = \frac{3(-5)}{-1} = \frac{-15}{-1} = 15$

7. $a^3 - b^3 = (3)^3 - (5)^3 = 27 - 125 = -98$

8. $ay + by = 3(2) + 5(2) = 6 + 10 = 16$

9. $(5x - 5z) + ab = [5(-1) - 5(-4)] + (3)(5) = (-5 + 20) + 15 = 15 + 15 = 30$

10. $3a^2b - 6 = 3(3)^2(5) - 6 = 3(9)(5) - 6 = 135 - 6 = 129$

11. $3x(xy - b) = 3(-1)[(-1)(2) - 5] = 3(-1)(-7) = 21$

12. $\frac{y}{x} + yz = \frac{2}{-1} + 2(-4) = -2 + (-8) = -10$

13. $a(7 - a)^2 = 3(7 - 3)^2 = 3(4)^2 = 3(16) = 48$

14. $\frac{bc - 5a}{b} = \frac{(5)(6) - 5(3)}{5} = \frac{30 - 15}{5} = \frac{15}{5} = 3$

15. $\frac{3(y + x)}{x} = \frac{3(2 + -4)}{-1} = \frac{3(2 - 4)}{-1} = \frac{3(-2)}{-1} = \frac{-6}{-1} = 6$

16. $\frac{a}{b} + \frac{b}{c} = \frac{3}{5} + \frac{5}{6} = \frac{18}{30} + \frac{25}{30} = \frac{43}{30} = 1\frac{13}{30}$

One-Step Equations Practice (page 60)

1. $x = 3$
2. $k = 63$
3. $x = 13$
4. $x = 5$
5. $y = 40$
6. $y = 25$
7. $y = 24$
8. $x = 9$
9. $x = 11$
10. $x = 44$

11. $3x = -21$
$\frac{3x}{3} = \frac{-21}{3}$
$x = -7$

12. $-5x = 5$
$\frac{-5x}{-5} = \frac{5}{-5}$
$x = -1$

13. $\frac{a}{7} = -2$
$7\left(\frac{a}{7}\right) = -2(7)$
$a = -14$

14. $\frac{-b}{2} = -9$
$-2\left(\frac{-b}{2}\right) = -9(-2)$
$b = 18$

15. $z + 3 = -4$
$z + 3 - 3 = -4 - 3$
$z = -7$

16. $12 + x = 1$
$12 - 12 + x = 1 - 12$
$x = -11$

17. $-19 + n = 34$
$-19 + 19 + n = 34 + 19$
$n = 53$

18. $p - 14 = -14$
$p - 14 + 14 = -14 + 14$
$p = 0$

19. $9x = 0$
$\frac{9x}{9} = \frac{0}{9}$
$x = 0$

20. $\frac{q}{5} = 0$
$5\left(\frac{q}{5}\right) = 0(5)$
$q = 0$

21. $12n = 36$
$\frac{12n}{12} = \frac{36}{12}$
$n = 3$

UNIT 2

22.
$$n + 10 = 80$$
$$n + 10 - 10 = 80 - 10$$
$$n = 70$$

23.
$$n - 6 = 2$$
$$n - 6 + 6 = 2 + 6$$
$$n = 8$$

24.
$$24 + n = 144$$
$$24 - 24 + n = 144 - 24$$
$$n = 120$$

25.
$$2n + 126$$
$$\frac{2n}{2} = \frac{126}{2}$$
$$n = 63$$

26.
$$n + 14 = 42$$
$$n + 14 - 14 = 42 - 14$$
$$n = 28$$

27.
$$n - 12 = 18$$
$$n - 12 + 12 = 18 + 12$$
$$n = 30$$

28.
$$4n = 60$$
$$\frac{4n}{4} = \frac{60}{4}$$
$$n = 15$$

29.
$$n + 40 = 84$$
$$n + 40 - 40 = 84 - 40$$
$$n = 44$$

30.
$$n - 13 = 39$$
$$n - 13 + 13 = 39 + 13$$
$$n = 52$$

Solving Two-Step Equations (page 61)

1.
$$4x + 7 = 11$$
$$4x + 7 - 7 = 11 - 7$$
$$4x = 4$$
$$\frac{4x}{4} = \frac{4}{4}$$
$$x = 1$$

2.
$$6x - 13 = 17$$
$$6x - 13 + 13 = 17 + 13$$
$$6x = 30$$
$$\frac{6x}{6} = \frac{30}{6}$$
$$x = 5$$

3.
$$\frac{x}{8} + 9 = 10$$
$$\frac{x}{8} + 9 - 9 = 10 - 9$$
$$\frac{x}{8} = 1$$
$$8\left(\frac{x}{8}\right) = 1(8)$$
$$x = 8$$

4.
$$\frac{x}{2} - 6 = 2$$
$$\frac{x}{2} - 6 + 6 = 2 + 6$$
$$\frac{x}{2} = 8$$
$$2\left(\frac{x}{2}\right) = 8(2)$$
$$x = 16$$

5.
$$-8x + 12 = 36$$
$$-8x + 12 - 12 = 36 - 12$$
$$-8x = 24$$
$$\frac{-8x}{-8} = \frac{24}{-8}$$
$$x = -3$$

6.
$$\frac{-x}{9} - 7 = 3$$
$$\frac{-x}{9} - 7 + 7 = 3 + 7$$
$$\frac{-x}{9} = 10$$
$$-9\left(\frac{-x}{9}\right) = 10(-9)$$
$$x = -90$$

7.
$$5 - 5x = -10$$
$$5 - 5 - 5x = -10 - 5$$
$$-5x = -15$$
$$\frac{-5x}{-5} = \frac{-15}{-5}$$
$$x = 3$$

8.
$$14 + \frac{x}{4} = -2$$
$$14 - 14 + \frac{x}{4} = -2 - 14$$
$$\frac{x}{4} = -16$$
$$4\left(\frac{x}{4}\right) = -16(4)$$
$$x = -64$$

9.
$$25 + 10x = 75$$
$$25 - 25 + 10x = 75 - 25$$
$$10x = 50$$
$$\frac{10x}{10} = \frac{50}{10}$$
$$x = 5$$

10.
$$-8 - 2x = -4$$
$$-8 + 8 - 2x = -4 + 8$$
$$-2x = 4$$
$$\frac{-2x}{-2} = \frac{4}{-2}$$
$$x = -2$$

11.
$$-1 + \frac{x}{3} = 2$$
$$-1 + 1 + \frac{x}{3} = 2 + 1$$
$$\frac{x}{3} = 3$$
$$3\left(\frac{x}{3}\right) = 3(3)$$
$$x = 9$$

12.
$$17 - \frac{x}{10} = 5$$
$$17 - 17 - \frac{x}{10} = 5 - 17$$
$$-\frac{x}{10} = -12$$
$$-10\left(-\frac{x}{10}\right) = -12(-10)$$
$$x = 120$$

Solving Multi-Step Equations (page 62)

1.
$$100 + 7x = 250 - 18x$$
$$100 - 250 + 7x - 7x = 250 - 250 - 18x - 7x$$
$$-150 = -25x$$
$$6 = x$$

2.
$$5n - 6 = 4n + 2$$
$$5n - 4n - 6 + 6 = 4n - 4n + 2 + 6$$
$$n = 8$$

3. Multiply and remove the parentheses before solving the equation.
$$3(x - 4) - 2(x - 8) = 1$$
$$3x - 12 - 2x + 16 = 1$$
$$x + 4 = 1$$
$$x + 4 - 4 = 1 - 4$$
$$x = -3$$

4.
$$14x - x + 1 = 14$$
$$13x + 1 = 14$$
$$13x + 1 - 1 = 14 - 1$$
$$13x = 13$$
$$x = 1$$

5.
$$5x + 8 = 4x - 12$$
$$5x - 4x + 8 - 8 = 4x - 4x - 12 - 8$$
$$x = -20$$

6.
$$5x - 75 = 3x + 7$$
$$5x - 3x - 75 + 75 = 3x - 3x + 7 + 75$$
$$2x = 82$$
$$x = 41$$

7.
$$10(x - 3) - 7x = 0$$
$$10x - 30 - 7x = 0$$
$$3x - 30 = 0$$
$$3x - 30 + 30 = 0 + 30$$
$$3x = 30$$
$$x = 10$$

8.
$$16 + 3x = x + 32$$
$$16 - 16 + 3x - x = x - x + 32 - 16$$
$$2x = 16$$
$$x = 8$$

9.
$$3x + 1 = 25 - x$$
$$3x + x + 1 - 1 = 25 - 1 - x + x$$
$$4x = 24$$
$$x = 6$$

10.
$$36 = 18x - 12x + 6$$
$$36 = 6x + 6$$
$$36 - 6 = 6x + 6 - 6$$
$$30 = 6x$$
$$5 = x$$

11.
$$4x + 4 = 20$$
$$4x + 4 - 4 = 20 - 4$$
$$4x = 16$$
$$x = 4$$

12.
$$9x - 6 = 48$$
$$9x - 6 + 6 = 48 + 6$$
$$9x = 54$$
$$x = 6$$

13.
$$2x + 10 = 3x + 14$$
$$2x - 2x + 10 = 3x - 2x + 14$$
$$10 - 14 = x + 14 - 14$$
$$-4 = x$$

14.
$$5x - 4 = 3x + 4$$
$$5x - 3x - 4 = 3x - 3x + 4$$
$$2x - 4 = 4$$
$$2x - 4 + 4 = 4 + 4$$
$$2x = 8$$
$$x = 4$$

15.
$$5(x + 3) = x + 15$$
$$5x + 15 = x + 15$$
$$5x - x + 15 = x - x + 15$$
$$4x + 15 = 15$$
$$4x + 15 - 15 = 15 - 15$$
$$4x = 0$$
$$\frac{4x}{4} = \frac{0}{4}$$
$$x = 0$$

Solving Word Problems (page 63)

1.
Let n = 1st consecutive number
Let $n + 1$ = 2nd consecutive number
$$n + (n + 1) = 111$$
$$2n + 1 = 111$$
$$2n + 1 - 1 = 111 - 1$$
$$2n = 110$$
$$n = 55$$
$$n + 1 = 56$$
check: $55 + 56 = 111$

2.
$$\text{Let } n = \text{Pam's age}$$
$$\text{Let } n + 4 = \text{Marion's age}$$
$$n + (n + 4) = 32$$
$$2n + 4 = 32$$
$$2n + 4 - 4 = 32 - 4$$
$$2n = 28$$
$$n = 14$$
$$n + 4 = 14 + 4 = 18$$
$$\text{check: } 14 + 18 = 32$$

3.
$$\text{Let } n = \text{smaller number}$$
$$\text{Let } 3n = \text{larger number}$$
$$3n + n = 180$$
$$4n = 180$$
$$n = 45$$
$$3n = 3(45) = 135$$
$$\text{check: } 45 + 135 = 180$$

4.
$$\text{Let } n = \text{cost of blouse}$$
$$n + \$3 = \$26$$
$$n + \$3 - \$3 = \$26 - \$3$$
$$n = \$23$$
$$\text{check: } \$23 + \$3 = \$26$$

5.
$$\text{Let } n = \text{smaller number}$$
$$\text{Let } 6n = \text{larger number}$$
$$n + 6n = 98$$
$$7n = 98$$
$$n = 14$$
$$6n = 6(14) = 84$$
$$\text{check: } 14 + 84 = 98$$

6. Let n = number of hours Eleanor worked
Let $n + 10$ = number of hours Evelyn worked
$$n + (n + 10) = 36$$
$$2n + 10 = 36$$
$$2n + 10 - 10 = 36 - 10$$
$$2n = 26$$
$$n = 13$$
$$n + 10 = 13 + 10 = 23$$
$$\text{check: } 13 + 23 = 36$$

Solving Word Problems (page 64)

1. (4) 1
$$\text{Let } x = \text{the number}$$
$$12(x + 2) = 36$$
$$12x + 24 = 36$$
$$12x = 12$$
$$x = 1$$

2. (2) 40 You are asked for <u>Jerry's</u> laps.
$$\text{Let } x = \text{Bill's laps}$$
$$2x = \text{Jerry's laps}$$
$$2x + x = 60$$
$$3x = 60$$
$$x = 20$$
$$2x = 2(20) = 40$$

3. (4) 9
$$\text{Let } x = \text{1st number}$$
$$x + 1 = \text{2nd number}$$
$$x + 2 = \text{3rd number}$$
$$x + x + 1 + x + 2 = 24$$
$$3x + 3 = 24$$
$$3x = 21$$
$$x = 7$$
$$x + 2 = 7 + 2 = 9$$

4. (3) \$420
$$\text{Let } x = \text{Sue's money}$$
$$3x = \text{Mary's money}$$
$$x + 3x = 560$$
$$4x = 560$$
$$x = 140$$
$$3x = 3(\$140) = \$420$$

5. (2) 5
$$\text{Let } x = \text{the number}$$
$$3(20 - x) = 45$$
$$60 - 3x = 45$$
$$-3x = -15$$
$$x = 5$$

6. (3) 300 miles
$$\text{Let } x = \text{3rd day's miles}$$
$$2x = \text{2nd day's miles}$$
$$3x = \text{1st day's miles}$$
$$3x + 2x + x = 600$$
$$6x = 600$$
$$x = 100$$
$$3x = 3(100) = 300$$

7. (3) 6
$$\text{Let } x = \text{the first number}$$
$$x + 2 = \text{the second number}$$
$$x + 4 = \text{the third number}$$
$$x + (x + 2) + (x + 4) = 2(x + 4)$$
$$3x + 6 = 2x + 8$$
$$x = 2$$
The largest number is $x + 4$. Substitute.
$$x + 4 = 2 + 4 = 6$$

8. (4) 8
$$\text{Let } x = \text{the number of quarters}$$
$$x = \text{the number of nickels also}$$
$$2x = \text{the number of dimes}$$
$$x + x + 2x = 16$$
$$4x = 16$$
$$x = 4 \text{ and } 2x = 8$$

GED Practice: Ratios and Proportions (pages 66–67)

1. **(5) $381.25**

   Let x = Tate Construction's money

   $3x$ = subcontractor's money

   $3x + x = \$1,525$

   $4x = \$1,525$

   $x = \$381.25$

2. **(3) 28**

   $\dfrac{\text{margarine}}{\text{flour}} = \dfrac{\text{margarine}}{\text{flour}}$

   $\dfrac{3}{3\frac{1}{2}} \times \dfrac{24}{x}$ Cross multiply.

   $3x = 24\left(3\frac{1}{2}\right)$

   $3x = 84$

   $x = 28$ cups

3. **(3) 120**

   Let $3x$ = 1st student's score

   $4x$ = 2nd student's score

   $2x$ = 3rd student's score

   $3x + 4x + 2x = 270$

   $9x = 270$

   $x = 30$

   $4x = 4(30) = 120$

4. **(2) $539.25**

   $\dfrac{\$35.95}{2} \times \dfrac{x}{30}$ Cross multiply.

   $2x = 30(\$35.95)$

   $2x = \$1078.50$

   $x = \$539.25$

5. **(2) $1\frac{1}{5}$ gallons of concentrate**

   $\dfrac{\text{concentrate}}{\text{water}} = \dfrac{\text{concentrate}}{\text{water}}$

   $\dfrac{2}{5} \times \dfrac{x}{3}$

   $5x = 6$

   $x = \dfrac{6}{5} = 1\frac{1}{5}$ gallons of concentrate

6. **(5) $1,500**

   $\dfrac{\$375}{3} \times \dfrac{x}{12}$

   $3x = 12(\$375)$

   $3x = \$4,500$

   $x = \$1,500$

7. **(4) $366**

   $\dfrac{\text{hours}}{\text{earnings}} = \dfrac{\text{hours}}{\text{earnings}}$

   $\dfrac{5}{\$45.75} \times \dfrac{40}{x}$

   $\$1,830 = 5x$

   $\$366 = x$

8. **(5) $22.50**

   $\dfrac{\text{cost}}{\text{value of policy}}$

   $\dfrac{\$.75}{\$1,000} \times \dfrac{x}{\$30,000}$

   $\$1,000x = \$22,500$

   $x = \$22.50$

9. **(3) $2,812.50**

   Let $3x$ = 1st person's money

   $5x$ = 2nd person's money

   $3x + 5x = \$4,500$

   $8x = \$4,500$

   $x = \$562.50$

   $5x = 5(\$562.50) = \$2,812.50$

10. **(2) $9.12**

    $\dfrac{\text{tax}}{\text{purchase}} = \dfrac{\text{tax}}{\text{purchase}}$

    $\dfrac{\$.48}{\$8} \times \dfrac{x}{\$152}$

    $8x = \$72.96$

    $x = \$9.12$

11. **(4) $14.75**

    $\dfrac{\text{cost}}{\text{words}} \times \dfrac{\text{cost}}{\text{words}}$

    $\dfrac{\$2.95}{15} = \dfrac{x}{75}$

    $\$221.25 = 15x$

    $\$14.75 = x$

12. **(4) 455**

    $\dfrac{\text{teacher}}{\text{students}} = \dfrac{\text{teacher}}{\text{students}}$

    $\dfrac{2}{35} \times \dfrac{26}{x}$

    $2x = 910$ students

    $x = 455$

13. **(4) 25**

    $\dfrac{\text{gallons}}{\text{miles}} = \dfrac{\text{gallons}}{\text{miles}}$

    $\dfrac{1}{25} \times \dfrac{x}{625}$

    $25x = 625$

    $x = 25$ gallons of gasoline

14. **(1) 30**

    $\dfrac{\text{mother's age}}{\text{daughter's age}} = \dfrac{\text{mother's age}}{\text{daughter's age}}$

    $\dfrac{5}{2} \times \dfrac{x}{12}$

    $2x = 60$

    $x = 30$

15. (2) $1,125

$$\frac{\text{rent}}{\text{total budget}} = \frac{\text{rent}}{\text{total budget}}$$
$$\frac{1}{5} = \frac{\$225}{x}$$
$$x = \$1,125$$

16. (2) 60

$$\frac{\text{person}}{\text{ounces}} = \frac{\text{person}}{\text{ounces}}$$
$$\frac{1}{8} = \frac{240}{x}$$
$$x = 1,920 \text{ ounces}$$

Change ounces to quarts: 32 ounces = 1 quart.
$$\frac{1,920}{32} = 60 \text{ quarts}$$

17. (2) 600

$$\frac{\text{time}}{\text{distance traveled}} = \frac{\text{time}}{\text{distance traveled}}$$
$$\frac{1.5}{90} = \frac{10}{x}$$
$$1.5x = 900$$
$$x = 600 \text{ miles}$$

18. (4) 1,000

$$\frac{\text{inches}}{\text{miles}} = \frac{\text{inches}}{\text{miles}}$$
$$\frac{.5}{200} = \frac{2.5}{x}$$
$$.5x = 500$$
$$x = 1,000 \text{ miles}$$

Formula Problems (pages 68–70)

1. (4) 6 hours

$d = 40$
$r = 7$
$$t = \frac{d}{r}$$
$$= \frac{40}{7}$$
$$= 5.71 \text{ rounds to } 6$$

2. (4) 600

$c = \$1,500$
$r = \$2.50$
$$n = \frac{c}{r}$$
$$= \frac{\$1,500}{\$2.50}$$
$$= 600$$

3. (4) 7%

$i = \$56$
$p = \$800$
$t = 1 \text{ year}$
$$r = \frac{i}{pt} = \frac{\$56}{\$800 \times 1 \text{ yr.}} = .07 = 7\%$$

4. (4) $1,276.50

$p = \$1,200$
$r = 8\frac{1}{2}\% = .085$
$t = 9 \text{ mos.} = \frac{3}{4} \text{ year}$
$$i = prt$$
$$= \$1,200 \times .085 \times \frac{3}{4} = \frac{306}{4} = \$76.50$$

$$\begin{array}{r} p = \$1,200.00 \\ i = +76.50 \\ \hline \$1,276.50 \end{array}$$

5. (2) $8

$c = \$8,000$
$n = 1,000 \text{ frames}$
$$r = \frac{c}{n}$$
$$= \frac{\$8,000}{1,000}$$
$$= \$8$$

6. (4) $1,622.50

$n = \text{number of books} = 550$
$r = \text{cost per book} = \$2.95$
$$c = nr$$
$$= 550(\$2.95)$$
$$= \$1,622.50$$

7. (3) 217 miles

$r = 124 \text{ miles per hour}$
$t = 1\frac{3}{4} \text{ hours}$
$$d = rt$$
$$= 124 \times 1\frac{3}{4}$$
$$= \frac{124}{1} \times \frac{7}{4} = \frac{868}{4}$$
$$= 217$$

8. (5) $4,625

$i = \$370$
$r = 8\%$
$t = 1 \text{ year}$
$$p = \frac{i}{rt}$$
$$= \frac{\$370}{.08 \times 1}$$
$$= \frac{\$370}{.08}$$
$$= \$4,625$$

9. (2) 3 years

$i = \$577$
$p = \$2,750$
$r = 7\%$
$$t = \frac{i}{pr}$$
$$= \frac{\$577}{\$2,750 \times .07}$$
$$= \frac{\$577.00}{\$192.50}$$
$$= 2.99 \text{ rounds to } 3$$

10. (4) 65 mph

$d = 390$ miles

$t = 6$ hours

$$r = \frac{d}{t}$$

$$= \frac{390}{6}$$

$$= 65$$

11. (2) \$255

$p = \$3{,}000$

$r = 8\frac{1}{2}\%$

$t = 1$ year

$$i = prt$$

$$= \$3{,}000 \times .085 \times 1$$

$$= \$255$$

12. (5) \$5,400

$i = \$513$

$r = 4\frac{3}{4}\%$

$t = 2$ years

$$p = \frac{i}{rt}$$

$$= \frac{\$513}{.0475 \times 2}$$

$$= \frac{\$513}{.095}$$

$$= \$5{,}400$$

13. (3) 51 mph

$d = 306$

$t = 6$

$$r = \frac{d}{t}$$

$$= \frac{160 + 146}{4 + 2}$$

$$= \frac{306}{6}$$

$$= 51$$

14. (3) 316.5

Car:	Truck:
$r = 55$ mph	$r = 50.5$ mph
$t = 3$ hours	$t = 3$ hours
$d = rt$	$d = rt$
$= 55 \times 3$	$= 50.5 \times 3$
$= 165$	$= 151.5$

$$165 + 151.5 = 316.5$$

15. (5) \$1,737.50

$n = 250$

$r = \$6.95$

$$c = nr$$

$$= 250 \times \$6.95$$

$$= \$1{,}737.50$$

16. (4) \$.63

$c = \$12.60$

$n = 20$

$$r = \frac{c}{n}$$

$$= \frac{\$12.60}{20}$$

$$= \$.63$$

17. (2) 10

$c = \$25$

$r = \$2.50$

$$n = \frac{c}{r}$$

$$= \frac{\$25}{\$2.50}$$

$$= 10$$

18. (3) \$67.50

$p = \$1{,}000$

$r = 6\frac{3}{4}\%$

$$i = prt = \$1{,}000 \times .0\,675 = \$67.5\,000$$

19. (1) 5%

$i = \$120$

$t = 1$ year

$p = \$2{,}400$

$$r = \frac{i}{pt}$$

$$= \frac{120}{(\$2{,}400)(1\text{ yr.})} = \frac{120}{\$2{,}400} = .05 = 5\%$$

20. (3) 637.5

$r = 85$ miles per hour

$t = 7.5$ hours

$$d = rt$$

$$= 85 \times 7.5$$

$$= 637.5$$

21. (3) $1\frac{1}{2}$ hours

$$\frac{25}{50} + \frac{65}{65} = \frac{1}{2} + 1 = 1\frac{1}{2}$$

22. (4) \$1.65

First find the rate or price per unit.

$$r = \frac{c}{n} = \frac{\$10.80}{12} = \$.90$$

Then add the profit to the price to find the actual selling price.

$\$.90 + \$.75 = \$1.65$

Inequalities (page 71)

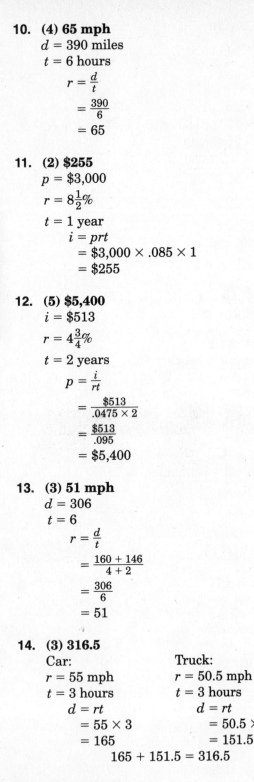

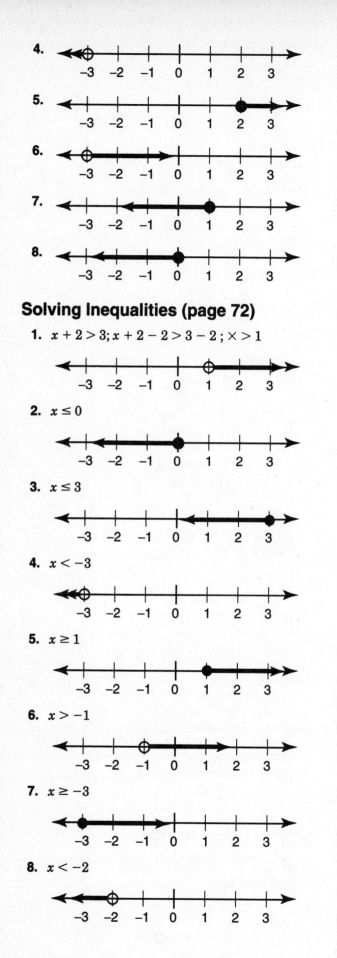

4.

5.

6.

7.

8.

Solving Inequalities (page 72)

1. $x + 2 > 3; x + 2 - 2 > 3 - 2; x > 1$

2. $x \le 0$

3. $x \le 3$

4. $x < -3$

5. $x \ge 1$

6. $x > -1$

7. $x \ge -3$

8. $x < -2$

UNIT 2

Solving Quadratic Equations by Substitution (page 73)

1. **(2) 7 and 2**

Substitute 7	Substitute 2
$x^2 - 9x + 14 = 0$	$x^2 - 9x + 14 = 0$
$7^2 - 9(7) + 14 = 0$	$2^2 - 9(2) + 14 = 0$
$49 - 63 + 14 = 0$	$4 - 18 + 14 = 0$
$0 = 0$	$0 = 0$

2. **(4) 2 and 6**

Substitute 2	Substitute 6
$x^2 - 8x + 12 = 0$	$x^2 - 8x + 12 = 0$
$2^2 - 8(2) + 12 = 0$	$6^2 - 8(6) + 12 = 0$
$4 - 16 + 12 = 0$	$36 - 48 + 12 = 0$
$0 = 0$	$0 = 0$

3. **(4) −5 and −4**

Substitute −5
$$p^2 + 9p + 20 = 0$$
$$(-5)^2 + 9(-5) + 20 = 0$$
$$25 - 45 + 20 = 0$$
$$0 = 0$$

Substitute −4
$$p^2 + 9p + 20 = 0$$
$$(-4)^2 + 9(-4) + 20 = 0$$
$$16 - 36 + 20 = 0$$
$$0 = 0$$

4. **(3) −3 and 8**

Substitute −3	Substitute 8
$a^2 - 5a - 24 = 0$	$a^2 - 5a - 24 = 0$
$(-3)^2 - 5(-3) - 24 = 0$	$(8)^2 - 5(8) - 24 = 0$
$9 + 15 - 24 = 0$	$64 - 40 - 24 = 0$
$0 = 0$	$0 = 0$

GED Review: Algebra (pages 74–75)

1. **(2) $10\frac{1}{4}$ hours**

$$d = 615$$
$$r = 60$$
$$d = rt$$
$$615 = 60t$$
$$10\frac{1}{4} = t$$

2. **(5) $c \le 5$**

$$3c - 8 \le 7$$
$$3c - 8 + 8 \le 7 + 8$$
$$3c \le 15$$
$$c \le 5$$

3. **(5) $-\frac{5}{2}$**

$$\frac{m - m^2 n}{3n} = \frac{3 - (3^2)(2)}{3(2)} =$$
$$\frac{3 - 9(2)}{6} = \frac{3 - 18}{6} = \frac{-15}{6} = \frac{-5}{2} = -\frac{5}{2}$$

4. **(1) 1**

$3q = 6$

$\dfrac{3q}{3} = \dfrac{6}{3}$

$q = 2$

$\dfrac{1}{2}q = \dfrac{1}{2} \cdot \dfrac{2}{1} = \dfrac{2}{2} = 1$

5. **(2) 5**

$\dfrac{\text{inch}}{\text{miles}} = \dfrac{\text{inch}}{\text{miles}}$

$\dfrac{1}{450} = \dfrac{x}{2,250}$

$450x = 2,250$

$x = 5$

6. **(2) 13**

Let n = Paul's hours

Let $n + 10$ = Rhonda's hours

$n + (n + 10) = 36$

$2n + 10 = 36$

$2n + 10 - 10 = 36 - 10$

$2n = 26$

$n = 13$

7. **(2) 25%**

$\$15,000 - 12,000 = \$3,000$

$\dfrac{\$3,000}{\$12,000} = \dfrac{1}{4} = 25\%$

8. **(4) 5a**

$a + a + a + a + a = 5a$

9. **(4) 162**

Let $3x$ = 1st typist's pages

Let $5x$ = 2nd typist's pages

Let $12x$ = 3rd typist's pages

$3x + 5x + 12x = 360$

$20x = 360$

$x = 18$

3rd typist $12x = 12(18) = 216$ pages

1st typist $3x = 3(18) = 54$ pages

$216 - 54 = 162$

10. **(1) 5**

$3(x - 1) = 2(x + 1)$

$3x - 3 = 2x + 2$

$3x - 2x - 3 + 3 = 2x - 2x + 2 + 3$

$x = 5$

11. **(3) 32**

Let x = Kim's age

Let $4x$ = Sylvia's age

$4x - x = 24$

$3x = 24$

$x = 8$

Sylvia = $4x = 4(8) = 32$ years old

12. **(5) any of the three factors**

Any number times zero equals zero.

13. **(3) 7**

$c + 21 = 4c$

$c - c + 21 = 4c - c$

$21 = 3c$

$7 = c$

14. **(4) $980**

First find the interest he will earn.

$i = prt$

$ = \$800(.045)(5)$

$ = \$180$

Then find the total amount.

$\$800 + \$180 = \$980$

15. **(3) y > 1**

$4y + 14 > 18$

$4y + 14 - 14 > 18 - 14$

$4y > 4$

$y > 1$

16. **(5) −3**

$\dfrac{5}{y} - x + \dfrac{4}{2} + 6x$

$\dfrac{5}{4} - (-1) + \dfrac{4}{2} + 6(-1) =$

$\dfrac{5}{4} + 1 + \dfrac{4}{2} - 6 =$

$\dfrac{5}{5} + \dfrac{4}{2} - 6 =$

$1 + 2 - 6 = -3$

17. **(2) 3:10**

decimal problems:total problems

$15:50 = 3:10$

18. **(2) 4**

$2a^3 - 3ab$

$2(-1)^3 - 3(-1)(2) =$

$2(-1) - 3(-2) =$

$-2 + 6 = 4$

19. **(2) 17**

Let a = 1st number

Let $a + 5$ = 2nd number

$a + (a + 5) = 39$

$2a + 5 = 39$

$2a + 5 - 5 = 39 - 5$

$2a = 34$

$a = 17$

UNIT 3: GEOMETRY

Solving Geometric Figure Problems (pages 81–82)

1.

$125° + \angle T = 180°$

$125° - 125° + \angle T = 180° - 125°$

$\angle T = 55°$

2. $\angle X + \angle Y = 180°$

$\angle X + \angle Y$ form a straight line, 180°

3. $\angle Y + 26° = 90°$

$\angle Y + 26° - 26° = 90° - 26°$

$\angle Y = 64°$

4. $\angle A + 30° + 40° = 180°$

$\angle A + 70° = 180°$

$\angle A + 70° - 70° = 180° - 70°$

$\angle A = 110°$

5. $\angle Z + 38° + 16° = 180°$

$\angle Z + 54° = 180°$

$\angle Z + 54° - 54° = 180° - 54°$

$\angle Z = 126°$

6. First find $\angle RTS$.

$180° = 45° + 20° + \angle RTS$

$180° = 65° + \angle RTS$

$180° - 65° = 65° - 65° + \angle RTS$

$115° = \angle RTS$

Then find $\angle RTU$.

$\angle RTS + \angle RTU = 180°$

$115° + \angle RTU = 180°$

$115° - 115° + \angle RTU = 180° - 115°$

$\angle RTU = 65°$

7. $2x = 70°$

$x = 35°$

8.

Larger Triangle	=	Smaller Triangle
$\dfrac{\overline{AE}}{\overline{AC}}$	=	$\dfrac{\overline{BC}}{\overline{BD}}$
$\dfrac{9}{12}$	=	$\dfrac{3}{x}$
$9x$	=	36
$\dfrac{9x}{9}$	=	$\dfrac{36}{9}$
x	=	4

9. Triangles A and C may be congruent because they seem to have the same size and shape.

10. $\dfrac{\overline{AB}}{\overline{BC}} = \dfrac{\overline{XY}}{\overline{YZ}}$

$\dfrac{2}{3} = \dfrac{\overline{XY}}{12}$

$3\overline{XY} = 24$

$\overline{XY} = 8$

11. $\dfrac{\overline{AB}}{\overline{BC}} = \dfrac{\overline{PR}}{\overline{PQ}}$

$\dfrac{40}{24} = \dfrac{60}{\overline{PQ}}$

$40\overline{PQ} = 1,440$

$\overline{PQ} = 36$

12. Let $5x$ = one angle

Let $7x$ = other angle

$5x + 7x = 90°$

$12x = 90°$

$x = 7\frac{1}{2}°$

Larger angle = $7x = 7(7\frac{1}{2}°) = 52\frac{1}{2}°$

13. Let $2x$ = one angle

Let $3x$ = other angle

$2x + 3x = 180°$

$2x + 3x = 180°$

$5x = 180°$

$x = 36°$

14. $\angle A + \angle B + \angle C = 180°$

$90° + \angle B + 28° = 180°$

$\angle B + 118° = 180°$

$\angle B + 118° - 118° = 180° - 118°$

$\angle B = 62°$

15. $\angle L + \angle M + \angle N = 180°$

$40° + 90° + \angle N = 180°$

$130° + \angle N = 180°$

$130° - 130° + \angle N = 180° - 130°$

$\angle N = 50°$

16. Base angles of isosceles triangles are equal. Therefore, $\angle A = \angle B$.

$\angle B = 180° - 121° = 59°$.

$\angle A = 59°$ because $\angle A = \angle B$

GED Practice: Formula Problems (pages 85–86)

1. **(5) 156 ft.** Add 2×7 ft. to each side of pool.

$P = 2l + 2w$

$= 2(32 + 14) + 2(18 + 14)$

$= 2(46) + 2(32)$

$= 92 + 64$

$= 156$ ft.

2. **(3) 600 sq. ft.**

$A = lw$

$= 32 \cdot 18 = 576$ sq. ft.

600 sq. ft. is the next larger size to 576 sq. ft.

3. **(4) 48 sq. ft.**

$A = \frac{1}{2}ab$

$= \frac{1}{2}(12)(8) = \frac{96}{2} = 48$ sq. ft.

4. **(1) $(15 \times 20) + (15 \times 20)$**

Total Area = Area A + Area B

$= (15 \times 20) + (15 \times 20)$

5. **(4) $1,500**

Total Area = Area A + Area B
$$= (15 \times 20) + (15 \times 20)$$
$$= 300 \times 300 = 600 \text{ sq. ft.}$$
$c = nr = 600 \times \$2.50 = \$1,500$

6. **(1) 392 sq. in.**

First find the width.
$$P = 2l + 2w$$
$$84 = 2(28) + 2w$$
$$84 = 56 + 2w$$
$$84 - 56 = 56 - 56 + 2w$$
$$28 = 2w$$
$$14 \text{ in.} = w$$
$A = lw = 28 \times 14 = 392 \text{ sq. in.}$

7. **(2) 3.14 × 345 × 345**

Determine total radius:

radius of center $= \frac{1}{2} \times 450 = 225$ ft.

3 tracks each 40 ft. wide = 120 ft.
Total radius = 225 + 120 = 345 ft.
$A = \pi r^2 = 3.14 \times 345 \times 345$

8. **(1) 2,166.6 ft.**

Determine diameter.
Diameter is twice the radius found in Item 7:
$$2 \times 345 \text{ ft.} = 690 \text{ ft.}$$
OR lanes + center + lanes =
$$120 + 450 + 120 = 690$$
$c = \pi d = 3.14 \times 690 \text{ ft.} = 2,166.6 \text{ ft.}$

9. **(4) 452.16 sq. in.**

Radius is $\frac{1}{2}$ of the diameter of 24.

Radius = 12 in.
$A = \pi r^2 = 3.14 \times 12 \times 12 = 452.16 \text{ sq. in.}$

10. **(1) 24 cm**

Find the area of the rectangle.
$A = lw = 24 \times 8 = 192$ cm
Since A(rectangle) = A(triangle),
A(triangle) = 192.

$$A = \frac{1}{2} bh$$
$$192 = \frac{1}{2} (16)h$$
$$192 = 8h$$
$$24 = h$$

11. **(4) 139 cu. ft.**

Change 9 in. to $\frac{3}{4}$ of a foot.

$$V = lwh = 14\frac{1}{2} \times 12\frac{3}{4} \times \frac{3}{4}$$
$$= 14.5 \times 12.75 \times .75 = 139 \text{ cu. ft.}$$

12. **(2) 46**

$$V = \pi r^2 h = 3.14 \times 11 \times 11 \times 28$$
$$= 10,638.32 \text{ cu. in.}$$
$10,638.32 \div 231 = 46.05$ rounds to 46 gallons

GED Practice: Ratio and Proportion (pages 87–88)

1. **(3) 9 in.**

Large Picture   Smaller Picture

$$\frac{\text{width}}{\text{length}} = \frac{\text{width}}{\text{length}}$$
$$\frac{12}{16} = \frac{x}{12}$$
$$16x = 144$$
$$x = 9 \text{ inches}$$

2. **(4) 1:4**

rise:span
5:20
1:4

3. **(3) $37\frac{1}{2}$ ft.**

$$\frac{\text{pole height}}{\text{shadow}} = \frac{\text{tree height}}{\text{shadow}}$$
$$\frac{6}{4} = \frac{x}{25}$$
$$4x = 150$$
$$x = 37\frac{1}{2} \text{ ft.}$$

4. **(2) 54 ft.**

$$\frac{\text{seedling height}}{\text{shadow}} = \frac{\text{tree height}}{\text{shadow}}$$
$$\frac{3}{4} = \frac{x}{72}$$
$$4x = 216$$
$$x = 54 \text{ ft.}$$

5. **(4) 25 ft.**

First find $\overline{AB}$.

$$\frac{\overline{AB}}{\overline{BC}} = \frac{2}{3}$$
$$\frac{\overline{AB}}{15} = \frac{2}{3}$$
$$3\overline{AB} = 30$$
$$\overline{AB} = 10 \text{ ft.}$$

$$\begin{array}{r} 10 \text{ ft.} \\ +15 \text{ ft.} \\ \hline 25 \text{ ft.} \end{array}$$

6. **(2) similar** Proportional triangles are similar.

7. **(2) 60 ft.** Use the Pythagorean relationship.
$$c^2 = a^2 + b^2$$
$$c^2 = 48^2 + 36^2$$
$$c^2 = 2,304 + 1,296$$
$$c^2 = 3,600$$
$$c = \sqrt{3,600}$$
$$c = 60 \text{ ft.}$$

UNIT 3

8. (2) 40 ft. $\triangle ABC$ and $\triangle CDE$ are similar. Thus,

$$\frac{AB}{BC} = \frac{DE}{CE}$$

$$\frac{8}{10} = \frac{x}{50}$$

$$10x = 400$$

$$x = 40 \text{ ft.}$$

9. (5) 1,000 miles

$$1\tfrac{7}{8} + \tfrac{5}{8} = 1\tfrac{12}{8} = 2\tfrac{4}{8} = 2\tfrac{1}{2} \text{ inches}$$

Change $2\tfrac{1}{2}$ to 2.5

$$\frac{2.5}{x} = \frac{.25}{100}$$

$$.25x = 250$$

$$x = 1,000 \text{ miles}$$

10. (3) 20 cm Since the triangles are similar,

$$\frac{\overline{AC}}{\overline{AB}} = \frac{\overline{EC}}{\overline{EF}}$$

$$\frac{36}{40} = \frac{18}{x}$$

$$36x = 720$$

$$x = 20 \text{ cm}$$

11. (3) 9

$$a^2 + b^2 = c^2$$

$$a^2 + 12^2 = 15^2$$

$$a^2 + 144 = 225$$

$$a^2 + 144 - 144 = 225 - 144$$

$$a^2 = 81$$

$$a = \sqrt{81} = 9$$

12. (3) $\sqrt{3^2 + 4^2}$ Look at the right triangle formed by the roof. The width of the roof is the hypotenuse (c) of this triangle. The height is given as 4 ft. The base is $\tfrac{1}{2}$ the width of the shed, or 3 ft. These are the legs of the right triangle.
Thus, $c = \sqrt{a^2 + b^2} = \sqrt{3^2 + 4^2}$

13. (4) $\sqrt{225 - 121}$

$$a^2 + b^2 = c^2$$

$$11^2 + b^2 = 15^2$$

$$b^2 = 15^2 - 11^2$$

$$b = \sqrt{15^2 - 11^2} = \sqrt{225 - 121}$$

14. (4) 15 ft.

$$c^2 = a^2 + b^2$$

$$c^2 = 5^2 + 12^2$$

$$c^2 = 25 + 144$$

$$c^2 = 169$$

$$c = \sqrt{169} = 13$$

The ladder must be 13 ft. + 2 ft. or 15 ft. long.

15. (3) 40 ft.

$$c^2 = a^2 + b^2$$

$$c^2 = 24^2 + 32^2$$

$$c^2 = 576 + 1024$$

$$c^2 = 1600$$

$$c = \sqrt{1600} = 40$$

Coordinate System (page 90)

1.–5.

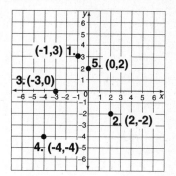

6. $A\,(3, 1)$

7. $B\,(-3, 3)$

8. $C\,(-5, -2)$

9. $D\,(3, -4)$

10. $E\,(0, 4)$

11. $d = \sqrt{(x_2 - x_1)^2 + (y_2 - y_1)^2}$
$d = \sqrt{(6 - (-6))^2 + (-2 - (-7))^2}$
$d = \sqrt{(12)^2 + (5)^2}$
$d = \sqrt{144 + 25}$
$d = \sqrt{169} = 13$

12. $d = \sqrt{(x_2 - x_1)^2 + (y_2 - y_1)^2}$
$d = \sqrt{(-7 - (-7))^2 + (-9 - 7)^2}$
$d = \sqrt{(0)^2 + (-16)^2}$
$d = \sqrt{256} = 16$

13. $d = \sqrt{(x_2 - x_1)^2 + (y_2 - y_1)^2}$
$d = \sqrt{(4 - (-8))^2 + (5 - (-4))^2}$
$d = \sqrt{(12)^2 + (9)^2}$
$d = \sqrt{144 + 81}$
$d = \sqrt{225} = 15$

14. $d = \sqrt{(x_2 - x_1)^2 + (y_2 - y_1)^2}$
$d = \sqrt{(7 - (-5))^2 + (4 - 4)^2}$
$d = \sqrt{(12)^2 + (0)^2}$
$d = \sqrt{144} = 12$

15. $d = \sqrt{(x_2 - x_1)^2 + (y_2 - y_1)^2}$
$d = \sqrt{(-10 - 10)^2 + (-6 - 9)^2}$
$d = \sqrt{(-20)^2 + (-15)^2}$
$d = \sqrt{400 + 225}$
$d = \sqrt{625}$
$d = 25$

Graphing Linear Equations (page 91)

1.–4.

Line 1: $x + y = 4$
if $x = 0, y = 4\ (0, 4)$
if $y = 0, x = 4\ (4, 0)$

Line 2: $x - y = -4$
if $x = 0, -y = -4$
$y = 4\ (0, 4)$
if $y = 0, x = -4\ (-4, 0)$

Line 3: $x - y = 4$
if $x = 0, -y = 4$
$y = -4\ (0, -4)$
if $y = 0, x = 4\ (4, 0)$

Line 4: $x + y = -4$
if $x = 0, y = -4\ (0, -4)$
if $y = 0, x = -4\ (-4, 0)$

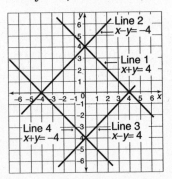

Graphing Problems (page 93)

1.–5.

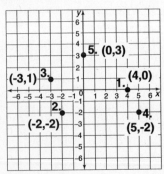

6. $A\ (-2, 5)$

7. $B\ (-3, 0)$

8. $C\ (-3, -4)$

9. $D\ (3, -2)$

10. $E\ (4, 3)$

11. $d = \sqrt{(x_2 - x_1)^2 + (y_2 - y_1)^2}$
$d = \sqrt{(5 - (-3))^2 + (6 - 0)^2}$
$d = \sqrt{(8)^2 + (6)^2}$
$d = \sqrt{64 + 36}$
$d = \sqrt{100} = 10$

12. $d = \sqrt{(x_2 - x_1)^2 + (y_2 - y_1)^2}$
$d = \sqrt{(3 - (-6))^2 + (-6 - 6)^2}$
$d = \sqrt{(9)^2 + (-12)^2}$
$d = \sqrt{81 + 144}$
$d = \sqrt{225} = 15$

13. $d = \sqrt{(x_2 - x_1)^2 + (y_2 - y_1)^2}$
$d = \sqrt{(8 - (-4))^2 + (0 - (-5))^2}$
$d = \sqrt{(12)^2 + (5)^2}$
$d = \sqrt{144 + 25}$
$d = \sqrt{169} = 13$

14. **(4) (3, 2)** Substitute each pair.
$x + 2y = 7$
$3 + 2(2) = 7$
$3 + 4 = 7$
$7 = 7$

15. **(3) (0, –9)** The y-intercept always has 0 for the x-coordinate. Choice (3) is the only choice with a zero for the x-coordinate that satisfies the equation.
Check: $2x - y = 9$
$2(0) - (-9) = 9$
$0 + 9 = 9$

16. **(5) (–2, 0)** The x-intercept always has 0 for the y-coordinate. Since choices (1), (3), and (5) have zeros for the y coordinate, we must find the x-intercept by letting $y = 0$ in the equation and solving for x.
$3y - 4x = 8$
$3(0) - 4x = 8$
$-4x = 8$
$\dfrac{-4x}{-4} = \dfrac{8}{-4}$
$x = -2$
Choice (5) has the correct coordinates, $(-2, 0)$.

17. **(5)** $\frac{1}{3}$
$m = \dfrac{y_2 - y_1}{x_2 - x_1}$
$m = \dfrac{2 - 0}{3 - (-3)}$
$m = \dfrac{2}{6} = \dfrac{1}{3}$

GED Review: Geometry (pages 94–95)

1. **(4) II and III only**

2. **(3) 42 ft.**
$$\frac{\overline{AC}}{\overline{AB}} = \frac{\overline{XZ}}{\overline{XY}}$$
$$\frac{21}{7} = \frac{x}{14}$$
$$7x = 294$$
$$x = 42$$

3. **(5) 1.39 in.**

    27.14 outer diameter $\frac{2.78}{2} = 1.39$ in.
    -24.36 inner diameter
      2.78 thickness of 2 walls

4. **(2) 1:8**

Original	Doubled dimensions
$V = lwh$	$V = lwh$
$= 2 \times 3 \times 4$	$= 4 \times 6 \times 8$
$= 24$ cu. in.	$= 192$ cu. in.

            Original:New
              24:192
               1:8

5. **(5) 30 in.**
$$c^2 = a^2 + b^2$$
$$c^2 = 18^2 + 24^2$$
$$c^2 = 324 + 576$$
$$c^2 = 900$$
$$c = \sqrt{900} = 30$$

6. **(1) –1**
$$m = \frac{y_2 - y_1}{x_2 - x_1} = \frac{-4 - 1}{3 - (-2)} = \frac{-5}{5} = -1$$

7. **(3) $(15 \times 15) - (7 \times 9)$**
$A(\text{Section I}) - A(\text{Section II})$
$(15 \times 15) - (7 \times 9)$

8. **(3) $2(15 + 15) - 2(7 + 9)$**
$P(\text{Section I}) - P(\text{Section II})$
$2(l + w) - 2(l + w)$
$2(15 + 15) - 2(7 + 9)$

9. **(4) 18 ft.**
$$P = 84$$
$$l = 24$$
$$P = 2l + 2w$$
$$84 = 2(24) + 2w$$
$$84 = 48 + 2w$$
$$84 - 48 = 48 - 48 + 2w$$
$$36 = 2w$$
$$18 = w$$

10. **(2) $19\frac{1}{2}$ ft.** Change 20 feet 6 inches to $20\frac{1}{2}$ feet.
$$P = 2l + 2w$$
$$80 = 2(20\tfrac{1}{2}) + 2w$$
$$80 = 41 + 2w$$
$$80 - 41 = 41 - 41 + 2w$$
$$39 = 2w$$
$$19\tfrac{1}{2} = w$$

11. **(3) 125** The face of a cube is a square. If the area of the face is 25 sq. ft., 5 feet is the measurement of each side. Therefore, since all sides of a cube are equal:
$$V = lwh$$
$$= 5 \times 5 \times 5$$
$$= 125 \text{ cu. ft.}$$

12. **(2) 65°**
$$\angle a + \angle b = 180°$$
$$115° + \angle b = 180°$$
$$115° - 115° + \angle b = 180° - 115°$$
$$\angle b = 65°$$

13. **(5) $\angle g$** $\angle c$ corresponds with $\angle g$. $\angle c$ and $\angle b$ are vertical angles. $\angle c$ and $\angle f$ are alternate interior angles.
$$\angle c = \angle g = \angle b = \angle f$$

14. **(4) 14 ft.** Use the Pythagorean relationship to find the height of the triangle.
$$a^2 + b^2 = c^2$$
$$a^2 + 8^2 = 10^2$$
$$a^2 + 64 = 100$$
$$a^2 + 64 - 64 = 100 - 64$$
$$a^2 = 36$$
$$a = \sqrt{36} = 6$$
Add the height of the triangle to the height of the side of the barn. Since 6 ft. + 8 ft. = 14 ft., the height of the center of the roof is 14 ft.

SIMULATED TEST A
(pages 96–105)

1. **(1) $9.28** (Measurement)
Sale price = 100% − 40% = 60% = .60
Sales price = $144 × .60 = $86.40
Sales tax = $86.40 × .05 = $4.32
Total cost = $86.40 + $4.32 = $90.72
Change = $100.00 − $90.72 = $9.28

2. **(4) 5:1** (Number relationships)
If you have 5 raisin cookies to every 1 sugar cookie, the total number of cookies will be some multiple of 6 (5 + 1) and thus will not equal 20. The totals of the other option proportions divide evenly into 20.

3. **(3) 8** (Measurement)

$\frac{1}{3} \times \frac{18}{1} = 6$ tokens for her sister

$18 - 6 = 12$ tokens left

$12 \times \frac{1}{3} = 4$ tokens for her brother

$12 - 4 = 8$ tokens left for Harriet

4. **(4) $13k + 6$** (Algebra)

$3(4k + 2) + k =$

$12k + 6 + k =$

$13k + 6$

5. **(1) $\frac{9.5 + 8.7 + 8.8}{3}$** (Data Analysis)

The mean is the sum of the scores divided by the number of scores.

6. **(1) 1,200** (Data Analysis)

$3,600 - 2,400 = 1,200$

OR $6(600) - 4(600) = 2(600) = 1,200$

7. **(2) $\frac{9(600)}{3(600)}$** (Data Analysis)

8. **(5) Not enough information is given.**

(Geometry) To determine the size of angle y, the size of angle x would be needed.

9. **(3) 8** (Geometry)

$P = (\text{\# of sides}) \times (\text{length of side})$

$56 = 7s; s = 8$

10. **(2) $\frac{1}{2}$ of 100** (Number relationships)

$.49$ rounds to $.5$ or $\frac{1}{2}$

97 rounds to 100

Therefore, $.49 \times 97$ is closest to $\frac{1}{2}$ of 100.

11. **(5) 605** (Measurement)

$.2 = 20\%$

121 miles is 20% of entire trip

$121 \div .2 = 605$

OR 20% of what number equals 121?

$.2x = 121$

$x = 121 \div .2 = 605$

12. **(4) $(2\frac{1}{2} + 3\frac{1}{2} + 1\frac{1}{2} + 3) \div 10$**

(Data analysis) Add the four distances, then divide by 10 to find the miles covered per hour.

13. **(3) $36.12** (Measurement)

$10\% + 20\% = 30\%$

$\$12.90 \times .30 = \$3.87 = \text{Discount}$

$\$12.90 - \$3.87 = \$9.03 = \text{Sale price}$

$\$9.03 \times 4 = \$36.12 \text{ cost of 4 yds on sale}$

14. **(3) $\frac{\$8,590}{24} = x$** (Algebra)

$\frac{\text{total cost}}{\text{months financed}} = \text{monthly payment} = x$

$\frac{\$8,590}{24} = x$

15. **(4) 12** (Algebra)

$$y - 14 = 10 - y$$
$$y - 14 + 14 + y = 10 + 14 - y + y$$
$$2y = 24$$
$$\frac{2y}{2} = \frac{24}{2}$$
$$y = 12$$

16. **(2) 256** (Data Analysis)

$40 + 90 + 204 + 10 = 344$

$600 - 344 = 256$

17. **(3) 90 minutes** (Algebra)

$\$15.00 = \text{total bill}$

$- \quad 4.50 = \text{total for 1st 20 minutes}$

$\overline{\$10.50} = \text{balance of call}$

$\frac{\$.75}{5} = \frac{\$10.50}{x}$

$\$.75x = \$52.50 \qquad \quad 20 \text{ 1st 20 minutes}$

$x = 70 \text{ minutes} \quad \underline{+70 \text{ additional minutes}}$

$\qquad\qquad\qquad\qquad 90 \text{ total minutes}$

18. **(1) $36** (Measurement)

$\frac{\$8.50}{10} = \frac{x}{1}$

$10x = \$8.50$

$x = \$.85$

$12 \times 10 \text{ dozen} = 120 \text{ glasses}$

$120 \times \$.85 = \$102.00$

$120 \times \$.55 = \$66.00$

$\$102.00 - 66.00 = \$36.00$

19. **(1) 356 ($\frac{1}{4}$)** (Measurement)

20. **(1) $5(20) - \frac{20 \times 5}{2}$** (Measurement)

$A(\text{parallelogram}) - A(\text{triangle}) = bh - \frac{1}{2}bh =$

$20(5) - \frac{1}{2}(20)(5)$

21. **(2) 40** (Algebra)

$(5x - 5z) + ab$

$5(1) - 5(-4) + (3)(5)$

$5 + 20 + 15 = 40$

22. **(1) $(12\frac{3}{4})(\$1.69)$** (Measurement)

23. **(2) $-12x + 4$** (Algebra)

24. **(4) 528,815** (Data Analysis) Arrange in order from smallest to largest.

383,000
493,509
509,386 ⎫
548,244 ⎭—middle values
903,084
3,164,632

Add the two middle values:
509,386 + 548,244 = 1,057,630
Find the average of the two values:
1,057,630 ÷ 2 = 528,815

25. **(5) 2,781,632** (Data Analysis)

$$\begin{array}{r} 3,164,632 \\ -\ \ 383,000 \\ \hline 2,781,632 \end{array}$$

26. **(4) $\frac{2}{20}, \frac{32}{64}, \frac{15}{18}, \frac{28}{32}, \frac{32}{36}$** (Number relationships)

$\frac{2}{20} = \frac{1}{10} = .10$

$\frac{32}{64} = \frac{1}{2} = .5$

$\frac{15}{18} = \frac{5}{6} = .83\frac{1}{3}$

$\frac{28}{32} = \frac{7}{8} = .875$

$\frac{32}{36} = \frac{8}{9} = .88\frac{8}{9}$

27. **(1) A** (Algebra)
1.6 + 1.2 − 7.8 = −5.0 = point A

28. **(5) 177** (Algebra)
x = 1st volunteer's hours
$2x$ = 2nd volunteer's hours
$3x$ = 3rd volunteer's hours
$6x$ = 4th volunteer's hours
$x + 2x + 3x + 6x = 354$
$12x = 354$
$\frac{12x}{12} = \frac{354}{12}$
$x = 29.5$
$6(29.5) = 177$ hours

29. **(5) ∠4 and ∠5 are alternate interior angles** (Geometry)

30. **(3) −4** (Algebra)
$(-2)^3 - 2(-2) =$
$-8 - (-4) =$
$-8 + 4 = -4$

31. **(1) I only** (Measurement)
$P = 2l + 2w$
$160 = 2l + 2w$
I: $2(60) = 120$
II: $2(80) = 160$
III: $2(100) = 200$
II and III are too large; only I would allow
$P = 160 = 2l + 2w$ to be true.

32. **(3) $6x + 4 = 22$** (Algebra)

33. **(1) (1.00 − .53) (3,000)** (Data analysis)
(100% − 53% girls) (total student population)
(1.00 − .53) (3,000)

34. **(5) 1,400** (Measurement)
Change $\frac{1}{4}$ to .25.

$\frac{.25}{140} = \frac{2.5}{x}$
$.25x = 2.5(140)$
$x = 10(140) = 1,400$

OR change 2.5 to $2\frac{1}{2}$
$2\frac{1}{2} \div \frac{1}{4} = \frac{5}{2} \div \frac{1}{4} =$
$\frac{5}{2} \times \frac{4}{1} = \frac{20}{2} = 10$
$140 \times 10 = 1,400$

35. **(2) $5n - 6 = 49$** (Algebra)

36. **(1) acute** (Geometry)
$2x$ = 1st angle
$3x$ = 2nd angle
$4x$ = 3rd angle
$2x + 3x + 4x = 180°$
$9x = 180°$
$x = 20°$
$2x = 2(20°) = 40°$
$3x = 3(20°) = 60°$
$4x = 4(20°) = 80°$

All of the angles are less than 90°; therefore, the triangle is an acute triangle.

37. **(1) $d = 30h$** (Algebra)
$d = rt; r = 30, t = h$

38. **(3) ∠DAB** (Geometry)

39. **(2) supplementary** (Geometry)
∠2 + ∠3 = 180°. Two angles whose sum equal 180° are supplementary.

40. **(3) $19,980** (Measurement)
$1,665 × 12 = $19,980

41. **(5) 14** (Algebra)
$x^2 + y^2 + z^2$
$(-3)^2 + (2)^2 + (-1)^2$
$9 + 4 + 1 = 14$

42. **(4) 38** (Measurement)
A = πr^2
= 3.14 × 3.5 × 3.5
= 38.465 rounds to 38 square feet

43. **(4) 5** (Algebra)
$$3x - 6 = x + 4$$
$$3x - x - 6 + 6 = x - x + 4 + 6$$
$$2x = 10$$
$$x = 5$$

44. **(2) positive** (Geometry) The line slants upward to the right so the slope is positive.

Check: $m = \dfrac{y_2 - y_1}{x_2 - x_1} = \dfrac{4 - 0}{0 - (-5)} = \dfrac{4}{5}$

45. **(2) 20** Measurement)

$$\begin{array}{r} 14{,}446 \\ -14{,}138.2 \\ \hline 307.8 \end{array} \div 15.4 = 19.9 \text{ rounds to } 20$$

46. **(3) the cost of a gallon of gas** (Measurement)

47. **(3) \$6.75** (Measurement)

$$\begin{array}{r} \$\ 450 \\ \times\ \ .015 \\ \hline 2250 \\ 450 \\ \hline \$6.750 \end{array} \quad (1.5\% = .015)$$

48. **(2)** $\sqrt{36}$ (Number relationships)

$$\sqrt{1} = \sqrt{1^2}$$
$$\sqrt{4} = \sqrt{2^2}$$
$$\sqrt{9} = \sqrt{3^2}$$
$$\sqrt{16} = \sqrt{4^2}$$
$$\sqrt{25} = \sqrt{5^2}$$

The square of 6 is 36: $\sqrt{6^2} = \sqrt{36}$

49. **(5) 5 ft. 4 in.** (Algebra)

$$\dfrac{\text{Amanda shadow}}{\text{height}} = \dfrac{\text{Statue shadow}}{\text{height}}$$

$$\dfrac{4}{x} = \dfrac{12}{16}$$
$$12x = 64$$
$$x = 5\dfrac{4}{12} = 5\dfrac{1}{3} \text{ feet}$$

Change $\dfrac{1}{3}$ foot to inches:

$$\dfrac{1}{3} \times 12 \text{ in.} = \dfrac{1}{3} \times \dfrac{12}{1} = \dfrac{12}{3} = 4 \text{ inches}$$

Therefore, $5\dfrac{1}{3}$ feet is 5 feet 4 inches.

50. **(5) 105** (Algebra)

$$\dfrac{\text{minutes}}{\text{gallons}} = \dfrac{\text{minutes}}{\text{gallons}}$$

$$\dfrac{15}{45} = \dfrac{35}{x}$$
$$15x = 1{,}575$$
$$x = 105$$

51. **(2)** $r = \dfrac{i}{pt}$ (Measurement)

52. **(4)** $(15 \times 18) \div (3 \times 3)$ (Geometry)
area of patio ÷ area of one concrete block

53. **(4)** $\angle BCE$ (Geometry)
All four angles at vertex E are right angles.

54. **(5) Not enough information is given.**
(Geometry)

55. **(2)** 8×10^4 (Algebra)
$$111{,}111 + n = 191{,}111$$
$$111{,}111 - 111{,}111 + n = 191{,}111 - 111{,}111$$
$$n = 80{,}000$$
$$n = 8 \times 10^4$$

56. **(2)** $\$1{,}140 \times 3 \times .055$ (Measurement)
Use interest formula $i = prt$.

SIMULATED TEST B
(pages 107–116)

1. **(2)** $2\dfrac{1}{2}\%$ (Measurement)

part ÷ base = percent

$$30 \div 1{,}200 = .025 = 2\dfrac{1}{2}\%$$

2. **(4)** $\dfrac{1}{4}$ (Data analysis)

Since there are two desired outcomes out of 8 possible outcomes, the probability is $\dfrac{2}{8}$ or $\dfrac{1}{4}$.

3. **(2)** $\dfrac{15}{3} = \dfrac{30}{10}$ (Number relationships)

$$\dfrac{15}{3} \overset{?}{=} \dfrac{30}{10}$$
$$15 \times 10 \overset{?}{=} 3 \times 30$$
150 is not equal to 90

4. **(5) parallel lines** (Geometry)

5. **(5) New York** (Number relationships)

6. **(2) Mexico City** (Number relationships)

7. **(5) New York** (Data analysis)

8. **(4) 49 thousand per square mile** (Number relationships)
To find density, divide the population (in thousands) by the number of acres.

$$\begin{array}{r} 49 \text{ (in thousands)} \\ 342{\overline{\smash{\big)}\,16{,}792}} \\ \underline{13{,}68\ \ } \\ 3{,}112 \\ \underline{3{,}078} \\ 34 \end{array}$$

9. **(1) 11 thousand per square mile.** (Number relationships) Divide the number of thousands of people by the number of square miles.

$$\begin{array}{r} 11.4 \text{ rounds to } 11 \text{ (thousands)} \\ 1274\overline{)14648.0} \\ \underline{1274} \\ 1908 \\ \underline{1274} \\ 634\,0 \\ \underline{509\,6} \\ 124\,4 \end{array}$$

10. **(4) 33%** (Number relationships)

$$\frac{(27{,}872 - 20{,}899)}{20{,}899} = \frac{6{,}973}{20{,}899}$$

Round to $\frac{7{,}000}{21{,}000} = \frac{1}{3} = .333$

.333 rounded to the nearest percent is 33%

11. **(4) $\frac{3}{10}$% of 70** (Number relationships)

$6\frac{3}{4}$% of 50 = .0675 × 50 = 3.375

8% of 90 = .08 × 90 = 7.2

50% of 100 = .50 × 100 = 50

$\frac{3}{10}$% of 70 = .003 × 70 = .21

$\frac{3}{4}$% of 240 = .0075 × 240 = 1.8

12. **(5) 20** (Algebra)

$$\frac{\text{newspapers}}{\text{time}} = \frac{\text{newspapers}}{\text{time}}$$

Change $1\frac{1}{4}$ to 1.25.

$$\frac{125}{1.25} = \frac{2{,}000}{x}$$

$125x = 2{,}500$

$x = 20$ hours

13. **(5) $24,840** (Number relationships)

$$\begin{array}{r} \$\ 21{,}600 \\ \times \quad\quad .15 \\ \hline 1\,080\,00 \\ 2\,160\,0 \\ \hline \$3{,}240.00 \end{array} \qquad \begin{array}{r} \$21{,}600 \\ +\ \ 3{,}240 \\ \hline \$24{,}840 \end{array}$$

14. **(1) $(1\frac{1}{4} + 1 + 4\frac{1}{2})$($1.69)** (Measurement)

Change 1 foot 3 inches to $1\frac{1}{4}$ feet.

Change 4.5 feet to $4\frac{1}{2}$ feet.

$$\left(1\frac{1}{4} + 1 + 4\frac{1}{2}\right)(\$1.69)$$

15. **(4) 1,650** (Measurement)

$\frac{1}{2}$ dozen = 6 eggs

275 × 6 = 1,650

16. **(4) 4(1,000) + 7(100) + 25** (Number relationships)

$4.6 \times 10^3 + 125 =$

$4.6 \times 1{,}000 + 125 =$

$4{,}600 + 125 = 4{,}725$

$4{,}725 = 4{,}000 + 700 + 25$

$= 4(1{,}000) + 7(100) + 25$

17. **(2) $x < 7$** (Algebra)

The open circle with the arrow pointing left means all numbers less than 7 are in the solution set.

18. **(4) 55 $2 books and 45 $3 books** (Algebra)

Let x = $2 books

$100x$ = $3 books

$(2)x + (3)(100x) = 245$

$2x + 300 - 3x = 245$

$-x = -55$

$x = 55$ and $100 - x = 45$

19. **(1) $\frac{1}{2}$** (Data analysis)

There are only 2 possible outcomes.

20. **(4) 200** (Measurement)

20 is 10% of total graduates: $\frac{20}{.10} = 200$

OR 10% of what number equals 20?

$.10x = 20; x = 200$

21. **(4) 18 in.** (Algebra)

Let x = width

Let $2x - 2$ = length

$2x + 2(2x - 2) = 56$

$2x + 4x - 4 = 56$

$6x - 4 + 4 = 56 + 4$

$6x = 60$

$\frac{6x}{6} = \frac{60}{6}$

$x = 10$

$2x - 2 = 2(10) - 2 = 18$

22. **(4) 50** (Geometry)

$c^2 = a^2 + b^2$

$c^2 = 30^2 + 40^2$

$c^2 = 900 + 1{,}600$

$c^2 = 2{,}500$

$c^2 = \sqrt{2{,}500}$

$c = 50$

23. **(1) $\frac{1}{4}x - \frac{1}{6}x = 18$** (Algebra)

Let $\frac{1}{4}x$ = first number

Let $\frac{1}{6}x$ = second number

$\frac{1}{4}x - \frac{1}{6}x = 18$

24. (5) $\frac{9}{20}$ (Number relationships)

$$\frac{\text{responses}}{\text{questionnaires}} = \frac{225}{500} = \frac{9}{20}$$

25. (2) 4 (Algebra)

$2a^3 - 3ay$
$2(-1)^3 - 3(-1)(2)$
$2(-1) + (3)(2)$
$-2 + 6 = 4$

26. (5) .15 (Number relationships)

.0015
.005
.015
.05
.15

Compare the first digit to the right of the decimal point: .15 is the largest value.

27. (3) $1,640 (Algebra)

Let $(x + \$640)$ = student leader's money
Let x = $ for each of the other four students
$(x + \$640) + 4x = \$5,640$
$5x + \$640 = \$5,640$
$5x + \$640 - \$640 = \$5,640 - \$640$
$5x = \$5,000$
$x = \$1,000$
student leader = $x + \$640$
$\$1,000 + \$640 = \$1,640$

28. (5) Not enough information is given.
(Measurement)
The dimensions of the wall unit pieces are not given on the diagram or in the passage.

29. (1) $143.20 (Measurement)

$A = lw$
$14 \times 10 = 140$ sq. ft.
1 yd. $\times$ 1 yd. = 3 ft. $\times$ 3 ft. = 9 sq. ft. =
1 sq. yd.
$\frac{140 \text{ sq. ft.}}{9 \frac{\text{sq. ft.}}{\text{sq. yd.}}} = 15\frac{1}{2} = 16$ sq. yd.

$8.95 rounds to 9
$9 \times 16 = \$144$

30. (3) 62% (Measurement)

$\begin{array}{r} \$3,250 \\ -\ 1,250 \\ \hline \$2,000 \end{array}$

.615 rounds to 62%
$\begin{array}{r} 3,250\overline{)2,000.000} \\ 1\ 950\ 0 \\ \hline 50\ 00 \\ 32\ 50 \\ \hline 17\ 500 \\ 16\ 250 \\ \hline 1\ 250 \end{array}$

31. (2) $(3.14 \times 14 \times 14 \times 60)$ +
$(3.14 \times 7 \times 7 \times 30)$ (Geometry)

32. (2) 3 (Algebra)

$10x + 7 - 8x = 13$
$2x + 7 = 13$
$2x + 7 - 7 = 13 - 7$
$2x = 6$
$x = 3$

33. (3) 6,606 (Measurement)

$\frac{26,424}{1} \times \frac{1}{4} = \frac{26,424}{4} = 6,606$

34. (4) 190 (Algebra)

Let n = number of boxes that they must sell.
$\$2n = \$380$
$n = 190$

35. (1) $600 - (125 + 50 + 105 + 100)$
(Measurement)

36. (5) 145 (Measurement)

$d = rt = 50 \times 15\frac{1}{2}$
$\frac{50}{1} \times \frac{31}{2} = \frac{1,550}{2} = 775$
$775 - 630 = 145$

37. (3) $\frac{1}{5}n + n = \$14.40$ (Algebra)

If n = Judy's, $\frac{1}{5}n$ = Diane's.
If n = Diane's, $5n$ = Judy's.
Added together the sum is $14.40.

38. (2) 12 ft. (Geometry)

$\frac{\overline{AB}}{\overline{AC}} = \frac{\overline{DE}}{\overline{DF}}$
$\frac{6}{3} = \frac{x}{6}$
$3x = 36$
$x = 12$ ft.

39. (1) $\frac{\$54}{(.06)}$ (Measurement)

$i = prt; r = \frac{i}{pt} = \frac{\$54}{.06(1)}$

40. (5) 135° (Geometry)

$\angle y + 45° = 180°$
$\angle y + 45° - 45° = 180° - 45°$
$\angle y = 135°$

Angle x is vertical to angle y, and vertical angles are equal, so $\angle x = \angle y = 135°$.

41. (5) −16 (Algebra)

$x = (n + 5)(n - 5)$
$= (-3 + 5)(-3 - 5)$
$= (+2)(-8)$
$= -16$

42. **(2) 20%** (Measurement)

$25
$\underline{-\ \ 20}$
$ 5 = savings

$$\frac{\text{savings}}{\text{regular price}} = \frac{5}{25} = \frac{20}{100} = .20 = 20\%$$

43. **(1) $5x + 9 = x - 25$** (Algebra)

44. **(5) $(-4, 4)$** (Geometry)
Option (1) (4,3) = point B; Option (2) (4 −3) = point A; Option (3) (−3,−6) = point E; Option (4) (−4,−3) = point C; point D = (3,6). So Option (5) (−4,4) is not one of the points.

45. **(4) 6** (Geometry)
Since the line is vertical, from $y = -3$ to $y = 0$ is 3, from $y = 0$ to $y = 3$ is 3; $3 + 3 = 6$
OR point A = (4,−3) and point B = (4,3)
$$d = \sqrt{(x_2 - x_1)^2 + (y_2 - y_1)^2}$$
$$d = \sqrt{(4 - 4)^2 + (3 - (-3))^2}$$
$$d = \sqrt{0^2 + 6^2} = \sqrt{6^2}$$
$$d = \sqrt{36} = 6$$

46. **(3) $6 \times 2(63 + 48) \div 36$** (Measurement)
One window $P = 2l + 2w$
$P = 2(63 + 48)$ inches
Six windows = Multiply by 6.
$6 \times 2(63 + 48)$ inches
There are 36 inches in a yard, therefore, divide by 36.
$[6 \times 2(63 + 48)] \div 36$

47. **(4) $25.53** (Measurement)
$[6 \times 2(l + w)] \div 36$
$[6 \times 2(63 + 48)] \div 36$
$[6 \times 2(111)] \div 36$
$[6 \times 222] \div 36$
$1,332 \div 36 = 37$
$.69 \times 37 = 25.53

48. **(4) $101.25** (Measurement)
$225\% = 2.25$
$\$45.00 \times 2.25 = \$101.25$

49. **(2) 60 ft.** (Algebra)
$$\frac{\text{Lester's height}}{\text{shadow}} = \frac{\text{street light's height}}{\text{shadow}}$$
$$\frac{6}{4} = \frac{x}{40}$$
$$4x = 240$$
$$x = 60$$

50. **(2) $250($4.50 − $.50)$** (Measurement)
Coupons × discount price of meal
$250(\$4.50 - \$.50)$

51. **(5) $\angle H$** (Geometry)
$\angle A$ and $\angle H$ are alternate exterior angles, and alternate exterior angles are equal.

52. **(3) 100°** (Geometry)
$$\text{Let } x = \angle G$$
$$\text{Let } x + 20° = \angle E$$
$$x + (x + 20°) = 180°$$
$$2x + 20° = 180°$$
$$2x + 20° - 20° = 180° - 20°$$
$$2x = 160°$$
$$\frac{2x}{2} = \frac{160°}{2}$$
$$x = 80° \angle G$$
Substituting:
$\angle E = x + 20° = 80° + 20° = 100°$

53. **(1) 40°** (Geometry)
First find the measurement of $\angle ABD$. $\angle ABD$ is vertical to $\angle CBE$; therefore, $\angle ABD = 50°$
$\angle ABD + \angle ABD = 90° + 50° = 140°$
Subtracting from the number of degrees in a triangle:
$180° - 140° = 40°$ for $\angle DAB$

54. **(4) 130°** (Geometry)
$\angle DBC$ is the supplementary angle to $\angle CBE$; therefore, $180° - 50° = 130°$.

55. **(1) 85°, 35°, and 90°** (Geometry)
$85° + 35° + 90° = 210°$
The number of degrees in a triangle must equal 180°.

56. **(2) 130°** (Geometry)
$180° - 50° = 130°$ = sum of 2 base angles
Base angles of an isoceles triangle are equal.
So, $130° \div 2 = 65°$ = each base angle.

Answer Sheet

GED Mathematics Test

Name: _____ Class: _____ Date: _____

○ Simulated Test A   ○ Simulated Test B

1 ①②③④⑤   11 ①②③④⑤   21 ①②③④⑤   31 ①②③④⑤   41 ①②③④⑤   51 ①②③④⑤

2 ①②③④⑤   12 ①②③④⑤   22 ①②③④⑤   32 ①②③④⑤   42 ①②③④⑤   52 ①②③④⑤

3 ①②③④⑤   13 ①②③④⑤   23 ①②③④⑤   33 ①②③④⑤   43 ①②③④⑤   53 ①②③④⑤

4 ①②③④⑤   14 ①②③④⑤   24 ①②③④⑤   34 ①②③④⑤   44 ①②③④⑤   54 ①②③④⑤

5 ①②③④⑤   15 ①②③④⑤   25 ①②③④⑤   35 ①②③④⑤   45 ①②③④⑤   55 ①②③④⑤

6 ①②③④⑤   16 ①②③④⑤   26 ①②③④⑤   36 ①②③④⑤   46 ①②③④⑤   56 ①②③④⑤

7 ①②③④⑤   17 ①②③④⑤   27 ①②③④⑤   37 ①②③④⑤   47 ①②③④⑤

8 ①②③④⑤   18 ①②③④⑤   28 ①②③④⑤   38 ①②③④⑤   48 ①②③④⑤

9 ①②③④⑤   19 ①②③④⑤   29 ①②③④⑤   39 ①②③④⑤   49 ①②③④⑤

10 ①②③④⑤   20 ①②③④⑤   30 ①②③④⑤   40 ①②③④⑤   50 ①②③④⑤

Copyright © 1996 by Steck-Vaughn Company. GED Mathematics Exercise Book. Permission granted to reproduce for class